THE DOJ INVESTIGATION
OF THE CHICAGO
POLICE DEPARTMENT

THE DOJ INVESTIGATION OF THE CHICAGO POLICE DEPARTMENT

THE COMPLETE REPORT BY THE UNITED STATES DEPARTMENT OF JUSTICE

UNITED STATES DEPARTMENT OF JUSTICE CIVIL RIGHTS DIVISION

AND

UNITED STATES ATTORNEY'S OFFICE NORTHERN DISTRICT OF ILLINOIS

FOREWORD BY CURTIS BLACK

Racehorse Publishing

First Racehorse Publishing edition 2017

Foreword © 2017 by Racehorse Publishing
Text by Curtis Black

Racehorse Publishing books may be purchased in bulk at special discounts for sales
promotion, corporate gifts, fund-raising, or educational purposes. Special editions can also
be created to specifications. For details, contact the Special Sales Department, Skyhorse
Publishing, 307 West 36th Street, 11th Floor, New York, NY 10018
or info@skyhorsepublishing.com.

Racehorse Publishing™ is a pending trademark of Skyhorse Publishing, Inc.®,
a Delaware corporation.

Visit our website at www.skyhorsepublishing.com.

10 9 8 7 6 5 4 3

Cover artwork by Michael Short
Images courtesy of the public domain

Print ISBN: 978-1-63158-210-3
E-Book ISBN: 978-1-63158-212-7

Printed in the United States of America

TABLE OF CONTENTS

Foreword by Curtis Black vii

EXECUTIVE SUMMARY 1

BACKGROUND **21**

    A. Chicago, Illinois 21
    B. Chicago Police Department 21
    C. Chicago's Accountability Systems 22
    D. Historical Background of Reform in Chicago 23
    E. Federal Involvement in Chicago 25
    F. Investigation of the Chicago Police Department 26

**CPD ENGAGES IN A PATTERN OR PRACTICE OF
UNCONSTITUTIONAL USE OF FORCE** **29**

    A. CPD Uses Deadly Force in Violation of the Fourth
       Amendment and Department Policy 31
    B. CPD Uses Less-Lethal Force in Violation of the Fourth
       Amendment and Department Policy 39
    C. Video Evidence Suggests a Broader Pattern or Practice
       of Unconstitutional Use of Force 44
    D. CPD Does Not Effectively Use Crisis Intervention
       Techniques to Reduce the Need for Force 45
    E. CPD's Failure to Accurately Document and Meaningfully
       Review Officers' Use of Force Perpetuates a Pattern of
       Unreasonable Force 50
    F. CPD's New De-escalation Training and Proposed
       Policy Revisions Should be Expanded and Sustained 55

**CHICAGO'S DEFICIENT ACCOUNTABILITY SYSTEMS
CONTRIBUTE TO CPD'S PATTERN OR PRACTICE OF
UNCONSTITUTIONAL CONDUCT** **57**

    A. Chicago's Systems for Investigating Police Conduct 59
    B. The City Has Put in Place Policies and Practices that
       Impede the Investigation of Officer Misconduct 61
    C. Investigations That CPD Does Conduct Are Neither
       Complete Nor Fair 69

D. Insufficient Staffing Contributes to IPRA's Investigative Deficiencies 86

E. Investigations Lack Timely Resolutions, Undermining the Quality of Investigations and Credibility of the Process 89

F. CPD and the City Do Not Take Sufficient Steps to Prevent Officers from Deliberately Concealing Misconduct 91

G. The City's Discipline System Lacks Integrity and Does Not Effectively Deter Misconduct 97

H. Chicago's Police Board 103

I. The City's Police Accountability Ordinance and Similar Efforts to Correct the Problems Our Investigation Identified 112

CPD DOES NOT PROVIDE OFFICERS WITH SUFFICIENT DIRECTION, SUPERVISION, OR SUPPORT TO ENSURE LAWFUL AND EFFECTIVE POLICING **114**

A. Training 114

B. Supervision 127

C. Officer Wellness and Safety 143

D. Data Collection and Transparency 150

E. Promotions 156

CPD MUST BETTER SUPPORT AND INCENTIVIZE POLICING THAT IS LAWFUL AND RESTORES TRUST AMONG CHICAGO'S MARGINALIZED COMMUNITIES **162**

A. CPD's Move to Restore True Community Policing Will Be Difficult But Is Promising 163

B. CPD Must Change Practices to Restore Trust and Ensure Lawful Policing 168

C. A Trust-Building, Community-Focused Approach to Policing Will Better Promote Lawful Policing and Public Safety 181

RECOMMENDATIONS **182**

A. Use of Force 182

B. Accountability 186

C. Training 188

D. Supervision 189

E. Officer Wellness and Safety 190

F. Data Collection and Transparency 191

G. Promotions 192

H. Community Policing 193

Endnotes 195

FOREWORD

This report on the Chicago Police Department, the product of a pattern and practice investigation by the Civil Rights Division of the U.S. Justice Department, is a historic document—the final and, by some accounts, the largest such investigation by the Obama administration, issued just days before a new administration under President Donald Trump took office with a new direction.

Its roots go back two decades, to the Los Angeles riots following the beating of Rodney King, which led to the passage of a law authorizing such investigations. The Obama administration expanded the number of investigations to an unprecedented level, particularly after events in Ferguson, Missouri, and elsewhere put a spotlight on the issue of police killings of unarmed African Americans.

Its roots in the history of Chicago are also deep. Complaints of abusive behavior, excessive force, and unwarranted killings of African Americans and Latinos by Chicago police go back decades. There have been high-water marks where attention was focused—on the assassination of Black Panther leaders Fred Hampton and Mark Clark in 1969, abusive treatment of black professionals and working people investigated by U.S. Representative Ralph Metcalfe in 1972, and the police torture ring led by Commander Jon Burge in the 1980s and '90s. There have been multiple official and nonofficial inquiries and reports, whose recommendations were generally ignored. The backdrop to all this was a steady stream of protests against questionable shootings, going back to the 1960s and '70s.

But the immediate impetus to this investigation was the killing of Laquan McDonald on October 20, 2014, one month past his seventeenth birthday. McDonald's short life was "complicated," according to a review of his juvenile court records by the *Chicago Tribune*. As a child, he was shuttled between foster care—including one placement where he said he was beaten and sexually abused—and various relatives. He was diagnosed with learning disabilities and multiple mental health issues, including post-traumatic stress disorder. He was prone to angry outbursts and fights with peers. He had three psychiatric hospitalizations by the time he was thirteen. He became involved with drugs and gangs, though apparently not with gang violence. He was arrested numerous times, including seven cases that went to juvenile court, all for possession of small amounts of drugs.

Judges and child welfare officials repeatedly gave him the benefit of the doubt. According to the *Tribune*, they saw potential in the young McDonald, noting his "honesty, charisma, and love for his family" and repeatedly referring to his "resilience." At the time of his death, he was enrolled in an alternative high school, where officials said he was participating in class, and teachers reported he had a warm and gentle side.

It's unclear what McDonald was doing in a desolate area of warehouses, commercial strips, and vacant lots on Chicago's Southwest Side the night he died. Child welfare officials said he was upset at the time about a family dispute. At 9:45 p.m. dispatchers got a 911 call about a person breaking into vehicles at a truck depot, according to an analysis of police transmissions of the incident by the *Chicago Sun-Times*. Within five minutes, two beat officers arrived. McDonald ignored their order that he drop the three-inch knife he held and walked away from them. They reacted calmly and appropriately— using the kind of tactics that this Justice Department report recommends— and tailed him, one officer in an SUV and the other on foot, while calling for backup and requesting an officer with a Taser. When another squad car arrived, officers tried to use the two vehicles to box McDonald in against a fence along Pulaski Avenue. McDonald stabbed the tire of one vehicle and tried to smash its windshield. The officers continued following him as he walked down the center of Pulaski.

The situation changed dramatically when Officer Jason Van Dyke and his partner arrived. Van Dyke immediately jumped out of his vehicle and within seconds began shooting at McDonald, who was pronounced dead at a nearby hospital at 10:42 p.m. A police union spokesperson at the scene told reporters McDonald was shot in the chest after he refused to drop his knife and "lunged" at officers, and his account framed short newspaper articles about the shooting. Van Dyke and his partner filed a report saying McDonald threatened Van Dyke, who backpedaled as he shot McDonald, continuing to do so as McDonald appeared to attempt to get up with his knife pointed at Van Dyke. Other officers at the scene gave reports which either backed Van Dyke's version or said they hadn't seen the shooting. A command review of the incident declared the shooting was justified. An investigation was opened by the Independent Police Review Authority, which looks into all police shootings.

So far this was a standard police shooting, with the standard police narrative, the standard press coverage, and the standard bureaucratic response. But there was a difference: there was a videotape.

About a month after the shooting, a whistleblower from law enforcement went to Craig Futterman of the University of Chicago's Mandel Legal Aid Clinic and told him there was a dash cam video that clearly contradicted the official story. Futterman and his longtime collaborator, journalist Jamie Kalven of the Invisible Institute, issued a call for the city to release all video footage of the incident.

In February 2015, Kalven reported on the results of McDonald's autopsy, which he'd received through a freedom of information request. Instead of a single shot to the chest, McDonald had been shot sixteen times, in the head, neck, chest, arms, legs, and back. "It's very difficult to square the police narrative with the facts established by the silent testimony of Laquan McDonald's corpse," Kalven commented.

That spring, as Mayor Rahm Emanuel faced a difficult reelection campaign, lawyers for McDonald's family began negotiations with the city's law department, which agreed to a $5 million settlement on April 15—before any lawsuit was filed. A condition of the settlement was that the video be kept secret until all investigations were complete, a process that could take years. After Corporation Counsel Steve Patton discussed the video in a hearing of the City Council's finance committee—saying it supported the family's contention that McDonald was walking away and posed no immediate threat when he was shot—the Council approved the settlement with no debate. *Sun-Times* columnist Mary Mitchell wrote a series of articles calling for the release of the video. In one, she related a description of the video by the family's attorney. He couldn't release it, he said, but he could talk about it.

Later that month, the *Tribune* reported that Van Dyke had received seventeen civilian complaints, including several for excessive force and one accusing him of making racially biased remarks. In one complaint, the city paid nearly $500,000 to settle a lawsuit charging excessive force. None of Van Dyke's complaints resulted in any disciplinary action.

In May, freelance journalist Brendon Smith filed a freedom of information request for the video. When it was denied, Smith filed a lawsuit seeking the video's release, and on November 19, Judge Franklin Valderrama ordered the video released in one week. It was released on November 24, 2015.

Reaction was intense. Despite the descriptions of the video that had been in the news, the actual images were, in the word many people used, horrific. McDonald is jogging down the street and slows to a fast stride, almost jaunty, veering away from police cars. Van Dyke steps toward him, and McDonald falls to the ground and twitches as bullets pound his body. After that, a police officer steps into the frame and kicks the knife out of McDonald's hand as he lays motionless.

Despite earlier claims by State's Attorney Anita Alvarez that she was conducting a "highly complex" investigation, and the city's argument that the ongoing investigation precluded release of the video, Alvarez announced Van Dyke's murder indictment on the very day the video was released. It looked like the people of Chicago had been subjected to a big legal and bureaucratic stall—or a cover-up.

Outrage erupted, with daily demonstrations calling for the resignation of Emanuel and Alvarez, continuing for weeks. (Alvarez would be resoundingly defeated for reelection in the Democratic primary in March.) Jesse Jackson and other civil rights leaders demanded a federal investigation. On December 1, the mayor fired Police Superintendent Garry McCarthy, saying "the public trust in the leadership of the department has been shaken." The same day, he announced he would appoint a blue-ribbon police accountability task force, headed by Police Board President Lori Lightfoot, to focus on the police department's discredited accountability system.

Also that same day, Illinois Attorney General Lisa Madigan made public a letter to U.S. Attorney General Loretta Lynch requesting a comprehensive investigation of CPD by the Justice Department's Civil Rights Division, calling on the feds to investigate whether there is a pattern of "discriminatory policing," how the department handles misconduct allegations, and how it trains and supervises its officers. Emanuel called Madigan's request "misguided" on December 2, but, the same day, Democratic presidential candidate Hillary Clinton seconded the call for a federal investigation, and Emanuel reversed course the next day and welcomed the inquiry.

Lynch came to Chicago on December 7, 2015, to announce a pattern and practice investigation of the Chicago police, focusing on use of force and racial bias. She emphasized the importance of trust between communities and police, and said the investigation would seek input from a broad cross section of officials and experts, community members, and rank-and-file cops.

Much happened in the thirteen months of the Justice Department's investigation. There were dozens of community hearings. Headlines depict the tenor of the Justice Department's hearings: "RESIDENTS BERATE POLICE, MAYOR." and "ANGER, SHOUTS GREET JUSTICE DEPT. TEAM." Skepticism over yet another official probe was expressed there and in hearings by the mayor's task force, which reported heartfelt and poignant testimony about "daily, pervasive transgressions" by police that prevent people in communities of color "from having basic freedom of movement in their own neighborhoods." Hearings were also held by the Progressive Caucus of the City Council and by the Grassroots Alliance for Police Accountability, a coalition of community groups.

The mayor's Police Accountability Task Force issued a report that the media characterized as "scathing" in April. "Chicago's police accountability system does not work," it stated baldly, reviewing the long-standing failure to discipline misconduct and concluding that, along with contracts with police unions, the system reinforces a "code of silence" in the police department. A range of recommendations addressed failures in the department's accountability, supervisory, and training systems, and proposed a transparency policy under which videos of police shootings would be released within sixty days. Mayor Emanuel quickly adopted the video release policy.

The task force also reported the profound lack of trust for police in minority communities. Among its conclusions: "CPD's own data gives validity to the widely held belief that the police have no regard for the sanctity of life when it comes to people of color." And: "The community's lack of trust in CPD is justified."

A special prosecutor was appointed to handle Van Dyke's case, and another to investigate a possible police cover-up. Eddie Johnson, the new police superintendent, moved to fire Van Dyke, his partner, and three other officer witnesses—and pushed the chief of detectives and a deputy chief to resign in order to avoid discipline—after an inspector general's report looked into the reports filed by officers on the scene. The *Tribune* reported that Johnson and McCarthy were among a group of top brass that viewed the McDonald video days after the incident and decided the shooting was justified. In September, one civilian witness to the shooting sued the city, saying she and other witnesses were detained for hours after the incident and pressured to change their accounts of what they saw; her cell phone, on which she'd attempted to record the incident, was taken from her.

As the Justice Department's inquiry got underway, Emanuel and Johnson began announcing initiatives to address recommendations of the task force or respond to new crises, and the Justice Department report comments on a number of these efforts, sometimes quite critically. Officers were equipped with body cameras without adequate policies for their use, according to the report. After initially postponing action, Emanuel bowed to community pressure and agreed to an ordinance creating a new oversight agency to replace the wholly discredited IPRA. The Justice Department echoes some of the concerns of advocates like Futterman that the ordinance doesn't go far enough to ensure adequate staffing resources—a key problem for IPRA—or to correct problems with the disciplinary process.

Other examples touch on the overarching issue of inadequate training. After McDonald's shooting, when calls by officers on the scene for a Taser were in vain, Emanuel declared that every Chicago officer would be equipped with a Taser and trained in its use. The report—which notes that CPD policy "permits the use of Tasers in situations where it is unreasonable," and criticizes planned revisions to department policy as inadequate—is devastating in describing a hastily mounted training, which was completely ineffective.

In early 2016, the mayor announced an expansion of the department's Crisis Intervention Team program, which details specially trained officers to handle people in mental health crisis. That was in response to the fatal shooting by police—just a month after the McDonald video was released—of Quintonio LeGrier, a distressed college student who called 911 to request assistance and then met police officers holding a baseball bat, and Bettie Jones, a neighbor who opened the door for police. The report criticizes CPD for rolling out the expansion with insufficient data and analysis, for overburdening an inadequate CIT staff, and for making participation mandatory in a program that requires well-screened volunteers.

The report also sheds light on one of the major controversies of 2016—one that made its way into the presidential campaign. Gun violence escalated dramatically in the weeks after the video release and homicide rates remain at levels not seen since the 1990s. The reasons for this are complex; homicides also climbed in other cities, though the uptick in Chicago was precipitous.

It became common to blame the surge of violence on a sharp decrease in the number of street stops by police at the end of 2016 following a legal agreement with the ACLU. A study by that group of stops that didn't result in arrests found a "shocking number"—a quarter million over the summer of 2015—heavily concentrated in the black community. On the contact cards then in use, officers either gave no reason for the stop or gave a reason that didn't pass constitutional muster for nearly half the stops.

Thus the decrease in the number of stops could have reflected more judicious—and constitutional—use of the tactic. (And it should be noted that crime rates fell after police in New York City curtailed street stops.) But officers complained about the new investigatory stop report forms they were required to fill out under the settlement, suggesting that it impeded their ability to be proactive and that it was a significant factor in the increase in gun violence. By summer, Republican presidential candidate Donald Trump was decrying Chicago's murder rate; in the first debate that fall he gave his solution: "You have to have stop-and-frisk."

The Justice Department report notes that investigatory stop reports are standard in other police departments. However, in Chicago, the new form "was quickly rolled out without a thoughtful, comprehensive training plan." Training focused on how to fill out the form, not how to conduct lawful stops and searches, and left officers feeling the change was politically driven instead of "an integral part of policing the community safely and effectively." The backlash against the new forms "could have been minimized if CPD had appropriately planned this training," the report concludes.

With Trump's upset victory in the November election, the circumstances surrounding the Justice Department investigation changed completely. Trump had referred repeatedly to crime in Chicago during the campaign, at one point saying he believed the violence could be stopped "in one week" with "tough police tactics." The Justice Department bore down to complete its report before Trump's inauguration. Sources told the *Sun-Times* that Emanuel was resisting Justice Department pressure to sign an agreement in principle to seek a consent decree with a court-appointed monitor to enforce the recommendations of the forthcoming report.

The report was issued on January 13, one week before Trump's inauguration, and Emanuel and Deputy Assistant Attorney General for Civil Rights Vanita Gupta signed a letter of agreement. Federal and city attorneys began meeting to negotiate a consent decree, but with the confirmation of Jeff Sessions as attorney general, prospects for court enforcement grew remote.

A longtime critic of civil rights litigation against police departments, Sessions in his confirmation hearing reiterated his concern that departments were being punished for the misdeeds of individual officers, which "can undermine respect for police officers." At the end of February, Sessions said he was still deciding whether to negotiate a consent decree, adding that he had seen summaries of the report, and "some of it was pretty anecdotal and not so scientifically based."

Pointing out that Sessions had admitted he hadn't actually read the report, *Mother Jones* provided some of its salient, "scientifically based" statistics: CPD uses force almost ten times more often against blacks than against whites; only one out of six recent police academy graduates "came close" to properly articulating the legal standard for use of force; IPRA received more than thirty thousand police misconduct complaints over five years, but fewer than 2 percent of those were sustained or resulted in discipline; IPRA investigated 409 police shootings over the same period, but found only two to be unjustified; and white residents were more than three times more likely to have a misconduct complaint sustained than black residents. The report also includes extensive and detailed discussion of policy and of organizational problems; the dissection of CPD's two early warning systems, which are supposed to identify officers in need of correction—neither of which is functional—could go in a management textbook.

And, as Sessions noted, the report contains many "anecdotes"—example after example of excessive force, a completely broken accountability system, a remarkably shoddy training program, and a dysfunctional department. But these are not a weakness; they are perhaps the greatest strength of the report. They put meat on the bones of the policy discussions. They add the human dimension.

They are presented in dry and straightforward prose, with no identifying details. It might help to know that the individual in the first "anecdote" under deadly force—the unarmed man who was shot by police forty-five times, with an assault rifle and other weapons—was named Calvin Cross: he had just turned nineteen, he was a member of his church's choir, he had helped a young friend find a job, and the city paid $2 million to settle a wrongful death lawsuit by his family. (Alex Kotlowitz reported on Cross's killing in the *New Yorker*; the *Chicago Reporter* annotated the Justice Department report, noting media accounts to flesh out its examples.)

But no one with the slightest imagination and human feeling can fail to be moved by the stories here—the sixteen-year-old girl beaten and Tased while being removed from school because she had a cell phone, and the naked, unarmed, sixty-five-year-old schizophrenic woman who had broken no laws but was Tased because she "ignored verbal commands." The "anecdotes" about the way investigations are handled—and false statements tolerated—are simply scandalous. The "anecdotal" insights of police officers into the failures of the department's trainings and supervision give compelling credibility to the report's analyses of shortcomings.

The anecdotes of racial discrimination—the black officer whose wife is called a "fucking nigger" by a white officer and others—are crucial to document this central aspect of the problem. Statistics can show disparities in use of force or street stops, but only stories reflecting the testimony of community residents and officers can reveal the existence of and tolerance for racial bias in the department.

To Sessions's larger point: individual officers come in for implicit criticism in many cases in this report. But it makes perfectly clear, and repeatedly emphasizes, that the essential failing is one of leadership and management. It's not just that racism and unjustified killings are tolerated, but that they flow from the department's failure to provide supervision and require accountability. If there are "good cops" and "bad cops," this report makes it clear that CPD has failed the good cops. Like the cops who patiently tailed Laquan McDonald, who called for a Taser and backup, and who now may face firing and prosecution because they felt they weren't in a position to tell the truth about what happened.

Eddie Johnson had a human reaction: parts of the report were "difficult to read," he said when it was released. And a few days later: "To think that we failed [our police officers] is a difficult pill to swallow."

This report was issued twenty years after the first patterns and practices investigation was initiated by the Justice Department in Pittsburgh. In those years the department opened seventy investigations and reached forty legal settlements, mainly during the Clinton and Obama administrations. "For the most part"—and despite some "backsliding" by individual departments—those agreements have "been successful in improving seriously troubled law enforcement agencies," according to policing expert Sam Walker in a recent review of the record.

Under Obama—and the pressure of increased attention on police killings by Black Lives Matter and others—the scope of those investigations and the reach of the settlements have grown substantially. Walker credits the Obama Justice Department with several major advances: the introduction of constitutional policing standards backed by a set of best practices; the consistent focus on institutional failings underlying individual police misconduct; and the involvement of community residents, rank-and-file officers, and police unions in investigations and the implementation of settlements.

In Walker's view, this unprecedented effort identified a key to the mystifying problem of transforming "police culture." The investigations consistently found inadequate reporting of force incidents and a failure of supervisors to review force reports critically. That's certainly true in the Chicago investigation, which devotes a long discussion to the issue, including the non-specificity of CPD's Tactical Response Reports and the automatic approval given to them by sergeants and lieutenants.

Merely revising use-of-force policies is insufficient, says Walker. To get officers to comply with a new policy it is necessary to establish detailed reporting and review requirements. He calls this "the heart and soul" of accountability and departmental transformation.

In October 2016, CPD issued a draft of a revised use-of-force policy for public comment, which is praised in this report—although reform advocates subsequently criticized the second iteration of the policy that followed the comment period. In a reform framework issued in March 2017, CPD said it planned to revise its Tactical Response Report and develop a system for supervisory review of force incidents in ways that appear to respond to the Justice Department's criticisms.

If actually implemented, that's going to require a lot more work from sergeants and other supervisors—and as this report makes clear, that's going to require a lot more supervisors. The issue of resources runs throughout this report: huge ratios of patrol officers to sergeants; inadequate staffing at IPRA, in the training department, at the Crisis Intervention Team, and in the department's counseling service. This is a key challenge for Mayor Rahm Emanuel, who since 2011 has run a city in fiscal crisis with a strategy heavily reliant on budget cuts. In his first year he ordered CPD's budget cut by $190 million—more than 10 percent. He closed police stations. He laid off civilian employees—and this report notes that one issue for sergeants is the amount of administrative work required of them that would be better handled by civilians.

In response to the surge of violence, Emanuel is now moving to fulfill a 2011 campaign promise to hire one thousand more officers. A coalition of criminal justice and anti-violence groups recently noted, "It is unclear whether adding more police into an unreconstructed system of inequitable deployment and insufficient oversight and training can positively impact violence."

The other question for Emanuel is that of political will and leadership. He is a reluctant reformer. He embraces change when forced to—as when a court ruling opening police misconduct records to public inspection became inevitable, or the drumbeat of wrongful convictions from the Burge torture ring became unavoidable. But in his first term, he also directed his law department to oppose a court ruling finding a code of silence in CPD, and he backed McCarthy when he promoted a lieutenant with a record number of abuse complaints. He endorsed the notion of a "Ferguson effect"—that increased public scrutiny was ruining morale in police departments—which is essentially the point of view of Jeff Sessions today.

Emanuel's political standing hit rock bottom after the release of the Laquan McDonald video, when many accused him of keeping it under wraps in order to save his reelection campaign. He has publicly embraced the recommendations of his task force and of the Justice Department, though he has moved slowly on some items and has not always followed through on promised actions; and it is not clear that he has fully embraced the idea that police reform is key to improving law enforcement and reducing violence. Most recently he has backed away from his previous commitment to seek a federal consent decree with an independent monitor and court oversight, and has opposed a lawsuit seeking a consent decree by Black Lives Matter and other community groups. He has also made dramatic announcements of initiatives that weren't quite ready for prime time; the rollout of Tasers and body cameras discussed in this report are two examples. Many reform advocates wonder whether his politically driven style of governance is capable of providing the sustained attention needed. It's a question this report raises repeatedly, as when it concludes:

"Our investigation found that the reforms the city already plans to implement, as well as the additional reforms our investigation found necessary, will likely not happen or be sustained without the reform tools of an independent monitoring team and a court order."

Regardless of the attitude of the Trump administration, criminologist Sam Walker argues, the momentum for police reform across the country will continue—in part due to the deepening understanding these issues by police leadership in many departments. The momentum in Chicago is likely to continue as well, with or without a federal consent decree—if not driven by political and departmental leadership, then by pressure from human rights advocates and community residents. But the challenges are great, as documented by this report. And regardless of the role played by the federal government going forward, this report sets a standard by which all of Chicago's future reform efforts will be measured.

—*Curtis Black*

EXECUTIVE SUMMARY

On December 7, 2015, the United States Department of Justice (DOJ), Civil Rights Division, Special Litigation Section, and the United States Attorney's Office for the Northern District of Illinois, jointly initiated an investigation of the City of Chicago's Police Department (CPD) and the Independent Police Review Authority (IPRA). This investigation was undertaken to determine whether the Chicago Police Department is engaging in a pattern or practice of unlawful conduct and, if so, what systemic deficiencies or practices within CPD, IPRA, and the City might be facilitating or causing this pattern or practice.

Our investigation assessed CPD's use of force, including deadly force, and addressed CPD policies, training, reporting, investigation, and review related to officer use of force. The investigation further addressed CPD's and IPRA's systems of accountability both as they relate to officer use of force and officer misconduct, including the intake, investigation, and review of allegations of officer misconduct, and the imposition of discipline or other corrective action. We also investigated racial, ethnic, or other disparities in CPD's force and accountability practices, and assessed how those disparities inform the breakdown in community trust.

We opened this investigation pursuant to the Violent Crime Control and Law Enforcement Act of 1994, 42 U.S.C. § 14141 (Section 14141), Title VI of the Civil Rights Act of 1964, 42 U.S.C. § 2000d (Title VI), and the Omnibus Crime Control and Safe Streets Act of 1968, 42 U.S.C. 3789d (Safe Streets Act). Section 14141 prohibits law enforcement agencies from engaging in a pattern or practice of conduct that violates the Constitution or laws of the United States. Title VI and its implementing regulations and the Safe Streets Act prohibit law enforcement practices that have a disparate impact based on protected status, such as race or ethnicity, unless these practices are necessary to achieve legitimate, non-discriminatory objectives.

This investigation was initiated as Chicago grappled with the aftermath of the release of a video showing a white police officer fatally shooting black teenager Laquan McDonald. This aftermath included protests, murder charges for the involved officer, and the resignation of Chicago's police superintendent. The McDonald incident was widely viewed as a tipping point—igniting longstanding concerns about CPD officers' use of force, and the City's systems for detecting and correcting the unlawful use of force.

Over the year-plus since release of that video, and while we have been conducting this investigation, Chicago experienced a surge in shootings and homicides. The reasons for this spike are broadly debated and inarguably

1

complex. But on two points there is little debate. First, for decades, certain neighborhoods on Chicago's South and West Sides have been disproportionately ravaged by gun violence. Those same neighborhoods have borne the brunt of the recent surge of violence. And second, for Chicago to find solutions—short- and long-term—for making those neighborhoods safe, it is imperative that the City rebuild trust between CPD and the people it serves, particularly in these communities. The City and CPD acknowledge that this trust has been broken, despite the diligent efforts and brave actions of countless CPD officers. It has been broken by systems that have allowed CPD officers who violate the law to escape accountability. This breach in trust has in turn eroded CPD's ability to effectively prevent crime; in other words, trust and effectiveness in combating violent crime are inextricably intertwined.

The aim of this investigation was to conduct a thorough, independent, and fair assessment of CPD's and IPRA's practices. To accomplish this goal, we relied on several sources of information.

First, we reviewed thousands of pages of documents provided to us by CPD, IPRA, and the City, including policies, procedures, training plans, Department orders and memos, internal and external reports, and more. We also obtained access to the City's entire misconduct complaint database and data from all reports filled out following officers' use of force. From there, we reviewed a randomized, representative sample of force reports and investigative files for incidents that occurred between January 2011 and April 2016, as well as additional incident reports and investigations. Overall, we reviewed over 170 officer-involved shooting investigations, and documents related to over 425 incidents of less-lethal force.

We also spent extensive time in Chicago—over 300 person-days—meeting with community members and City officials, and interviewing current and former CPD officers and IPRA investigators. In addition to speaking with the Superintendent and other CPD leadership, we met with the command staff of several specialized units, divisions, and departments. We toured CPD's training facilities and observed training programs. We also visited each of Chicago's 22 police districts, where we addressed roll call, spoke with command staff and officers, and conducted over 60 ride-alongs with officers. We met several times with Chicago's officer union, Lodge No. 7 of the Fraternal Order of Police, as well as the sergeants', lieutenants', and captains' unions. All told, we heard from over 340 individual CPD members, and 23 members of IPRA's staff.

Our findings were also significantly informed by our conversations with members of the Chicago community. We met with over ninety community organizations, including non-profits, advocacy and legal organizations, and faith-based groups focused on a wide range of issues. We participated in several community forums in different neighborhoods throughout Chicago where we heard directly from the family members of individuals who were killed by CPD officers and others who shared their insights and experiences. We also met with several local researchers, academics, and lawyers who have studied CPD extensively for decades. Most importantly, however, we heard directly from individuals who live and work throughout the City about their interactions with CPD officers. Overall, we talked to approximately a thousand community members. We received nearly 600 phone calls, emails, and letters from individuals who were eager to provide their experiences and insights.

In addition to attorneys, paralegals, outreach specialists, and data analysts from the Civil Rights Division of the United States Department of Justice and the United States Attorney's Office for the Northern District of Illinois, 11 independent subject-matter experts assisted with this investigation. Most of these experts are current or former law enforcement officials from police departments across the country. Accordingly, these experts have decades of expertise in areas such as the use of force, accountability, training, supervision, community policing, officer-involved domestic violence and sexual misconduct, officer wellness, and more. These experts accompanied us on-site, reviewed documents and investigative files, and provided invaluable insights that informed both the course of this investigation and its conclusions.

During the year it took us to complete this investigation, the City of Chicago took action of its own. Following the release of dashboard-camera video capturing the death of Laquan McDonald, Mayor Rahm Emanuel established the Police Accountability Task Force (PATF). The Mayor charged the PATF with assessing the Police Department and making recommendations for change in five areas: community relations; oversight and accountability; de-escalation; early intervention and personnel concerns; and video release protocols. In April 2016, the PATF issued a report with over a hundred recommendations for improving transparency and accountability. In December of 2016, the City issued a progress report outlining the steps it has taken since April to meet the recommendations made by the PATF.

Perhaps most significantly, the City passed an ordinance creating the Civilian Office of Police Accountability (COPA), which is scheduled to replace IPRA in 2017. The ordinance also establishes a Deputy Inspector General for Public Safety, who is charged with auditing the entire police accountability system and identifying patterns that violate residents' constitutional rights. In June of 2016, the City issued a new "transparency policy" mandating the release of videos and other materials related to certain officer misconduct investigations. CPD also pledged to establish an anonymous hotline for CPD members to report misconduct; began an ambitious process to develop an early intervention system; and developed a draft disciplinary matrix to guide CPD in assigning appropriate discipline for various misconduct violations.

The City embarked on other initiatives during our investigation that are intended to improve policing in Chicago. In early 2016, the City began a pilot program for body-worn cameras, and reported recently that the expansion of the program will be accelerated so that all officers will be wearing these cameras by the end of 2017. In the last few months, CPD began an important force mitigation/de-escalation training course for officers, and revised several policies related to use of force. The City also committed to providing additional training on how officers and emergency dispatchers respond to individuals in mental health crisis, and to improving CPD's training more broadly. As part of its efforts to engage community members and improve police-community relations, the City established a Community Policing Advisory Panel that will help develop a new strategic plan for community policing. The City is also undertaking recruitment efforts aimed at increasing CPD's diversity, and recently retained a consultant to complete a staffing analysis to inform deployment decisions Department-wide.

Many of these planned or implemented reforms are discussed in detail in this Report, alongside our assessment of their impact on the problems our investigation found, and whether CPD and the City need to go further.

As noted, while our investigation was underway and the City moved forward with some reforms, Chicago experienced an unprecedented surge in shootings and homicides. In 2016, there were 762 homicides, nearly 300 more than the previous year and, according to the draft of a new study from the University of Chicago Crime Lab, the largest single-year homicide increase of the last 25 years among the five most populous United States cities. Overall, there were 3,550 shootings, with 4,331 shooting victims, in Chicago in 2016, approximately 1,100 more than in 2015. While shootings and homicides occurred in all parts of the City, they were largely concentrated in Chicago's South Side and West Side neighborhoods. Homicide clearance rates, the rate at which police identify the suspected killer, continued their years-long slide, with CPD clearing only 29% of all homicides, less than half the national clearance rate.

During our investigation, DOJ has enhanced its assistance with CPD's reform and violence-reduction efforts. DOJ has allocated additional funding to CPD to support its efforts, provided technical assistance, and continued and expanded its cooperation through DOJ's Violence Reduction Network (VRN), an innovative approach to support and enhance local violence reduction efforts. Since December 2014, CPD and DOJ, through the United States Attorney's Office in Chicago, have hosted nine Community Trust Roundtables across Chicago's most violence-plagued neighborhoods. These recent efforts build on the foundation of DOJ's longstanding collaborative initiatives with CPD.

It has never been more important to rebuild trust for the police within Chicago's neighborhoods most challenged by violence, poverty, and unemployment. As discussed below and throughout our Report, Chicago must undergo broad, fundamental reform to restore this trust. This will be difficult, but will benefit both the public and CPD's own officers. The increased trust these reforms will build is necessary to solve and prevent violent crime. And the conduct and practices that restore trust will also carry out an equally important public service: demonstrating to communities racked with violence that their police force cares about them and has not abandoned them, regardless of where they live or the color of their skin. That confidence is broken in many neighborhoods in Chicago.

At the same time, many CPD officers feel abandoned by the public and often by their own Department. We found profoundly low morale nearly every place we went within CPD. Officers generally feel that they are insufficiently trained and supported to do their work effectively. Our investigation indicates that both CPD's lawfulness and effectiveness can be vastly improved if the City and CPD make the changes necessary to consistently incentivize and reward effective, ethical, and active policing. While it will take time and concerted focus to implement all of the necessary changes, a strong sign of a genuine and unalterable commitment to such change could increase officer morale more quickly, especially among the countless good officers within CPD who police diligently every day, and who disapprove of some officer conduct they see—and many of whom quietly told us how eager they are for the kind of change that can come only from an investigation like the one we have just completed. It is within this current climate, and with these challenges in mind, that we conducted our investigation and make the following findings.

Force

We reviewed CPD's force practices mindful that officers routinely place themselves in harm's way in order to uphold their commitment to serve and protect the people of the City of Chicago, and that officers regularly encounter individuals who may be armed and determined to avoid arrest. We likewise recognize that officers have not only a right, but an obligation, to protect themselves and others from threats of harm, including deadly harm, which may arise in an instant.

But even within this context, we, in consultation with several active law enforcement experts, found that CPD officers engage in a pattern or practice of using force, including deadly force, that is unreasonable. We found further that CPD officers' force practices unnecessarily endanger themselves and others and result in unnecessary and avoidable shootings and other uses of force.

As discussed throughout this Report, this pattern is largely attributable to systemic deficiencies within CPD and the City. CPD has not provided officers with adequate guidance to understand how and when they may use force, or how to safely and effectively control and resolve encounters to reduce the need to use force. CPD also has failed to hold officers accountable when they use force contrary to CPD policy or otherwise commit misconduct. This failure to hold officers accountable results in some officers remaining with the Department when they should have been relieved of duty. These officers often continue their misconduct including, at times, again using unreasonable deadly force. More broadly, these failures result in officers not having the skills or tools necessary to use force wisely and lawfully, and they send a dangerous message to officers and the public that unreasonable force by CPD officers will be tolerated. We found further that CPD's failure to meaningfully and routinely review or investigate officer use of force is a significant factor in perpetuating the practices that result in the pattern of unlawful conduct we found. Each of these causal factors is discussed further in this Summary and the accompanying Report.

Our finding that CPD engages in a pattern or practice of force in violation of the Constitution is based on a comprehensive investigation of CPD's force practices and a close analysis of hundreds of individual force incidents. We reviewed CPD's policies related to the use, reporting, and investigation of force, including older versions of polices that were effective during our review period, and CPD's proposed revised policies. We spoke with officers at all ranks, including the Superintendent and the Chief and Deputy Chief of the Bureau of Patrol, to understand how officers are trained to use force, their view of when force is appropriate, and how the policies are interpreted in practice throughout CPD. We also did an in-depth review of officer reports of force, civilian complaints of force, and CPD's and IPRA's review of force, and investigations of allegations of excessive force. We reviewed all documents we were provided related to over 425 incidents of less-lethal force, including representative samples of officers' own reports of force, and of investigations of civilian complaints about officer force between January 2011 and April 2016. We also reviewed over 170 files related to officer-involved shootings.

The pattern of unlawful force we found resulted from a collection of poor police practices that our investigation indicated are used routinely within CPD. We found that officers engage in tactically unsound and unnecessary foot pursuits, and that these foot pursuits too often end with officers unreasonably shooting someone—including unarmed individuals. We found that officers shoot at vehicles without justification and in contradiction to CPD policy. We found further that officers exhibit poor discipline when discharging their weapons and engage in tactics that endanger themselves and public safety, including failing to await backup when they safely could and should; using unsound tactics in approaching vehicles; and using their own vehicles in a manner that is dangerous. These are issues that can and must be better addressed through training, accountability and ultimately cultural change.

Among the most egregious uses of deadly force we reviewed were incidents in which CPD officers shot at suspects who presented no immediate threat. CPD's use of less-lethal force also contributes to the pattern of unlawful conduct we found. We reviewed instances of CPD using less-lethal force, often Tasers, including in drive-stun mode, against people who posed no threat, and using unreasonable retaliatory force and unreasonable force against children. We found also that CPD officers use force against people in mental health crisis where force might have been avoided. These issues are further discussed, along with specific examples, in the Force Section of this Report.

CPD does not investigate or review these force incidents to determine whether its responses to these events were appropriate or lawful, or whether force could have been avoided. The City is currently taking steps to improve its response to persons in mental health or behavioral crisis, in part in response to the tragic shootings deaths of Quintonio LeGrier and Bettie Jones. While we applaud the steps the City has taken, as discussed in our Report, there are important additional steps the City needs to take. The City must do more to ensure that effective, well-trained "crisis intervention" officers respond to these events, and that mental-health or similar crises are analyzed to determine whether changes to the program or CPD's crisis response are warranted.

We found many circumstances in which officers' accounts of force incidents were later discredited, in whole or part, by video evidence. Given the numerous use-of-force incidents without video evidence, discussed further in Section II.C. of this Report, the pattern of unreasonable force is likely even more widespread than we were able to discern through our investigation.

In light of these incidents and many more like them, we support the City's decision to accelerate its plan to ensure that all CPD officers have body cameras so that all officers have them by the end of this year. While we urge the City to go forward with this plan, we hope the City will also heed the concerns set out later in our Report that it work with police unions and community groups on policies and protocols for body-camera usage, and that it develop the supervisory and accountability supports necessary to ensure that body cameras are effective, both at preventing misconduct and exonerating officers where they are wrongfully accused.

Our review further determined that CPD and IPRA do not adequately respond to incidents in which officers used unreasonable or unnecessary force—including force that resulted in a person's death and the officer's stated justification was at odds with the physical evidence. Although IPRA's deficiencies—discussed in the Accountability Section of our Report—have played a central role in allowing patterns of unconstitutional force to persist, IPRA cannot eliminate the pattern of misconduct we found unless CPD's force reporting and investigations change fundamentally as well. As an initial matter, formal and functional gaps in IPRA's jurisdiction mean that many incidents are inadequately investigated or not investigated at all. Where IPRA does act on its jurisdiction, we found that IPRA's ability to fairly investigate force pursuant to its mandate is compromised by deficiencies in how CPD reports force and gathers related evidence immediately after a force incident.

CPD policy requires officers to report force but, in practice, officers are not required to provide detail about the force they used that is sufficient for an adequate review, and most officer force is not reviewed or investigated. Although shootings where a person is struck are investigated, as discussed in the Accountability Section, those investigations are inadequate. As a result of so few force incidents being even nominally investigated, and the low quality of the force investigations that do occur, there is no meaningful, systemic accountability for officers who use force in violation of the law or CPD policy. Nor is there any opportunity for meaningful assessment of whether policies, training, or equipment should be modified to improve force outcomes in the future for officers or civilians. The failure to review and investigate officer use of force has helped create a culture in which officers expect to use force and not be questioned about the need for or propriety of that use. In this way, CPD's failure to adequately review officer use of force on a regular basis has combined with CPD's failure to properly train and supervise officers to perpetuate a pattern of unlawful use of force within CPD.

The City has acknowledged and begun to correct a number of deficiencies related to how officers use and are held accountable for force. In March 2016, CPD began a review of its force policies in an effort to provide clearer direction to officers on the appropriate use of force. CPD released the draft force policies in October 2016 for public comment. The proposed revisions address core force principles such as the sanctity of life; ethical behavior; objective and proportional use of force; use of deadly force; de-escalation; and force mitigation. CPD is reviewing the public feedback and, at the time of this drafting, "will in the very near future incorporate suggestions and improvements to prepare final versions of the policies." CPD also has begun providing all officers with force-mitigation training designed to better equip officers to de-escalate conflicts safely; recognize the signs of mental illness, trauma and crisis situations; and respond quickly and appropriately when force is necessary.

These steps are meaningful and important. But to fulfill their promise, this new approach to CPD use of force must be supported by leadership and enforced by supervisors. Moreover, they must be accompanied by changes to how force is reported and reviewed, not only so that officers can be held accountable when they misuse force, but so that CPD can learn from force incidents and make the policy, training, and equipment changes necessary to make officers and the public safer and more secure.

Accountability

Police accountability systems are vital to lawful policing. In combination with effective supervision, a robust accountability system helps identify, correct and ultimately prevent unreasonable and unnecessary uses of force. We also investigated the City's police accountability systems and their effectiveness in identifying police misconduct and holding officers responsible.

The City received over 30,000 complaints of police misconduct during the five years preceding our investigation, but fewer than 2% were sustained, resulting in no discipline in 98% of these complaints. This is a low sustained rate. In evaluating the City's accountability structures, we looked beneath these and other disconcerting statistics and attempted to diagnose the cause of the low sustained rates by examining the systems in place, the resources, and leadership involved with the City's accountability bodies, including CPD's Bureau of Internal Affairs (BIA), IPRA, and the Chicago Police Board. We reviewed their policies and practices, interviewed many current and former supervisors, investigators, and other members involved, and we reviewed hundreds of force and misconduct investigative files from an accountability standpoint. We discovered numerous entrenched, systemic policies and practices that undermine police accountability, as described below. We also took into account that the City has taken many steps during our investigation to address many of these accountability deficiencies, including creating COPA, which will replace IPRA as the independent agency responsible for investigating serious police misconduct. Although we commend the City for these and other recent reforms, they do not sufficiently address many of problems we discovered in the City's deeply flawed investigative system.

The City does not investigate the majority of cases it is required by law to investigate. Most of those cases are uninvestigated because they lack a supporting affidavit from the complaining party, but the City also fails to investigate anonymous and older misconduct complaints as well as those alleging lower level force and non-racial verbal abuse. Finally, and also contrary to legal mandates, IPRA does not investigate most Taser discharges and officer-involved shootings where no one is hit. Some of these investigations are ignored based on procedural hurdles in City agreements with its unions, but some are unilateral decisions by the accountability agencies to reduce case-loads and manage resources. And many misconduct complaints that avoid these investigative barriers are still not fully investigated because they are re-solved through a defective mediation process, which is actually a plea bargain system used to dispose of serious misconduct claims in exchange for modest discipline. Regardless of the reasons, this failure to fully investigate almost half of all police misconduct cases seriously undermines accountability. These are all lost opportunities to identify misconduct, training deficiencies, and problematic trends, and to hold officers and CPD accountable when miscon-duct occurs. In order to address these ignored cases, the City must modify its own policies, and work with the unions to address certain CBA provisions, and in the meantime, it must aggressively investigate all complaints to the extent authorized under these contracts.

Those cases that are investigated suffer from serious investigative flaws that obstruct objective fact finding. Civilian and officer witnesses, and even the accused officers, are frequently not interviewed during an investigation. The potential for inappropriate coordination of testimony, risk of collusion, and witness coaching during interviews is built into the system, occurs routinely, and is not considered by investigators in evaluating the case. The question-ing of officers is often cursory and aimed at eliciting favorable statements justifying the officer's actions rather than seeking truth. Questioning is often marked by a failure to challenge inconsistencies and illogical officer explana-tions, as well as leading questions favorable to the officer. Investigators rou-tinely fail to review and incorporate probative evidence from parallel civil and criminal proceedings based on the same police incident. And consistent with these biased investigative techniques, the investigator's summary reports are often drafted in a manner favorable to the officer by omitting conflicts in testimony or with physical evidence that undermine the officer's justification or by exaggerating evidence favorable to the officer, all of which frustrates a reviewer's ability to evaluate for investigative quality and thoroughness.

Investigative fact-finding into police misconduct and attempts to hold of-ficers accountable are also frustrated by police officers' code of silence. The City, police officers, and leadership within CPD and its police officer union acknowledge that a code of silence among Chicago police officers exists, ex-tending to lying and affirmative efforts to conceal evidence. Officers who may be inclined to cover up misconduct will be deterred from doing so if they understand that honesty is the most crucial component of their job and that the Department will aggressively seek to identify dishonest officers and appropriately discipline them. However, our investigation found that IPRA and BIA treat such efforts to hide evidence as ancillary and unexcep-tional misconduct, and often do not investigate it, causing officers to believe there is not much to lose if they lie to cover up misconduct. Investigators employ a higher standard to sustain claims against officers for making false statements under what is known as a Rule 14 charge and they rarely expand their investigations to charge accused and witness officers with lying to cover up misconduct. Nor, until recently, has the City focused much attention on officers' efforts to conceal by mishandling video and audio equipment or by retaliating against civilians who witness misconduct. The City's failure to prioritize Rule 14 investigations must change. When it is aware of information that an officer lied or otherwise covered up misconduct, the City must actively and aggressively investigate and consistently seek to discipline officers who do so.

We found that inadequate staffing contributes both to these investigative flaws and to the City's decisions to forego or short-circuit so many of the investigations it should be handling. The City has recently committed to providing more funding to IPRA when it becomes COPA, and the agency has already begun to hire additional staff. But COPA's range of responsibilities will also be much broader than IPRA's, and there has not been sufficient analysis to determine whether COPA will have the capacity to do any better than IPRA. We also found that poor training accounted for some of these investigative deficiencies. Investigators and leadership at IPRA acknowledged investigative training was inadequate, and IPRA/COPA is developing plans to revamp and increase training for all staff, especially investigators. While we commend IPRA for this reform, improved training is likewise necessary for BIA investigators as well. Such enhanced training is an important step towards improving the quality of misconduct investigations handled and changing the culture to one that is more determined to resolve investigations and reliably determine whether an officer committed misconduct. However, the depth and breadth of that training is unclear. It should not only cover general investigative techniques, but should include training to eliminate biased investigative techniques as well as training in specific areas, including unlawful entry and seizure, domestic violence and sexual assault, and false statement charges under Rule 14.

In the rare instances when complaints of misconduct are sustained, we found that discipline is haphazard and unpredictable, and is meted out in a way that does little to deter misconduct. Officers are often disciplined for conduct far less serious than the conduct that prompted the investigation, and in many cases, a complaint may be sustained, but the officer is not disciplined at all. The police discipline system, including the City's draft disciplinary matrix, fails to provide clear guidance on appropriate, fair, and consistent penalty ranges, thus undermining the legitimacy and deterrent effect of discipline within CPD.

Finally, we also found deficiencies with the Chicago Police Board's systems, which impair its ability to be an effective component of CPD's accountability structure. The Board should focus on improving its civil service commission function of providing due process to officers accused of misconduct and relinquish its role of providing community input into CPD's accountability system to the Community Oversight Board that the City has committed to creating. The fairness of Police Board hearings can be improved by modifying current rules that bar the officer's "negative" disciplinary history but allow the officer's "complimentary" history as well as favorable character evidence offered by the accused's supervisors. The City can further level the playing field by providing more experienced advocates to represent CPD before the Board and by offering better training for Board members. Allowing Board members to hear evidence directly, instead of a second-hand summary from the hearing officer, and increasing the Board's transparency will further instill community confidence in the Police Board.

Training and Supervision

CPD's pattern of unlawful conduct is due in part to deficiencies in CPD's training and supervision. CPD does not provide officers or supervisors with adequate training and does not encourage or facilitate adequate supervision of officers in the field. These shortcomings in training and supervision result in officers who are unprepared to police lawfully and effectively; supervisors who do not mentor or support constitutional policing by officers; and a systemic inability to proactively identify areas for improvement, including Department-wide training needs and interventions for officers engaging in misconduct.

Both at the outset and through the duration of their careers, CPD officers do not receive the quality or quantity of training necessary for their jobs. Pre-service Academy training relies on outmoded teaching methods and materials, and does not equip recruits with the skills, knowledge, and confidence necessary to serve Chicago communities. For example, we observed an Academy training on deadly force—an important topic, given our findings regarding CPD's use of force—that consisted of a video made decades ago, which was inconsistent with both current law and CPD's own policies. The impact of this poor training was apparent when we interviewed recruits who recently graduated from the Academy: only one in six recruits we spoke with came close to properly articulating the legal standard for use of force. Post-Academy field training is equally flawed. The Field Training Officer (FTO) Program, as currently structured, does not attract a sufficient number of qualified, effective leaders to train new probationary police officers (PPOs), has an insufficient number of FTOs to meet demand, and fails to provide PPOs with appropriate training, mentorship, and oversight. Finally, in-service training is not provided pursuant to any long-term training plan or strategy. Instead, CPD provides only sporadic in-service training, and does not think proactively about training needs Department-wide. Without a long-term training plan, CPD is often called upon to deliver ad-hoc trainings on tight timelines in response to crises. Consequently, in-service trainings are often incomplete and ineffective at teaching officers important skills and information. The recently-mandated Department-wide Taser training exemplifies CPD's problematic approach to in-service training. Large numbers of officers were cycled through this important training quickly in order to meet a deadline set by the City, without proper curriculum, staff, or equipment. This left many officers who completed the training uncomfortable with how to use Tasers effectively as a less-lethal force option—the very skill the training was supposed to teach.

The City recognizes the need for comprehensive reform of its training program. Its plans for reform are discussed in this Report. While laudable, these plans are still preliminary and amount to verbal commitments with uncertain dates for completion. Academy curriculum revisions, restructuring of the field training program, and development of a proactive, well-planned in-service training program are all needed. CPD must also evaluate whether it has the staff, equipment, and physical space to meet the training demands of the Department, and if not, proactively plan for how to meet training needs going forward. CPD must identify the resources necessary to make these changes, and obtain commitment from the City to provide what is needed.

We found that deficiencies in officer training are exacerbated by the lack of adequate supervision CPD provides to officers in the field, which further contributes to CPD's pattern or practice of unconstitutional policing. CPD does not sufficiently encourage or facilitate supervisors to provide meaningful supervision to officers. Overall, CPD does not hold supervisors accountable for performing certain basic supervisory tasks, including guiding officer behavior or reporting misconduct. Additionally, structural deficiencies in how CPD organizes supervision prevent effective oversight of officer activities. CPD requires supervisors to engage in non-supervisory tasks and manage too many officers at a time. CPD also structures its shift system in such a way that supervisors do not consistently work with the same groups of officers, which inhibits supervisors from learning the needs of officers under their watch. And, much like the deficiencies in CPD's officer training, CPD does not adequately train supervisors on how to provide appropriate supervision. Compounding its supervision problems, CPD does not have a meaningful early intervention system (EIS) to effectively assist supervisors in identifying and correcting problematic behavior. CPD's current behavior intervention systems are underused and inadequate, putting both officers and the public at risk.

Providing robust, meaningful supervision would not only better prevent officer misconduct, it would help CPD better prevent crime in the community. The City and CPD leadership must make the necessary reforms to supervision to protect public and officer safety.

Officer Wellness and Safety

Policing is a high-stress profession. Law enforcement officers often are called upon to deal with violence or crises as problem solvers, and they often are witnesses to human tragedy. In Chicago, this stress is particularly acute, for several reasons. Increasing levels of gun violence and neighborhood conditions take their toll on officers as well as residents. At the same time, the relationship between CPD officers and the communities they serve is strained; officers on the street are expected to prevent crime, yet they must also be the face of the Department in communities that have lost trust in the police. This makes it particularly difficult to police effectively. And these stresses animate the interactions officers have with the communities that they serve—both positively and negatively. As one CPD counselor explained, it is the "stress of the job that's the precursor to the crisis."

Our investigation found that these stressors can, and do, play out in harmful ways for CPD officers. CPD deals with officer alcoholism, domestic violence, and suicide. And as explained elsewhere in this Report, CPD officers engage in a pattern or practice of using force that is unjustified, disproportionate, and otherwise excessive. Although the pressure CPD officers are under is by no means an excuse for violating the constitutional rights of the citizens they serve, high levels of unaddressed stress can compromise officer well-being and impact an officer's demeanor and judgment, which in turn impacts how that officer interacts with the public. Some officers are able to manage the stress by shifting their focus to working even harder to do their jobs well. For others, it is more difficult. As these officers struggle with the stress of the job, they can close off and push away those they serve and those who want to help. As noted by the President's Task Force on 21st Century Policing, "an officer whose capabilities, judgment, and behavior are adversely affected by poor physical or psychological health not only may be of little use to the community he or she serves but also may be a danger to the community and to other officers." For precisely these reasons, law enforcement agencies can and should do everything they can to support officers' physical and psychological well-being.

Because of how officer wellness can impact officer behavior, and the uniquely tense circumstances facing CPD officers each day, CPD officers need greater support from the City and CPD leadership. CPD and the City should think meaningfully about how to better address the stressors CPD officers face, and how to create an overarching operational plan that includes robust counseling programs, comprehensive training, functioning equipment, and other tools to ensure officers are successful and healthy. CPD should move away from traditional strategies that fail to fully address the issue of officer wellness and react to the changing nature of policing in Chicago and the demographic changes in CPD's police force. CPD needs to transform its officer support system so that officer wellness is an integral part of the Department's operations and reinforces the values of wellness and a culture that encourages officers to seek assistance when needed. CPD also should work to overcome officers' concern that using officer wellness services will negatively impact their career, and to educate officers on the value of these services. In this way, CPD can better support its officers' success, personally and professionally.

Data Collection and Transparency

A lack of transparency regarding CPD's and IPRA's activities has contributed to CPD's failure to identify and correct unlawful practices and to distrust between CPD and the public. Since the start of our investigation, the City and CPD have instituted steps aimed at increasing transparency regarding CPD's and IPRA's work. For example, the current IPRA Chief Administrator significantly improved IPRA's public reporting by expanding the amount of information regarding misconduct investigations that is regularly posted on IPRA's website. And, following the PATF's recommendation, the City adopted a "transparency policy," which created a portal on IPRA's website where video and other evidence of certain types of police misconduct investigations are posted. These steps go beyond the measures many other agencies put in place.

Our investigation found that additional steps are necessary to ensure the City is as transparent as possible and uses its data to adequately address the patterns and practices identified in this investigation. The City and CPD must improve the ways in which they collect, organize, analyze, track, and report on available data and data trends. Currently, CPD's data collection systems are siloed and do not allow for meaningful cross-system data collection, evaluation, and tracking. As a result, CPD is unable to easily use the data at its disposal to identify trends, including trends in misconduct complaints, training deficiencies, and more. Improving these systems will allow CPD to better understand its operations, and more easily report CPD activities to the public.

The data that is collected and publicly reported by the City is also incomplete, and at times, inaccurate. IPRA reports only on how investigations are resolved by that agency; but, as discussed in this Report, the findings of IPRA investigators can be set aside, and its discipline recommendations greatly reduced. IPRA's reporting, therefore, does not give a full picture of how misconduct investigations are ultimately resolved. Independent evaluation of IPRA's publicly reported data regarding use of force found that the data was, at least historically, inaccurate. And, even though IPRA's public reporting is far more comprehensive now than it was before, CPD does not aggregate or publish the same information for investigations handled by BIA and the districts. Currently, very little information is published about those investigations, even though those entities handle roughly 70% of all misconduct complaints. Finally, the City should also release more information regarding settlements of officer misconduct lawsuits; publicly available data is, at present, limited to the general nature of the allegation (e.g., "excessive force" or "false arrest") and the settlement amount.

Finally, the City should actively engage the public in crafting solutions in this area. Recent public engagement efforts, such as soliciting public feedback on the video release policy, COPA ordinance, and new use-of-force policies, were important steps toward increasing solicitation of public input into contemplated reforms. Improving and expanding upon these recent initiatives will ensure that the public understands and supports, to the greatest extent possible, the additional reforms currently being considered by the City.

Promotions

Dedicated, highly qualified supervisors are vital to ensuring CPD officers are able to police safely while valuing and respecting the rights of all community members. Under CPD's current promotions system, officers can be promoted to detective, sergeant, or lieutenant based on test scores or evaluation of other merit-based criteria. The merit-based promotion track was created following several lawsuits challenging CPD's promotional exams as discriminatory. The merit promotions system was then later challenged, as part of larger litigation regarding City hiring practices, as unfairly promoting individuals based on political connections rather than true merit. All of these legal battles resulted in several important reforms, including the creation of a City Hiring Plan and corresponding policies intended to organize and structure the merit promotion process.

Despite these important reforms, however, officers we spoke with continue to express skepticism about CPD's promotions system. Much of this is because CPD does not effectively communicate the details of its promotions process to the rank-and-file, and does not provide sufficient transparency following promotional decisions to allay officer concerns. For example, officers are unaware of the metrics used to evaluate individuals who are nominated for merit promotions, or why the officers receiving those promotions were selected. By not sharing this information publicly, and not ensuring Department-wide understanding of the promotions system, CPD has perpetuated an atmosphere of doubt around the promotions process as a whole.

CPD can and should do several things to restore officer and public confidence in its promotions system, and to ensure that the best-qualified candidates are promoted in a fair, lawful, and transparent manner. Promotional exams must be reviewed regularly to ensure they are fair and lawful, and offered often enough to ensure well-qualified candidates have the opportunity to be promoted. Monitoring and oversight of compliance with CPD's merit promotion policies are also necessary to ensure those systems are working as intended, and that merit promotion decisions are as transparent as possible. Without regular review and increased transparency, CPD's promotion processes will continue to be viewed as unfair and ineffective.

Community-Focused Policing

A contributing factor to CPD's unreasonable use of force is CPD's approach to policing. CPD as a whole needs to support and provide incentives to policing practices that are lawful and restore trust among the City's marginalized communities. Within the past several months, CPD and the City have announced ambitious plans to revive community policing in Chicago. Superintendent Johnson has formed a Community Policing Advisory Panel to develop strategies for enhancing community policing within CPD. The Superintendent has pledged to remake the Department's Chicago Alternative Policing Strategy (CAPS), and the Department recently issued a directive expanding community involvement programs in several districts. CPD has several additional community policing-related initiatives underway. We commend CPD for these efforts. This policing approach, when implemented with fidelity to all its tenets, has been shown to be effective at making communities safer while incentivizing a policing culture that builds confidence in law enforcement.

Notwithstanding this recognition, community policing as a true CPD value and driving force fell away in Chicago many years ago, and past attempts to restore it have not been successful. To be successful this time, CPD must build up systems to support and bolster this community-focused approach to policing.

CPD has the officers it needs to make community policing work. During our investigation we observed many instances of diligent, thoughtful, and selfless policing, and we heard stories of officers who police this way every day. We know that there are many dedicated CPD officers who care deeply about the community, are affected by the violence they see, and work hard to build trust between the community and the Department. We heard about officers and command staff who are well-respected and beloved in the neighborhoods they patrol.

But for community policing to really take hold and succeed in Chicago, CPD must ensure that its supervision, training, promotions and account-ability systems incentivize and support officers who police in a manner that conveys to community members that CPD officers can be a trusted partner in protecting them, their families, and their neighborhoods. Community policing must be a core philosophy that is infused throughout the Department's policing strategies and tactics.

In recent years, community policing in Chicago has been relegated, through CAPS, to a small group of police officers and civilians in each district. We were told by CAPS staff that CAPS offices were understaffed, and that CAPS officers receive little training on how to accomplish their mandate. Community policing efforts are also poorly funded and institutionally neglected.

In addition to infusing the tenets of community policing throughout the Department, and creating support for community policing beyond the CAPS program, CPD must also change its policing practices so that it can restore trust and ensure lawful policing. The Department has to do more to ensure that officers police fairly in neighborhoods with high rates of violent crime, and in vulnerable communities. A striking feature of our conversations with members from Chicago's challenged communities was the consistency with which they expressed concern about the lack of respect in their interactions with police, whether those interactions come when they are targets of po-lice activity or when they or their family members are the victims of crime. Advocates and members of the Latino, Muslim, and transgender communi-ties each separately raised concerns with us about the Department's response to potential or apparent hate crimes against members of their communities. There was also a sense that CPD relies too heavily on specialized units, such as Tactical (TACT).

This may not be how CPD intends policing to be conducted or perceived in these neighborhoods, but these experiences impact individual dignity and residents' willingness to work with law enforcement, and should not be ignored. CPD must ensure that it is creating incentives and rewarding policing where building community trust is central to all crime-prevention efforts, whether this policing is done by specialized units, beat officers, or CAPS staff.

Additionally, the City must address serious concerns about systemic de-ficiencies that disproportionately impact black and Latino communities.

CPD's pattern or practice of unreasonable force and systemic deficiencies fall heaviest on the predominantly black and Latino neighborhoods on the South and West Sides of Chicago, which are also experiencing higher crime. Raw statistics show that CPD uses force almost ten times more often against blacks than against whites. As a result, residents in black neighborhoods suffer more of the harms caused by breakdowns in uses of force, training, supervision, accountability, and community policing.

Our investigation found also that CPD has tolerated racially discriminatory conduct that not only undermines police legitimacy, but also contributes to the pattern of unreasonable force. The pattern or practice of unreasonable force, coupled with the recurrence of unaddressed racially discriminatory conduct by officers further erodes community trust and police effectiveness. Our review of complaints of racially discriminatory language found repeated instances where credible complaints were not adequately addressed. Moreover, we found that some Chicago police officers expressed discriminatory views and intolerance with regard to race, religion, gender, and national origin in public social media forums, and that CPD takes insufficient steps to prevent or appropriately respond to this animus. As CPD works to restore trust and ensure that policing is lawful and effective, it must recognize the extent to which this type of misconduct contributes to a culture that facilitates unreasonable force and corrodes community trust. We have serious concerns about the prevalence of racially discriminatory conduct by some CPD officers and the degree to which that conduct is tolerated and in some respects caused by deficiencies in CPD's systems of training, supervision and accountability. In light of these concerns, combined with the fact that the impact of CPD's pattern or practice of unreasonable force fall heaviest on predominantly black and Latino neighborhoods, restoring police-community trust will require remedies addressing both discriminatory conduct and the disproportionality of illegal and unconstitutional patterns of force on minority communities.

Finally, during our investigation, we heard allegations that CPD officers attempt to gain information about crime using methods that undermine CPD legitimacy and may also be unlawful. In some instances, we were told, CPD will attempt to glean information about gang activity or other crime by arresting or detaining individuals, and refusing to release the individual until he provides that information. In other instances, CPD will take a young person to a rival gang neighborhood, and either leave the person there, or display the youth to rival members, immediately putting the life of that young person in jeopardy by suggesting he has provided information to the police. Our investigation indicates that these practices in fact exist and significantly jeopardize CPD's relationship with the community.

CPD must root out these practices that harm CPD's interaction with the community. Doing so will better support lawful policing, and allow CPD to gain legitimacy in the eyes of the public and more effectively address crime. With a community-focused approach that incentivizes and rewards officers for policing actively and in a manner that builds strong, positive community relationships, CPD will be better able to carry out its mission lawfully and effectively.

* * *

Finally, we find that, notwithstanding the City's recent efforts to address the broad problems within the Chicago Police Department, it is not likely to be successful in doing so without a consent decree with independent monitoring. Fixing the problems our investigation found will be neither easy nor quick. The root causes of these patterns of conduct and systemic deficiencies are complicated and entrenched, which is why they have persisted for so long despite repeated, concerted reform efforts by the City and community members from all walks. As Chicago's Mayor said in stating his intention to cooperate with our investigation, "We need a third party in this City because in the past instances . . . we've never, ever as a City measured up with the changes on a sustained basis to finally deal in whole cloth with that situation."

We applaud the City for this recognition and for agreeing to negotiate a set of comprehensive reforms that will be entered as a federal court order and assessed by a team of independent experts in policing and related fields. Through this commitment, the City has signaled its willingness to go further than any previous City administration to ensure that necessary reforms to the Chicago Police Department are made and take root.

We agree that such an approach is necessary. Our investigation found that the reforms the City already plans to implement, as well as the additional reforms our investigation found necessary, will likely not happen or be sustained without the reform tools of an independent monitoring team and a court order. An independent team of policing and other experts will be charged with assessing and publicly reporting on CPD's and the City's progress implementing reforms. A court-ordered, over-arching plan for reform that is overseen by a federal judge will help ensure that unnecessary obstacles are removed, and that City and police officials stay focused on carrying out promised reforms. Together, an independent monitor and court decree will make it much more certain that Chicago is finally able to eliminate patterns of unconstitutional conduct, and can bolster community confidence to make policing in Chicago more effective and less dangerous.

I. BACKGROUND

❦

A. CHICAGO, ILLINOIS

Chicago is the largest city in Illinois and the third largest metropolitan area in the United States with approximately 9.5 million residents, 2.7 million of whom live within the city limits. The City is racially diverse: 33% of current residents are black, 32% are white, 29% are Latino, and 8% identify as Asian or multi-racial. The median household income in Chicago is $48,522, which is below the national average of $53,889. 22% of the City's residents live below the federal poverty threshold. The unemployment rate for individuals living in Chicago is 5.5%. Black and Latino Chicago residents are disproportionately poor when compared to white Chicago residents. Approximately 35% of black residents and 25% of Latinos live below the poverty line, compared to less than 11% of white residents. The mean household income for black residents is $30,400, as opposed to $61,500 for whites.

Chicago is governed by a Mayor, who is the chief executive, and the City Council, which is the legislative body. The City Council is made up of 50 Alderman elected from each of the 50 wards of Chicago. The City Council is led by a President Pro Tempore, currently Margaret Laurino. The current Mayor, Rahm Emanuel, was elected in 2011 and re-elected to a second term in 2015.

In 2015, Chicago reported 24,663 violent crime incidents. 9,649 of those crimes were robberies, and aggravated assaults constituted over 13,000 reported incidents. The City recorded 478 homicides that year. In 2016, there were 762 homicides in Chicago. According to the draft of a new study from the University of Chicago Crime Lab, this is the largest single-year homicide increase of the last 25 years among the five most populous United States cities.

B. CHICAGO POLICE DEPARTMENT

CPD is the primary law enforcement agency in the City and the second largest municipal police department in the United States. The Department is led by a Superintendent and a First Deputy Superintendent who reports directly to the Superintendent. The Mayor appoints the Superintendent of CPD with the advice and consent of the City Council. Mayor Emanuel appointed the current Superintendent, Eddie Johnson, in March 2016. As of June 2016, CPD employed approximately 12,000 sworn officers.

CPD is divided into four major bureaus: Patrol, Detectives, Organized Crimes, and Support Services. There are 22 different police districts in Chicago, and three geographic patrol "areas"—Area North, Area Central, and Area South. Each Area is led by a deputy chief who reports to the Chief of the Bureau of Patrol. Each district is led by a district commander who reports to the Area deputy chief. Each district also has specialty units, including gang, saturation, and tactical teams. All officers employed by CPD are required to live within City limits.

There are several unions in Chicago that represent the interests of CPD officers and supervisors. The Fraternal Order of Police, Chicago Lodge 7, is the CPD officers' union. Sergeants, lieutenants, and captains are all separately unionized under the Policeman's Benevolent & Protective Association of Illinois, Unit 156. Each union has a separate collective bargaining agreement (CBA) with the City. These CBAs include detailed provisions establishing certain terms and conditions of employment. Several CBA provisions relate to areas addressed by our investigation and are specifically discussed within this Report. The supervisors' unions are currently renegotiating their CBAs with the City. The officers' union will begin renegotiating its CBA this year.

C.   Chicago's Accountability Systems

CPD's systems for reviewing misconduct allegations are unique and are explained in more detail later in this Report. The Independent Police Review Authority (IPRA), which is external to CPD, serves as the intake agency for all complaints of police misconduct. In 2015, IPRA intake totaled more than 5,000 cases, which were predominantly complaints filed by community members or other officers within CPD.

IPRA is led by a chief administrator, who is appointed by the Mayor and confirmed by the City Council. The Mayor appointed the current Chief Administrator, Sharon Fairley, in December 2015. IPRA's budget is set by the City Council. IPRA employs a staff of roughly 80 civilian investigators, supervisory investigators, attorneys, and support staff.

IPRA only has jurisdiction to investigate certain types of misconduct, including allegations of excessive force, domestic violence, biased-based verbal abuse, coercion, weapons discharges, and deaths in custody. Accordingly, IPRA handles roughly 30% of all complaints of misconduct filed against CPD officers.

On October 5, 2016, the Chicago City Council passed an ordinance establishing the Civilian Office of Police Accountability (COPA), which will replace IPRA in 2017. Because COPA is not yet in existence, this Report focuses on the work of IPRA, but will note changes that are anticipated as a result of the COPA ordinance.

The majority of misconduct complaints do not fall within IPRA's jurisdiction and are referred to CPD's Bureau of Internal Affairs (BIA). BIA is led by Chief Eddie Welch III. There are over 90 sworn personnel assigned to BIA, including officers, sergeants, lieutenants, and one commander. BIA handles investigations related to officer-involved criminal conduct and various rule violations, including abuse of CPD medical leave and CPD's policy requiring that CPD officers live within City limits. BIA also assigns some misconduct complaints to district commanders for investigation.

Chicago has a Police Board made up of nine private citizens appointed by the Mayor with the City Council's consent. The Police Board is not an investigatory body. Rather, it participates in finalizing CPD disciplinary decisions both by presiding over evidentiary hearings in discharge cases and by resolving discipline disputes between IPRA and the Superintendent, as described further below.

There is also an Inspector General for the City of Chicago who serves as the "watchdog for the taxpayers of the City, and has jurisdiction to conduct investigations and audits into most aspects of City government," including some parts of CPD operations. And the police accountability ordinance established a new Deputy Inspector General for Public Safety charged with auditing the police accountability system and identifying patterns and practices that violate residents' constitutional rights.

D. HISTORICAL BACKGROUND OF REFORM IN CHICAGO

The Chicago Police Department has cycled in and out of the national consciousness almost since its inception, and the last several decades have been no exception. In 1968, images of CPD officers beating protestors at the Democratic National Convention were captured and broadcast on national television. A commission convened in the aftermath of the event found that the violence amounted to a "police riot." No officers were prosecuted. In the 1980s and 1990s, a CPD detective, Jon Burge, and several officers under his command used severe interrogation tactics, such as physical force, suffocations, and electric shocks, to coerce confessions from predominantly black men living on Chicago's South and West Sides. Burge was ultimately fired, and in 2008, decades after the abuse began, he was arrested on charges of perjury and obstruction of justice. He was convicted on all counts, but was allowed to keep his pension from CPD and served only four-and-a-half years in prison. In the 1990s, CPD ran a special enforcement unit within the Patrol Division called the Special Operations Section (SOS). This unit improperly stopped and searched black and Latino community members and seized their cash and other property. Many of the officers working in that unit amassed numerous misconduct complaints. When the activities of the unit became publicly known, it was disbanded, and several officers involved were arrested and sent to prison for robbery and kidnapping. More recently, the circumstances of several officer-involved fatal shootings have generated coverage by national media, including the deaths of Rekia Boyd, Laquan McDonald, Quintonio LeGrier, and Bettie Jones.

In response to these and other incidents, the City has undertaken many reform efforts over the past several decades. In 1972, then-Mayor Richard J. Daley convened a blue ribbon panel that heard four days of public testimony regarding concerns about police abuse. Black and Latino residents testified about illegal stops and searches, excessive uses of force, and unjustified killings of Chicago residents by police officers. The panel issued a report containing several recommendations "for steps that should be taken to eliminate abusive police conduct and improve police performance in Chicago." In 1997, then-Mayor Richard M. Daley appointed the Commission on Police Integrity "in response to the indictment of seven members of [CPD] on charges of conspiracy, racketeering, and extortion." The Commission's charge "was to examine the root causes of police corruption . . . and to propose possible changes to department policies and procedures." The Commission's final report recommended changes to CPD's hiring standards, training program, early warning system, and other "management process improvements." More recently, the City asked a Chicago-based global consulting firm and a local law firm to jointly conduct an independent assessment "of what [CPD] is doing to prevent and address police misconduct and, specifically, to suggest ways the Department can improve." The conclusions of that review were released in 2014, and contained roughly 30 pages of recommendations for changes to CPD's accountability systems. In response to each of these panels and reports, the City and CPD chose to implement some recommendations, and rejected others. Some implemented recommendations lasted; others did not.

Most recently, in the wake of the shooting death of Laquan McDonald by a CPD Officer and the release of dashboard-camera video capturing the incident, Mayor Emanuel quickly responded to widespread community concern by establishing the Police Accountability Task Force (PATF). The Mayor charged the PATF with assessing the Police Department and making recommendations for change in five areas: community relations; oversight and accountability; de-escalation; early intervention and personnel concerns; and video release protocols. In April 2016, the PATF issued a report with over a hundred recommendations for improving transparency and accountability. In December 2016, the City issued a progress report outlining the steps it has taken since April to meet the recommendations made by the PATF. Too little time has passed to know whether the recommendations the City decided to implement will be sustained.

E. FEDERAL INVOLVEMENT IN CHICAGO

During the thirteen months of our investigation, and particularly in light of the tumultuous year Chicago saw in 2016, the United States Department of Justice (DOJ) has proactively enhanced its assistance with CPD's reform and violence-reduction efforts. Beginning in September 2014, Chicago became part of DOJ's Violence Reduction Network (VRN), an innovative approach to support and enhance local violence reduction efforts. This data-driven, evidence-based initiative complemented DOJ's Smart on Crime initiative through delivery of strategic, intensive training, and technical assistance. Through VRN, Chicago received federal support and resources including training, federal law enforcement support, technical assistance from subject-matter experts, and participation in peer exchanges. This support led to implementation of new strategies, policy enhancements, improved technology, and increased analytic capacity.

In October 2016, at the conclusion of the initial VRN program phase, DOJ extended its commitment to the City of Chicago by offering continued support, technical assistance, and resources through at least March 2017. This additional commitment builds on existing strategies that have shown promise in Chicago, such as focusing on high-risk individuals and high-crime neighborhoods; emphasizing timely inter-agency intelligence gathering and sharing; concentrating on homicides, gun violence, and gang activity; ensuring fidelity to agreed-upon strategies throughout each agency; and incorporating trust-building principles into CPD's violence-reduction efforts. DOJ also is facilitating technical assistance to CPD by federal law enforcement agencies and current and former high-ranking police executives with expertise in reducing violence while increasing community trust. The areas of focus for crime-fighting strategies include development and dissemination of a comprehensive crime fighting plan; assessment and managed evolution of the Compstat command accountability program; and enhancing partnerships with state, local, and federal law enforcement agencies.

Further, in October 2016, DOJ allocated additional funding through its Office of Justice Programs (OJP), which now has professionals working directly with the City and CPD to assess community needs and available services in high crime neighborhoods to identify areas that would benefit from multi-sector public and private investments. The new OJP resources are complementary to, and coordinated with, preexisting collaborative initiatives launched by DOJ and CPD to improve community trust. Since December 2014, CPD and DOJ, through the United States Attorney's Office in Chicago, have hosted nine Community Trust Roundtables across Chicago's most violence-plagued neighborhoods.

These recent efforts build on the foundation of DOJ's longstanding collaborative initiatives with CPD. The United States Attorney's Office and other federal law enforcement partners in Chicago, including the Federal Bureau of Investigation (FBI), Drug Enforcement Agency (DEA), Bureau of Alcohol, Tobacco, Firearms and Explosives (ATF), and the United States Marshals Service (USMS) work closely with CPD on a variety of ongoing enforcement initiatives. Last year, each of these federal agencies increased resources dedicated to working with CPD in an effort to tamp down on the current spike in gun violence. Indeed, the United States Attorney's Office charged more illegal firearms cases in total, and more as a percentage of its overall cases, last year than it has in any year since 2004. Further, longstanding collaborations include, among other programs: Project Safe Neighborhoods, which seeks to reduce gun violence through strategic enforcement, deterrence, and reentry; Chicago's Violence Reduction Strategy (VRS), which is a targeted deterrence partnership aimed at gangs and violent criminals; and Youth Outreach Forums, a DOJ-funded program aimed at helping at-risk youth, 13 to 17 years old.

F. Investigation of the Chicago Police Department

On December 7, 2015, the United States Department of Justice, Civil Rights Division, Special Litigation Section, and the United States Attorney's Office for the Northern District of Illinois, jointly initiated an investigation of CPD and IPRA. This investigation was undertaken to determine whether the Chicago Police Department is engaging in a pattern or practice of unlawful conduct and, if so, what systemic deficiencies or practices within CPD, IPRA, and the City might be facilitating or causing this pattern or practice.

We opened this investigation pursuant to the Violent Crime Control and Law Enforcement Act of 1994, 42 U.S.C. § 14141 (Section 14141), Title VI of the Civil Rights Act of 1964, 42 U.S.C. § 2000d (Title VI), and the Omnibus Crime Control and Safe Streets Act of 1968, 42 U.S.C. § 3789d (Safe Streets Act). Section 14141 prohibits law enforcement agencies from engaging in a pattern or practice of conduct that violates the Constitution or laws of the United States. Title VI and the Safe Streets Act prohibit law enforcement practices that have a disparate impact based on protected status, such as race or ethnicity, unless these practices are necessary to achieve legitimate, non-discriminatory objectives.

Our investigation assessed CPD's use of force, including deadly force, and addressed CPD policies, training, reporting, investigation, and review related to officer use of force. The investigation further addressed CPD's and IPRA's systems of accountability both as they relate to officer use of force and officer misconduct, including the intake, investigation, and review of allegations of officer misconduct, and the imposition of discipline or other corrective action. We also investigated racial, ethnic, or other disparities in CPD's force and accountability practices, and assessed how those disparities inform the breakdown in community trust.

We relied on several sources of information. First, we reviewed thousands of pages of documents provided to us by CPD, IPRA, and the City, including policies, procedures, training plans, Department orders and memos, internal and external reports, and more. We also obtained access to the City's entire misconduct complaint database and data from all reports filled out following officers' use of force. From there, we reviewed a randomized, representative sample of force reports and the investigative files for incidents that occurred between January 2011 and April 2016, as well as additional incident reports and investigations. Overall, we reviewed over 170 officer-involved shooting investigations, and documents related to over 425 incidents of less-lethal force, including representative samples of officers' own reports of force, and of investigations of civilian complaints about officer force between January 2011 and April 2016. We also reviewed documents provided to us by other City agencies, such as the Office of Inspector General and the City's Law Department.

We also spent extensive time in Chicago—over 300 person-days—meeting with community members and City officials, and interviewing current and former CPD officers and IPRA investigators. In addition to speaking with the Superintendent and other CPD leadership, we met with the command staff of several specialized units, divisions, and departments. We toured CPD's training facilities and observed training programs. We also visited each of Chicago's 22 police districts, where we addressed roll call, spoke with command staff and officers, and conducted over 60 ride-alongs with officers. We met several times with Chicago's officer union, Lodge No. 7 of the Fraternal Order of Police, as well as the sergeants', lieutenants', and captains' unions. All told, we heard from over 340 individual CPD members, and 23 members of IPRA's staff.

In addition to document review and conversations with CPD and IPRA, our findings were significantly informed by our conversations with members of the Chicago community. During the course of our investigation we met with over 90 community organizations, including non-profits, advocacy and legal organizations, and faith-based groups focused on a wide range of issues. Several of these groups set up meetings for us so that we could hear directly from their clients or membership. We participated in forums where we heard directly from the family members of individuals who were killed by CPD officers. We also met with several local researchers, academics, and lawyers who have studied CPD extensively for decades. Most importantly, however, we heard directly from individuals who live and work throughout the City about their interactions with CPD officers. Overall, we talked to approximately a thousand community members. We received nearly 600 phone calls, emails, and letters during the course of our investigation from individuals who were eager to provide their experiences and insights. We also held several community forums in different neighborhoods throughout Chicago, where community members were able to share their stories in person.

In addition to attorneys, paralegals, outreach specialists, and data analysts from the Civil Rights Division of DOJ and the United States Attorney's Office for the Northern District of Illinois, eleven independent subject matter experts assisted with this investigation. Most of these experts are current or former law enforcement officials from police departments across the country. Accordingly, these experts have decades of expertise in areas such as the use of force, accountability, training, supervision, community policing, officer-involved domestic violence and sexual misconduct, officer wellness, and more. These experts accompanied us on-site, reviewed documents and investigative files, and provided invaluable insights that informed both the course of this investigation and its conclusions.

We thank the City, CPD officials, union officials, and the rank-and-file officers who have cooperated with this investigation and provided us with insights into the operation of the Department. We are also grateful to the many members of the Chicago community who have met with us during this investigation to share their experiences.

II. CPD ENGAGES IN A PATTERN OR PRACTICE OF UNCONSTITUTIONAL USE OF FORCE

❦

We reviewed CPD's force practices mindful that officers routinely place themselves in harm's way in order to uphold their commitment to serve and protect the people of the City of Chicago, that officers regularly encounter individuals who may be armed and determined to avoid arrest, and that our inquiry should be guided by the perspective of the reasonable officer on the scene rather than perfect hindsight. We likewise recognize that officers have not only a right, but an obligation to protect themselves and others from threats of harm, including deadly harm, which may arise in an instant. We also recognize that the City has taken some steps that—if properly implemented—could represent meaningful improvements to the way that officers use force.

Nonetheless, we found reasonable cause to believe that CPD has engaged in a pattern or practice of unreasonable force in violation of the Fourth Amendment and that the deficiencies in CPD's training, supervision, accountability, and other systems have contributed to that pattern or practice. CPD has not provided officers with adequate guidance to understand how and when they may use force, or how to safely and effectively control and resolve encounters to reduce the need to use force. CPD often does not appropriately supervise officers to identify dangerous tactics or behaviors that may indicate officers need additional training or other intervention. CPD also does not review its force practices as a whole to identify problematic trends or patterns that endanger officers and others. When officers use force, CPD often does not adequately review those force incidents to determine whether the force used complied with the law or CPD policy, or whether the tactics the officer used were safe and effective. Consequently, officers are asked to perform a dangerous job with insufficient guidance as to whether their force practices are safe, effective, or legal. These failures have resulted in CPD engaging in a pattern or practice of using force in a manner that is unconstitutional, contrary to CPD policy, and unsafe. Inappropriate use of force by the police (even when no lasting physical injury is involved) results in fear and distrust from many of the people whom the police are committed to protect and whom the police need as partners in that effort.

The use of excessive force by a law enforcement officer violates the Fourth Amendment. *Graham v. Connor*, 490 U.S. 386, 394 (1989). "In determining whether police used excessive force under the Fourth Amendment, the relevant inquiry is 'whether the officers' actions [were] objectively reasonable in light of the totality of the circumstances.'" *Flournoy v. City of Chicago*, 829 F.3d 869, 874 (7th Cir. 2016) (citations omitted); *Fitzgerald v. Santoro*, 707 F.3d 725, 733 (7th Cir. 2013) (citing *Graham*, 490 U.S. at 396–97). In determining whether force used by a law enforcement officer is reasonable, courts look to "the severity of the crime at issue, whether the suspect poses an immediate threat to the safety of the officers or others, and whether he is actively resisting arrest or attempting to evade arrest by flight." *Id.* at 396. Whether a particular use of force is reasonable is "judged from the perspective of a reasonable officer on the scene, rather than with the 20/20 vision of hindsight." *Id.* Courts are mindful that "police officers are often forced to make split-second judgments—in circumstances that are tense, uncertain, and rapidly evolving—about the amount of force that is necessary in a particular situation." *Id.* at 396–97. An officer's use of force is unreasonable if, judging from the totality of the circumstances at the time of the arrest, the officer uses greater force than was reasonably necessary to effectuate the arrest. *Phillips v. Cmty. Ins. Corp.*, 678 F.3d 513, 519 (7th Cir. 2012) (citing *Gonzalez v. City of Elgin*, 578 F.3d 526, 539 (7th Cir. 2009)).

A pattern or practice of unreasonable force may be found where incidents of violations are repeated and are not isolated instances. *Int'l Bd. of Teamsters v. United States*, 431 U.S. 324, 336 n.16 (1977) (noting that the phrase "pattern or practice" "was not intended as a term of art," but should be interpreted according to its usual meaning "consistent with the understanding of the identical words" used in other federal civil rights statutes). Courts interpreting the term "pattern or practice" in similar statutes have established that statistical evidence is not required. *Coates v. Johnson & Johnson*, 756 F.2d 524, 533 (7th Cir. 1985) ("Neither statistical nor anecdotal evidence is automatically entitled to reverence to the exclusion of the other."). A court does not need a specific number of incidents to find a pattern or practice. *See United States v. W. Peachtree Tenth Corp.*, 437 F.2d 221, 227 (5th Cir. 1971) ("The number of [violations] . . . is not determinative. . . . In any event, no mathematical formula is workable, nor was any intended. Each case must turn on its own facts.").

Although a specific number of incidents and statistical evidence is not required, our investigation found that CPD officers use unnecessary and unreasonable force[1] in violation of the Constitution with frequency, and that unconstitutional force has been historically tolerated by CPD. This finding is based on a comprehensive investigation of CPD's force practices. We reviewed CPD's policies related to the use, reporting, and investigation of force, including older versions of polices that were effective during our review period, and CPD's proposed revised policies. We spoke with officers at all ranks, including the Superintendent and the Chief and Deputy Chief of the Bureau of Patrol, to understand how officers were trained to use force, their view of when force is appropriate, and how the policies are interpreted in practice throughout CPD and at each level. We also did an in-depth review of officer reports of force, civilian complaints of force, and CPD's and IPRA's reviews of force and investigations of allegations of excessive force. We reviewed over 425 incidents of less-lethal force, including representative samples of officers' own reports of force and of investigations of civilian complaints about officer force between January 2011 and April 2016.

We also reviewed over 170 IPRA files related to officer-involved shootings, which amounts to a significant portion of all officer-involved shootings. The City was not able to accurately identify how many people were shot by CPD officers. We were provided with a list of all incidents involving a weapons discharge between January 2011 and January 2016, but it was inaccurate and incomplete. By comparing this list to other data provided by the City, we were able to identify nine shooting incidents during that time period in which a person was struck that either were not on the list provided by the City or that were not categorized as hits of people. In all, we were able to identify 203 officer-involved shooting incidents in which at least one civilian was shot between January 1, 2011 and March 21, 2016. In those 203 incidents, 223 civilians were shot. We reviewed 151 of these, including all 134 for which the investigation was complete and the disposition was final as of June 2016. In addition to these 151 officer-involved shooting incidents, we also reviewed 22 shooting files that pertained to officer-involved shootings that CPD refers to as "no-hits," meaning that CPD is not aware of anyone being struck during the incident. As described below, the City does not investigate shootings in which it is not aware that a person was struck. Consequently, those files contain very little information about the circumstances of those shootings and did not provide sufficient information to determine whether the force was lawful.

The uses of excessive force we identified were not aberrational. Our holistic review of this information, combined with our investigation of CPD's training, supervision, accountability, and other systems, give us reasonable cause to believe that the unreasonable force we identified amounts to a pattern or practice of unlawful conduct. Below we describe some recurring categories of unreasonable force we identified. We also provide illustrative incidents. In all incidents, the description of events comes from CPD's and IPRA's own records.

A. CPD USES DEADLY FORCE IN VIOLATION OF THE FOURTH AMENDMENT AND DEPARTMENT POLICY

CPD's pattern or practice of unreasonable force includes the use of deadly force. Our review of CPD's deadly force practices identified several trends in CPD's deadly force incidents, including that CPD engages in dangerous and unnecessary foot pursuits and other unsound tactics that result in CPD shooting people, including those who are unarmed. We also saw a trend in dangerous and unnecessary shootings at vehicles and other unsafe tactics that placed officers and others in danger of being shot.

1. CPD's pattern or practice of unreasonable force includes shooting at fleeing suspects who present no immediate threat

We found numerous incidents where CPD officers chased and shot fleeing persons who posed no immediate threat to officers or the public. Such actions are constitutionally impermissible. *See Tennessee v. Garner*, 471 U.S. 1, 13 (1985) ("Where the suspect poses no immediate threat to the officer and no threat to others, the harm resulting from failing to apprehend him does not justify the use of deadly force to do so."). Moreover, "an officer does not possess the unfettered authority to shoot a member of the public simply because that person is carrying a weapon. Instead, deadly force may only be used by a police officer when, based on a reasonable assessment, the officer or another person is *threatened* with the weapon." *Cooper v. Sheehan*, 735 F.3d 153, 159 (4th Cir. 2013); *Curnow v. Ridgecrest Police Agency*, 952 F.2d 321, 324–25 (9th Cir. 1991) (deadly force unreasonable when suspect holding gun was not pointing it or facing officers). *Cf. Williams v. Ind. State Police Dep't*, 797 F.3d 468, 484–85 (7th Cir. 2015) (deadly force justified not merely by possession of weapon, but by suspect's actions).

In some cases, CPD officers initiated foot pursuits without a basis for believing the person had committed a serious crime. In these cases, the act of fleeing alone was sufficient to trigger a pursuit ending in gunfire, sometimes fatal. During subsequent review, almost without exception, officers' reports of these events were accepted at face value, even where there was contrary evidence.

In one case, a man had been walking down a residential street with a friend when officers drove up, shined a light on him, and ordered him to freeze, because he had been fidgeting with his waistband. The man ran. Three officers gave chase and began shooting as they ran. In total, the officers fired 45 rounds, including 28 rifle rounds, toward the man. Several rounds struck the man, killing him. The officers claimed the man fired at them during the pursuit. Officers found no gun on the man. However, officers reported recovering a handgun nearly one block away. The gun recovered in the vicinity, however, was later determined to be fully-loaded and inoperable, and forensic testing determined there was no gunshot residue on the man's hands. IPRA found the officers' actions were justified without addressing the efficacy of the pursuit or the number of shots fired.

In another case, a CPD officer chased and shot a man. The officer later claimed that during pursuit she ordered the man to stop, at which point the man turned and raised his right arm towards her. According to the officer, the man had pointed a gun at her earlier in the incident and, fearing he was doing so now, she fired. The only gunshot wounds were to the man's buttocks. No weapon was found on the man, but a gun was found on a nearby roof gutter. IPRA found the shooting justified without accounting for the wounds to the man's backside. In another case, a CPD officer chased a man who ran when an officer told him to stop, and then shot the man in the back of the leg. The officer claimed the man had turned to point a gun. After a thorough search of the scene, no gun was recovered. The man, who denied ever turning to face the officer, was found only with a cell phone.

In another case, a CPD officer fatally shot a fleeing, unarmed suspect in the back. The officer told investigators the suspect had turned around to point a black object. This account did not square with the location of the shooting victim's gunshot wounds and appeared contrary to video footage that showed the suspect running away from the officer. Again, IPRA accepted the officer's account, despite the conflicting evidence. IPRA's final report of the incident did not mention the existence of the video.

In another case, video evidence showed the tragic end of a foot pursuit of a man who was not a threat when an officer shot him in the back. The officer, who fired 16 shots, killing the man, claimed on his force report that the man was armed and the man "charged [him] with apparent firearm." The officer shot the man during the foot pursuit, and dashboard-camera footage showed that as the unarmed man lay on the ground, the officer fired three shots into his back. CPD stripped the officer of his police powers after this shooting—his third that year—and the City paid the man's family $4.1 million in settlement.

To be sure, foot pursuits are a necessary and sometimes important part of good policing. There are circumstances in which officers are legally authorized to engage in a foot pursuit, and should. That said, foot pursuits are also inherently dangerous and present substantial risks to officers and the public. Officers may experience fatigue or an adrenaline rush that compromises their ability to control a suspect they capture, to fire their weapons accurately, and even to make sound judgments. Consequently, officers caught up in the heat of a pursuit "often exhibit a tendency to rush into what can be described as 'the killing zone,' that is, within a 10-foot radius of the offender."[2] The adrenaline rush also may make it more difficult for the officer to decrease the amount of force used as the threat diminishes. CPD has long had detailed policies regarding vehicle pursuits. It does not have a foot pursuit policy. It should. In addition to not having a policy, CPD has not taken corrective action to address problematic foot pursuits. This puts officers and the public in danger and results in unreasonable uses of force.

2. <u>CPD's pattern or practice of unreasonable force includes firing at vehicles without justification</u>

We also reviewed incidents involving officers who either unlawfully fired at fleeing vehicles, or, in violation of CPD policy, who fired after recklessly positioning themselves in the path of a moving vehicle or refusing to move from the path of a moving vehicle. Shooting at a moving vehicle is inherently dangerous and almost always counterproductive. First, bullets fired at the vehicle itself are unlikely to stop or disable it. Second, the bullets may strike a passenger who is not a threat and may be a victim. Third, bullets fired into a vehicle may not result in surrender, but may instead provoke a fight-or-flight response in which the driver is even more determined to escape or stop the source of gunfire. Fourth, disabling the driver may result in a runaway vehicle that endangers the lives of officers or bystanders. Faced with a threat posed by a moving vehicle, the appropriate response ordinarily is to avoid the vehicle's path, take cover, and summon additional resources to maximize safety and obtain a tactical advantage. This approach likewise minimizes the risk of deadly force.[3]

CPD policy has long formally recognized the appropriate tactical response to officers facing threats from moving vehicles. Its deadly force policy for the period September 2002 to February 2015 provided, "When confronted with an oncoming vehicle and that vehicle is the only force used against them, sworn members will move out of the vehicle's path." Since February 2015, CPD policy expressly prohibits "[f]iring at or into a moving vehicle when the vehicle is the only force used against the sworn member or another person."

CPD did not enforce its 2002–2015 policy, however. For example, in one case, an off-duty officer witnessed a reckless driver cause a vehicle collision during a high-speed chase. The officer exited his vehicle and ran to the scene. The motorist, seeking to escape, backed up his car, managing to pin it between the officer's vehicle and a tree. The officer moved in front of the trapped car and fired two shots into the windshield, claiming he did so because he heard the car's engine revving. During the IPRA investigation, the officer was never asked to explain why he positioned himself in front of the car or why he could not have stepped out of the way if he believed the car was about to move forward. IPRA found the shooting justified, despite the apparent policy violation and insufficient factual record regarding the officer's claimed need to fire in self-defense.

Our review also included cases involving shots fired at moving vehicles that occurred after CPD's February 2015 change to its deadly force policy. Some of these matters remain under investigation. Absent accountability for violations, the 2015 revisions do not adequately address or resolve the unconstitutional pattern or practice.

3. <u>CPD officers exhibit poor discipline in discharging weapons</u>

We found repeated incidents where officers exhibited poor discipline in discharging their weapons, reflecting disregard for innocent bystanders and constitutional standards.[4] As noted above, for example, in one incident three CPD officers fired a total of 45 rounds, including 28 rifle rounds, at a man during a foot pursuit in a residential area. This man was shot several times, but dozens of the bullets were fired into this residential neighborhood.

In some incidents, officers appeared to fire their weapons merely because others had done so. For example, in one case, two officers chased a man they saw carrying a gun. During the foot pursuit, one officer told his partner he intended to shoot, and then fired 11 shots at the suspect. The partner then fired five shots of his own. Later recounting the incident to IPRA, the partner did not articulate any threatening actions by the man that prompted him to shoot. He stated that the suspect did not turn his body or raise his weapon. Instead, he explained that the first officer began shooting and so he did as well. IPRA did not pursue the matter further and found the use of deadly force justified.[5] On the evidence available to us, the shooting did not meet the constitutional standard because the officer was not responding to a specific, articulable threat.

4. <u>CPD officers make tactical decisions that unnecessarily increase the risk of deadly encounters</u>

We observed a trend in shootings resulting from CPD officers unnecessarily escalating confrontations or using reckless, untrained tactics, putting themselves in a position of jeopardy and limiting their force options to just deadly force. While these tactical decisions may not always result in uses of force that are unconstitutional, they do result in avoidable uses of force and resulting harm, including deaths. Moreover, these poor tactics are part of the systemic deficiencies that have led to the pattern or practice of excessive force.

a. Failure to await backup and use of unsound tactics in approaching vehicles

Deadly force incidents have occurred when CPD officers failed to await backup and unnecessarily injected themselves into high-risk situations where there was no exigent need to do so. Although not necessarily unconstitutional uses of force, these are avoidable uses of force that present an unnecessary risk to officer and public safety. In one case, an off-duty civilian-dressed CPD officer did not call for backup after witnessing two men exit a car, fire gunshots at an unknown target, and then drive off. Instead, after locating the car stopped in traffic, the officer approached it on foot and engaged the suspects. The officer fired his off-duty firearm at their car upon seeing an occupant of the car point a pistol at him. The officer fired 10 times, wounding but not disabling either suspect. The officer had fired all his ammunition, leaving him defenseless in the middle of the street. In addition, the CPD officer did this in a high-traffic area, thereby exposing bystanders to the risk of errant rounds from a shootout. And, a nearby uniformed state trooper conducting an unrelated traffic stop drew his gun on the CPD officer, because the trooper was unsure whether he had just witnessed an attempted murder.

In another case, two officers were flagged down by a woman reporting that someone in a car had pointed a shotgun at her. The officers spotted the car and radioed for assistance. They did not wait for backup and instead approached on foot alone. As one officer stood adjacent to the passenger side of the suspect's car, he reportedly saw the driver point a shotgun at him. Standing exposed at close range, the officer fired twice, wounding but not disabling the suspect. The suspect drove off without returning fire. Though the officer was justified in firing in self-defense, the violence may have been avoided altogether if the officers had observed sound tactics.

In another case, an off-duty CPD officer spotted the silhouette of a man in a vacant building and suspected the man was burglarizing it. The officer called 911, but did not wait for other officers to arrive. Instead, the off-duty officer summoned the man out of the building. According to a civilian witness, the burglary suspect angrily exited the building, yelling, "You're not a fucking cop." The suspect then advanced on the officer, who struck and kicked the suspect. According to the officer, the suspect then reached into his waistband and withdrew a shiny object, prompting the officer to fire twice, killing the man. No weapon was recovered. Instead, officers reported finding a silver watch near the man's body. IPRA found the shooting justified without addressing the officer's failure to await backup. According to press reports, in November 2016, this same officer shot a man in the back and killed him, claiming the man had pointed a gun at him during a foot pursuit. No gun was recovered.

We further found instances where CPD officers unnecessarily exposed innocent bystanders to deadly risks. In one case, three CPD officers were driving two civilian witnesses assisting in an assault investigation. Along the way, the officers heard gunshots from a nearby restaurant and saw a group of individuals running. The officers decided to confront the suspected gunmen themselves, with their unwilling civilian passengers in tow. The driver officer stopped the unmarked patrol car within a few yards of the suspects and issued police commands. According to the officers, one of the suspects drew a firearm and pointed it toward the officers and the side of the patrol car, where the two civilian witnesses sat exposed in the back seat. Both the driver officer and front passenger officer opened fire. During the IPRA investigation, both officers acknowledged that the confrontation had placed the civilian witnesses' lives at risk and sought to justify their use of deadly force in part because of that risk. While the suspect was indeed armed, one of the civilians in the backseat denied seeing the man point or raise the weapon at officers. IPRA found the shooting reasonable and justified with no stated concerns about the officers' tactics and without mentioning the civilian's contrary account in its final report.

b. Use of dangerous vehicle maneuvers

Other shooting incidents arose out of officers' use of high-risk, untrained vehicle maneuvers designed to box in suspects' cars. In one such incident, officers in two patrol vehicles tried to stop a car reportedly matching a description of suspected narcotics dealers with a gun hidden in the car. The first patrol car initiated the traffic stop by pulling in sideways in front of the suspects' car, thereby exposing the passenger officer to the risk of gunfire or serious injury if the driver had opted to ram the police car. The passenger officer exited the patrol car and fired upon the suspects as they attempted to drive away. Although it is unclear whether the officer's use of force was constitutional, it is clear that the poor stop tactics unnecessarily placed the officer at risk, thereby increasing the likelihood of a deadly force encounter.

On another occasion, officers used a variation of this box-in technique to trap a car in a high-traffic area. Again, an officer in the lead patrol car ended up firing into the suspect's vehicle, although in this case the car had not fled the scene. The officer acknowledged in his interview that they used the vehicle technique in the field despite never having been trained on the technique.

In another case, CPD officers used unmarked police cars to box in a car driven by an armed robbery suspect. After forcing the suspect to stop, the officer in the front patrol car exited and placed himself between his car and the driver's side of the suspect's vehicle. The suspect backed up, striking the rear police car. As this occurred, the front car officer moved in front of the suspect's car. The suspect then placed the car in drive, turned his wheels, and attempted to drive away. The officer from the front car fired a single shot into the driver's window, claiming he feared the suspect would run him over. The officer's bullet struck the suspect through the driver's window, causing the driver to crash his car into an occupied parked car. IPRA found the shooting justified without addressing the officers' tactics.

c. Reckless foot pursuits

As discussed above, we found repeated incidents of unreasonable uses of force stemming from foot pursuits that were initiated with an insufficient basis to conduct the pursuit. We also identified other cases in which foot pursuits were conducted in a tactically unsound, often reckless manner, some of which culminated in an officer-involved shooting. We found multiple instances in which officers began pursuit without first broadcasting over radio dispatch critical information like location and direction of travel. In addition, officers frequently engage in a dangerous tactic known as "partner-splitting," in which officers split off from one another to pursue one or more suspects. In some cases, one officer drives away from the foot chase, seeking to cut the suspect off from the other side of the block. Partner-splitting covers more territory, but it also can compromise the safety of officers who lose their ability to assist or effectively communicate with each other. It also increases the risk that the officers or innocent civilians will be caught in cross-fire. Because it is dangerous to officers and the public, this tactic should be used only when absolutely necessary to protect the public or officers from imminent harm.

Partner-splitting is not a trained CPD technique, but a practice developed in the field. As one CPD officer put it, "My partner and I have an agreement or we call it protocol, if you will, that if I'm driving, I stay in the vehicle and he is going to be the one that's going to pursue on foot." The officer offered this observation during an IPRA investigation of a partner-splitting foot pursuit that left him alone in a backyard with a man he claimed pointed a gun at him, resulting in a fatal shooting. The shooting was deemed justified, with no scrutiny of the tactics that precipitated the event.

This lack of policy, guidance, and oversight of foot pursuits presents not only constitutional and safety concerns, but also exposes the City to substantial damages claims in civil rights litigation. *See, e.g., Quintana v. City of Philadelphia*, Civ. No. 10–6088, 2011 WL 2937426 at *3 (E.D. Pa. July 21, 2011) ("[A]rming police officers without providing any training on the constitutional limitations of the use of deadly force may amount to deliberate indifference, as could failing to maintain any sort of foot pursuit or partner splitting policy for police officers involved in a foot pursuit.") (citations omitted); *Pelzer v. City of Philadelphia.*, 656 F. Supp. 2d 517, 535 (E.D. Pa. 2009) ("[F]oot pursuits tend to be strong in emotion, weak in tactics. . . . A reasonable jury could find the failure to establish [foot] pursuit policies creates a sufficiently obvious risk to the rights of pursuit subjects. . . . A jury may also be able to conclude that the issue of pursuit and patrol policies are the result of a policymaker's decision, and that the City's omission was the moving factor behind the plaintiff's injury.").

A contributing factor to many foot pursuits that end in unnecessary force is CPD's use of a particular stop technique, often called a "jump out." The practice involves groups of officers, frequently in plain clothes and riding in unmarked vehicles driving rapidly toward a street corner or group of individuals and then jumping out and rapidly advancing, often with guns drawn.

These actions often cause one of more members of the targeted group to walk away briskly or run from the scene. The officers then zero-in on the fleeing person, often with one officer tasked with chasing him on foot. Some of the most problematic shootings occurred when that sole officer closed in on the subject, thus greatly increasing the risk of a serious or deadly force incident.

Such techniques can be particularly problematic when deployed by CPD tactical or other specialized units using unmarked vehicles and plainclothes officers. It can be difficult, especially at night, to discern that individuals springing out of an unmarked car are police officers. In high-crime areas, residents may be particularly unwilling to stick around to find out. For example, in one case, a tactical officer in plain clothes jumped out of an unmarked car, chased a man who ran from him, and ultimately shot the man from behind. Officers claimed the man pointed a gun, but no weapon was recovered. The shooting victim explained to investigators that he ran because a sedan he did not recognize had raced through a stop sign and headed toward him. Similarly, in another case, two plainclothes officers dressed in black and in unmarked vehicles approached a man and his female passenger as they were getting into their car. According to the woman, the couple did not know they were officers and fled, and an officer shot at the side and rear of the vehicle, killing the man.

CPD should provide officers with guidance and support in conducting field operations in a tactically sound manner that reduces risk to officers and civilians alike. This does not mean a retreat from law enforcement, but rather a move toward practices that are more effective. Policy and guidance are the first step; scenario-based training is the next. As noted by trainers from the FBI Academy, "realistic and practical exercises can instill in officers the skills and mental preparedness that they can call on automatically when confronting offenders. Law enforcement agencies should ensure that officers receive training in such critical issues as formulating action plans, following established policies, knowing their physical and mental conditions, remaining aware of their surroundings, considering offender reactions, and exploring tactical options."

B. CPD USES LESS-LETHAL FORCE IN VIOLATION OF THE FOURTH AMENDMENT AND DEPARTMENT POLICY

Although CPD documents generally include insufficient detail of when and how officers use force, particularly less-lethal force, our review of CPD records made clear that CPD's pattern of unreasonable force includes unreasonable less-lethal force. As discussed in detail below, CPD does not require officers to provide detailed information about the amount and type of force they use. The form on which officers are to report force requires officers to indicate via check box, for example, that they used a Taser[6] or a "control instrument" without requiring them to explain the manner or circumstances in which the force was used. Officers also are not required to provide any details about the amount of resistance they encountered from suspects. Instead, officers use boilerplate, vague terminology like "actively resisted" or "attempted to defeat arrest." In reviewing officers' use of less-lethal force, supervisors generally do not conduct any follow-up investigation or request any additional information from officers to help them understand what happened. As a consequence, CPD's documentation for many uses of less-lethal force do not paint a complete or accurate picture of the amount of force used or why it was used. IPRA investigations of misconduct complaints regarding force are similarly deficient, as discussed in the Accountability Section of this Report.

In many cases we reviewed, due to insufficient information, we were not able to determine whether the force was reasonable. For example, if an officer reported that he used a "kick" because a subject "balled his fists" and actively resisted, we were unable to determine whether the force used was reasonable because we did not know how many times the officer kicked the subject, where on the body the subject was kicked, or whether it might have been necessary. In many cases, however, the information that was reported was sufficient to demonstrate that the force used was unreasonable. If, for example, an officer reported that he or she used a Taser against someone suspected of a minor property crime as the suspect fled, we determined that force to be unreasonable because, as described below, that level of force is unconstitutional on its face. Even using this conservative methodology—taking officers' reports of force at face value and not making inferences—we saw a clear pattern of unreasonable force.

1. <u>CPD's pattern or practice of unreasonable force includes the use of excessive less-lethal force against people who present no threat</u>

CPD's pattern or practice of unreasonable force includes using excessive force against people who do not present a threat and who are suspected only of low-level crimes or, in some cases, no crime at all. For example, officers used a Taser in "drive-stun mode" against a woman in mental health crisis and whose only documented actions were that she failed to follow verbal commands and that she stiffened.[7] Officers provided no narrative of the encounter other than to write that the woman was "a high risk mental" who needed to be transported to a hospital for a "mental evaluation." They noted on the form that the woman was engaged in passive, not active, resistance. This use of force against a woman who was not suspected of any crime was unreasonable and violated CPD policy, which prohibits the use of Tasers against people who only are passively resisting.

The use of unreasonable force to quickly resolve non-violent encounters is a recurrent issue at CPD. This is at least in part because CPD's policy permits the use of Tasers in situations where it is unreasonable, and allows the use of Tasers in drive-stun mode in any circumstance in which "probe mode" is allowed. CPD's policy permits use of a Taser (in any mode) to defeat active resistance, defined by CPD policy as "movement to avoid physical control," without regard to the severity of the crime or whether the person poses any danger to an officer, factors that must be considered in judging the reasonableness of a use of force. *Graham*, 490 U.S. at 396. CPD recently has proposed changes to its Taser policy. The proposed revised policy makes clearer that officers may not use a Taser unless it is objectively reasonable, necessary under the circumstances, and proportional to the threat or resistance of the subject. This is an important change, but the policy still does not place restrictions on the use of drive-stun mode. And, like any policy, it must be enforced in order to be effective.

Some CPD officers resort to Tasers as a tool of convenience, with insufficient concern or cognizance that it is a weapon with inherent risks that inflicts significant pain. Use of a Taser "is more than a *de minimis* application of force" and is a "very significant intrusion on [a person's] Fourth Amendment interests." *Abbott v. Sangamon County, Ill.*, 705 F.3d 706, 726, 730 (7th Cir. 2013). In an incident we reviewed, a man died after hitting his head when he fell while fleeing because a CPD officer shot him with a Taser. The man had been suspected only of petty theft from a retail store. IPRA deemed this use of a Taser justified. We saw other unnecessary uses of Tasers against people fleeing after committing minor violations, including a man who was suspected of urinating in public, and a 110-pound-juvenile who fled after officers caught him painting graffiti on a garage. In all of these instances, as in many others we reviewed, the officers articulated no basis to support a conclusion that the convenient but painful and at times dangerous use of Tasers, rather than a less severe use of force, was necessary.

As with lethal force, some officers escalate encounters unnecessarily. This includes incidents in which CPD officers use retaliatory force against people who object and claim that they were unlawfully stopped by CPD. In one incident, officers had searched and released a man they had detained to determine if he was armed (he was not). The man then yelled at the officers and put his left foot in front of the squad car tire, taunting them to run over his foot so he could sue them. Instead of backing up, going around the man, or trying verbal techniques to calm the man down, the officers got out of the car and ordered him to stop blocking their car. The man then yelled that he was going to beat and kill them. They arrested him for aggravated assault.

Officers reported that, during the arrest, he balled his fists and tried to pull away, so they punched and hit him and took him to the ground. In another incident, officers used pain compliance techniques and forcibly brought to the ground a man because he stiffened and locked his arms while they were arresting him for walking his dog without a leash and refusing to present identification. In both of these instances, officers provided no justification for the level of force they used, or why they did not attempt to resolve these situations with common de-escalation techniques.

2. CPD's pattern or practice of unreasonable force includes the use of excessive less-lethal force against children

CPD's pattern or practice of excessive force also includes subjecting children to force for non-criminal conduct and minor violations. In one incident, officers hit a 16-year-old girl with a baton and then Tasered her after she was asked to leave the school for having a cell phone in violation of school rules. Officers were called in to arrest her for trespassing. Officers claimed the force was justified because she flailed her arms when they tried to arrest her, with no adequate explanation for how such flailing met the criteria for use of a Taser. This was not an isolated incident. We also reviewed incidents in which officers unnecessarily drive-stunned students to break up fights, including one use of a Taser in drive-stun mode against a 14-year-old girl. There was no indication in these files that these students' conduct warranted use of the Taser instead of a less serious application of force.

CPD's Taser policy does not address the use of Tasers on children. It should. Prior to using a Taser on a child, officers should be required to factor into their decision the child's apparent age, size, and the threat presented. The use of a Taser in schools and on students should be discouraged and deployed only as a last resort. Tasers are painful and, because of a child's smaller size, children are especially vulnerable to greater injury from them. That is one reason the Police Executive Research Forum warns that Tasers should not be used against young children and that officers should consider a person's age in deciding whether use of a Taser is reasonable.[8] CPD policy contains no such admonition, and this is true even under CPD's proposed revised policies. Moreover, in several of the instances we reviewed, officers used the Taser in drive-stun mode, which as noted above is prone to abuse.

We also found instances in which force was used against children in a re-taliatory manner. In one incident, an officer's neighbor called to report that some boys were playing basketball on the officer's property. The officer, on duty, left his district to respond and found the teenage boys down the street on their bikes. The officer pointed his gun at them, used profanity, and threatened to put their heads through a wall and to blow up their homes. The boys claim that the officer forced them to kneel and lie face-down, handcuffed together, leaving visible injuries on their knees and wrists. Once released, one boy called his mother crying to tell her an officer had pointed a gun at his face; another boy went home and showed his mother his scraped leg and, visibly upset, said "the police did this to me." The mothers reported the incident to IPRA. The officer, who had not reported the use of force, accepted a finding of "sustained" and received a five-day suspension. The officer was never interviewed and his reasons for not contesting the allegations are not documented in the file.

In another case, a girl and a boy, both 15 years old, were crossing a street at the light, and one car had already stopped so they could proceed. A uniformed officer in an unmarked car braked hard and changed lanes to avoid the stopped car. The girl claimed the officer got out of the car and yelled profanity (calling her a "fucking idiot" among other things), drawing the attention of a female witness. The girl claimed that when she told the officer that they had the right of way, he pushed her in the back with both hands so hard she fell into a newspaper stand, after which he handcuffed her arms behind her back while she still wore her backpack, hurting her wrists, and did not loosen the cuffs when she complained. The officer called for backup, two officers responded, and the teens were released without charges. The girl reported this incident to IPRA. During the investigation, the officer, who had not reported using any force, claimed the teens were standing in the street obstructing traffic, causing him to slam on his brakes, prompting the teens to laugh at him. He said the teens cursed at him, and he handcuffed the girl for his and her safety because she "was becoming agitated and refused any and all direction." Despite the existence of four witnesses (the two officers, the boy, and the female witness at the very least), the IPRA investigator obtained a statement only from the accused officer. The investigator did not try to call the female witness until 26 months after the incident (yet wrote that she "did not cooperate with this investigation"). By the time the investigator concluded the investigation in April 2014 and deemed her allegations not sustained, the girl had turned 18.

In another case, an officer forcibly handcuffed a 12-year-old Latino boy who was outside riding a bike under his father's supervision. A plainclothes officer, responding to a report of "two male Hispanics running from" the area, detained the boy. According to the boy and his father, the officer approached the boy, ordered him to stop his bike, forcibly handcuffed him, pulled him off his bike, and placed him up against a fence. The boy reported he did not understand the man was a police officer or why he was being detained and told the officer he was only 12. According to the boy, the officer responded that the boy was "old enough to bang," meaning old enough to engage in gang violence. The boy's father approached the officer, explained that his son was only 12 years old, and asked what was going on. Records of 911 calls reflect a caller reporting that a plainclothes officer had a 12-year-old in handcuffs and was refusing to say why. The officer placed the boy in the back of a police vehicle before eventually releasing him. The officer's only apparent basis for this detention was the boy's race, which is constitutionally unreasonable. *United States v. Moore*, 983 F. Supp. 2d 1030, 1033 (E.D. Wis.

2013) ("[P]olice could not, consistent with the Fourth Amendment, stop every black male within their perimeter wearing a dark winter coat on a cold January day"); *United States v. Brown*, 448 F.3d 239, 248 (3d Cir. 2006) (reversing conviction where "about the only thing [defendant] had in common with the suspects was that they were black").

C. VIDEO EVIDENCE SUGGESTS A BROADER PATTERN OR PRACTICE OF UNCONSTITUTIONAL USE OF FORCE

Evidence suggests that the pattern of unreasonable use of force identified by our investigation may be even broader than that revealed through CPD documents alone. During our investigation, we reviewed numerous use-of-force incidents captured on video. In many of these incidents, the use of force was facially unreasonable and the videos undercut the officers' descriptions of the incidents. Given the large volume of reported incidents not captured on video, this suggests that the extent of unreasonable force by CPD officers may be larger than is possible to discern from CPD's scant force reports and force investigations alone. Indeed, the inaccurate descriptions of events that *were* undercut by video we reviewed bore striking similarities to descriptions provided by officers in numerous cases with no video.

In one incident captured on cell-phone video, an officer breaking up a party approached a man, grabbed him by the shirt, and hit him in the head with a baton. In his reports, the officer, using language very similar to that used in many other reports we reviewed, falsely claimed that the victim had tried to punch him. Before the video surfaced, the officer's supervisor had approved the use of force and the victim had pled guilty to resisting arrest. The officer has since been relieved of his police powers and is facing criminal charges for his conduct. In another video, a woman exited her car and placed her hands on her vehicle when officers threw her to the ground, hit her, and deployed a Taser against her. The video indicates that the officer's claim that she had refused to show her hands, thus justifying the force used, was false. Despite the existence of the video, IPRA deemed the force reasonable.

We also reviewed a video of an officer choking, hitting, and slapping a man who had refused an order to leave the area in front of a store where the man was shopping with his family. The officer had not reported having used any force at all, and an officer witness to the event did not report the choking. The man complained to IPRA. Investigators there obtained a copy of the store surveillance video, which confirmed the man's account. The officer was then suspended for 45 days.

In many of these cases, IPRA generally accepted the officer's version of events, which were later undercut by video evidence. The Laquan McDonald shooting is one such incident; our review found many others. In one incident, for example, officers justified unreasonable force by falsely claiming in their reports that a woman had attacked them. In the video, officers can be seen aggressively grabbing the woman, who was being arrested for a prostitution offense, throwing her to the ground, and surrounding her. After she is hand-cuffed, one officer tells another to "tase her ten fucking times." Officers call her an animal, threaten to kill her and her family, and scream, "I'll put you in a UPS box and send you back to wherever the fuck you came from" while hitting the woman—who was handcuffed and on her knees. Officers can then be seen discovering a recording device and discussing whether they can take it. Supervisors approved this use of force and the officers were not disciplined until after the woman complained to IPRA and produced surveillance video of the event. The City paid the woman $150,000 in settlement of her lawsuit.

Another video shows an officer punching a handcuffed man several times, apparently in retaliation for the man having earlier punched the officer. The officer claimed falsely in his report, again using language very similar to many other reports we read, that the man had been struggling and kicking and that the force had been necessary to control him. Unknown to the officer, the incident was captured on surveillance video of the hospital where officers had taken him for a psychiatric evaluation. The officer's partner also did not report this unlawful force, and supervisors deemed the use of force justified. It was only after the hospital staff who reviewed the video contacted IPRA that anyone was disciplined.

Video evidence is available in only a sliver of force incidents. This under-scores the potential value of body-worn cameras—and functioning in-car cameras—to ensuring that the true circumstances of officer uses of force are known, and that officers can be held accountable when they use unreasonable force. As discussed in the Accountability Section of this Report, the Mayor re-cently has announced that the provision of body-worn cameras to all officers will be accelerated. This is commendable, but must be made part of a broader system of accountability in which protocols are put in place to ensure such equipment is used appropriately and that videos are routinely and randomly reviewed by supervisors to determine whether an incident reveals deficiencies in officer use of force.

D. CPD DOES NOT EFFECTIVELY USE CRISIS INTERVENTION TECHNIQUES TO REDUCE THE NEED FOR FORCE

When individuals experience a mental or behavioral health crisis, law en-forcement officers often are the first responders. Officers who are well trained in interacting with people in crisis can reduce the need to use force, save lives, and keep officers and others safer. Chicago has adopted a Crisis Intervention Team (CIT) approach as a means to safely and effectively respond to incidents involving persons in crisis. However, our review of CPD's force reports revealed that CPD uses force against people in crisis where force might have been avoided had a well-trained CIT officer responded to the scene and employed de-escalation techniques. While not all of these avoidable uses of force are unconstitutional, a meaningful number were, and deficiencies in CPD's CIT response contributes to the pattern or practice of unconstitutional use of force.

CPD's documentation of these incidents is often insufficient to determine whether the force was necessary, appropriate, or lawful. Consequently, all we know are the broad contours of terribly sad events—that officers used force against people in crisis who needed help. In one case, officers used a Taser against an unarmed, naked, 65-year-old-woman who had bipolar disorder and schizophrenia. Officers used a Taser "to subdue a mental who ignored verbal commands" because he was believed to be a danger to himself and others. Officers twice drive-stunned a man who they then transported for a mental health evaluation. Officers used a Taser in probe and drive-stun mode against an unarmed suicidal man who pulled away from the responding officers. Officers, who were responding to a call that a woman was "off meds" and "not violent," Tasered an unarmed woman because she pulled away and "repeatedly moved [her] arm." CPD did not conduct any investigation or review of these incidents to determine whether its response to these events was appropriate or lawful, or whether force could have been avoided.

The shooting deaths of Quintonio LeGrier and Bettie Jones by CPD officers who responded to a call for help with a domestic disturbance laid bare failures in CPD's crisis response systems—the dispatcher did not recognize the call as one involving someone in crisis and did not ask questions that might have resulted in clues that it did; a crisis-trained officer was not dispatched to the scene; the officers did not use crisis intervention techniques; and the officers made tactical errors that resulted in the shooting death of a bystander who had simply opened her door. In part as a response to this tragic event, Mayor Emanuel in December 2015 called for a review of the City's crisis intervention program. The crisis response review led to the announcement of plans for reforms which, if effectively implemented and sustained, could result in important improvements to the City's CIT program. There are additional steps the City should take. The City should do more to ensure that effective, well-trained crisis intervention officers respond to these events, and that crisis incidents are analyzed to determine whether changes to the program or CPD's crisis response are warranted.

1. <u>CPD's crisis intervention team model needs more support to be sustainable</u>

Like many major city police departments, CPD has developed a CIT designed to respond to incidents involving someone in crisis, whether related to addiction, trauma, or mental health.[9] While no process is a guarantee against all poor outcomes, an effective crisis intervention approach can reduce the need for force, including deadly force, and prevent unnecessary entanglement of persons in crisis with the criminal justice system where mental health services will better serve the individual and public safety.

CPD purports to adhere to the "Memphis Model" of crisis intervention response consistent with the recommendations of CIT International.[10] While specialized training is the cornerstone of the Memphis Model, CIT is more than just training.[11] It requires a dedicated cadre of trained officer volunteers large enough to cover all shifts and all districts.[12] It also requires coordination between dispatch and police, policies that facilitate referrals to mental health providers, coordination with such mental health service providers, and continuous evaluation of CIT outcomes.[13]

CPD began developing its CIT program in 2002 and made initial laudatory steps. It created a dedicated CIT unit to coordinate the CIT program and training. CPD trained its first cadre of CIT police officers in October 2004. By 2005, CPD rolled out CIT to its first two pilot districts and, as of April 2016, had trained 2,200 officers—18% of CPD's approximately 12,000-member authorized strength. In a 2010 study, CPD personnel reported that CIT training was effective and valuable, and that CIT-certified officers were able to more effectively resolve encounters, noting lives saved and diversion to service providers.[14]

Over the years, however, CPD has reduced the number of personnel assigned to run the CIT unit, from a high of nine people in 2008–2009, to three people as of late 2016. Those three people now bear the burden of training more officers and administering a CIT program that is being asked to do more than ever. Despite the work of these dedicated individuals and the positive response CIT officers have expressed when employing their skills on scene, CPD has not dedicated adequate resources to the CIT unit, thereby limiting its effectiveness and failing to achieve the promises of effective crisis intervention. In 2016, CPD increased its number of CIT trained officers by approximately one-third and plans to have 35% of the officers in the Department's Bureau of Patrol certified in CIT by the end of 2017. The already overburdened three-member CIT unit has been tasked with training these officers, which has reduced the ability of these hardworking individuals to develop thoughtful, effective, and well-delivered training. And because the staff that comprises the three-member CIT unit is now consumed with increased training demands, it is even more difficult for them to perform other critical functions, including conducting evaluations and follow-up on CIT incidents.

2. CPD should improve its CIT selection process in conjunction with plans to increase the number of CIT officers

As noted, the City has recognized the need for an effective crisis intervention response and has recently announced an ambitious plan to quickly increase its cadre of officers who have received the 40-hour crisis intervention training. The City's commendable desire for a rapid development of the CIT program, however, should not come at the expense of the quality of its crisis intervention response.

Effective crisis response requires a police department to designate and train certain officers to be members of the CIT, and dispatch those officers to all crisis intervention calls. It is important that all CIT officers have volunteered for the assignment. Officers who volunteer are more likely to have a deeper interest in and commitment to working with people in crisis. And they are more likely to develop proficiency and expertise as they become more experienced responding to crisis calls. Volunteers should be screened to determine that they are qualified. Of course, all officers should receive some training in responding to persons in crisis, and it may be useful to provide the full 40-hour CIT training to officers who have not volunteered for or not been accepted to the CIT program. But these officers should not be considered designated CIT officers and should not be dispatched to a crisis call in lieu of a CIT officer.

CPD, understandably eager to improve its crisis response, has deviated from the use of volunteer officers who are dedicated to working with people in crisis. CPD has required certain categories of officers, including all field training officers and sergeants, to take crisis intervention training and has designated those officers as CIT officers. In addition, CPD has dropped most screening for volunteer officers and is simply accepting most volunteers. By making CIT participation mandatory rather than voluntary and failing to screen those who volunteer, CPD has not developed a CIT team consisting of officers optimally suited for this work. While it is true that CPD likely needs more CIT officers to meet the demand of CIT calls, training large numbers of officers who have not volunteered for the task is, in the long run, unlikely to achieve the City's goal of improved crisis intervention response.

The City does not yet know how many additional CIT officers are necessary or where they should be deployed. The City has provided dispatchers with training to recognize when a person is in crisis, and recently developed a straightforward way for dispatchers to identify CIT officers available for dispatch. Already, these laudable steps have resulted in a five-fold increase in the number of calls identified as being crisis related from 2015–2016. This is a positive development because it suggests that dispatchers are becoming adept at identifying these calls and more CIT officers are being directed to handle crisis situations. But it has greatly increased the demand on the small CIT unit and the current CIT officers. And the City does not currently collect data on CIT calls in a way that would allow it to make informed staffing and deployment decisions to ensure an adequate number of CIT officers to cover all shifts in all districts. It has announced plans to do so. Each of these announced improvements should be implemented, supported, and sustained.

3. CPD should analyze crisis incidents to determine whether CIT is functioning effectively

CPD does not have an effective system in place to evaluate its response to CIT calls. CPD has developed a Crisis Intervention Report that is designed to capture important information about its response to crisis calls, including whether the call was recognized and identified as a CIT call before the officer's arrival and whether crisis techniques were employed. Even under CPD's newly revised policies, however, officers do not complete this form if the incident requires any other reporting. Thus, if an officer uses force during the crisis call, the officer will be required to fill out a Tactical Response Report (TRR) and therefore is not required to fill out a Crisis Intervention Report. As discussed above, the TRRs provide very little information about a use of force and include almost none of the information necessary to evaluate whether the crisis response was appropriate. Consequently, CPD has no ability to analyze the most concerning crisis incidents to evaluate its response.

During our review of force incidents, we saw many examples of force, including deadly force, being used against individuals in crisis. We did not see any evidence that CPD had engaged in after-action analysis to determine whether: the force used was reasonable and necessary; the incident had been recognized as a crisis incident and if not, why not; a CIT officer was dispatched to the scene and, if not, whether there were any barriers to dispatching a CIT officer; the officer used crisis intervention techniques; or the incident demonstrated that improvements in policy or training are needed. CPD should develop an after-action review process that answers these questions so that it understands how its CIT team is functioning and can correct deficiencies and build on successes.

CPD also has no mechanism to evaluate the quality of its CIT officers. Once an officer receives the 40-hour training and is certified as a CIT officer, CPD does not evaluate that officer's performance to determine whether the officer is applying the CIT training and is effective in resolving crises, or whether the officer may need some refresher training or additional support, or is not working out as a CIT officer. Although the City is aware of this need, this improvement was not part of the City's recently announced plans for reform. Without analyzing these incidents and the skills and training of its officers, CPD has no way of knowing whether its CIT program is effective, whether refinements in policies and training are needed, and whether the performance of any individual officers should be addressed.

The City's plans to improve its CIT program—including by increasing and improving data collection, providing training to Office of Emergency Management and Communications dispatchers, and increasing the number of trained CIT officers—are important and long needed. But these steps by themselves are not sufficient. Until they are accomplished, the City cannot know how many CIT officers it truly needs. Similarly, until CPD requires officers to accurately document these events and engages in analysis and evaluation of this data, it cannot know whether its training is effective or in need of improvement. We applaud the City's desire to respond quickly to legitimate concerns about its CIT program, but it is important that the response be based on an understanding of the effectiveness of and challenges to its current program. Failure to develop that understanding may, in the long term, impede its ability to improve its crisis intervention response.

E. CPD'S FAILURE TO ACCURATELY DOCUMENT AND MEANINGFULLY REVIEW OFFICERS' USE OF FORCE PERPETUATES A PATTERN OF UNREASONABLE FORCE

CPD policy requires officers to report most uses of force, but in practice, officers are not required to provide sufficient detail about the force they used, and most officer force is not reviewed or investigated, notwithstanding CPD policy requirements.

In the most serious instances of force—where an officer discharges his firearm in a manner that could potentially hit someone—CPD responds to the scene to conduct a preliminary investigation, but IPRA has the authority to investigate whether the shooting was justified. Because of IPRA's central role in these cases, all aspects regarding the reporting and review of these uses of force—including CPD's initial response to the scene—is discussed in the Accountability Section of this Report.

Below, however, we discuss the reporting and review of other uses of force. CPD policy requires supervisors to investigate all reported uses of force, other than shootings, to determine whether they were in compliance with policy. In actuality, however, most force is not reviewed. As a result of so few force incidents being reported and even nominally investigated, and the low quality of the force investigations that do occur, there is no consistent, meaningful accountability for officers who use force in violation of the law or CPD policy. Nor is there any opportunity for meaningful assessment of whether policies, training, or equipment should be modified to improve force outcomes in the future. The failure to ensure the accurate reporting, review, and investigation of officers' use of force has helped create a culture in which officers expect to use force and never be carefully scrutinized about the propriety of that use.

1. <u>CPD does not require officers to accurately report uses of less-lethal force</u>

CPD's documentation of officer use of less-lethal force is consistently insufficient. Moreover, CPD and IPRA have accepted insufficient documentation even when officers' use of force is suspect, or when people complain about the force officers used against them.

CPD policy requires officers to complete a TRR anytime they use force, except for control holds to handcuff someone and techniques attendant to handcuffing or searching a person that do not result in injury or an allegation of injury.[15] As detailed earlier, TRRs do not require officers to provide a narrative but instead present a series of boxes officers check to indicate in standard terms the force used, such as "elbow strike" or "take down/emergency handcuffing," and the resistance encountered, such as "stiffened," "imminent threat of battery," or "attack with weapon." There is a small textbox on the form for the officer to include additional information, but it is too small to provide an actual narrative of the encounter and officers rarely use it at all. The design of the form also discourages officers from providing important details about the force they used. For example, an officer might check that the officer used "kicks," but the TRR contains no requirement that the officer state how many kicks were used, where these blows landed, any injuries they specifically caused, or the order in which events occurred. The form also does not require officers to indicate what alternatives to force they considered or tried, and why these efforts were or would be unsuccessful. If a subject is injured, they must check the box for "injured" but they need not and generally do not document what those injuries were. Officers do often include some description of the encounter either in the arrest report or the case report that is related to the TRR. In reviewing CPD's use of force, we reviewed all of the documents the City provided related to a particular TRR. Even with this additional information, however, the true details of a force encounter were often obscured by a lack of sufficient detail and the use of boilerplate language.

In one typical example, officers documented that they used force on a man who they alleged was trying to interfere with their arrest of his brother for domestic battery. According to the arrest report, the man kept approaching officers as they tried to make the arrest, despite repeated commands not to do so. The officers arrested him for resisting arrest and reported that he tightened his arms and tried to pull away while they were placing him in custody. On the TRRs, the officers checked off "arm bar," "pressure sensitive areas," "control instrument," and "takedown/emergency handcuffing" in describing the force they used. It is impossible for anyone, including these officers' supervisors charged with determining whether the force was reasonable and within policy, to know even approximately how much force these officers used. But what is described could very well be unreasonable—officers provided no details that would justify a takedown, and he appears to have merely been upset that his brother was being arrested. Indeed, in the box in which the supervisor is to document the subject's response to the use of force, the lieutenant wrote that the man said, "I don't know why they arrested me." CPD conducted no follow-up investigation of this use of force.

In many other instances, there are indications in the reports that the force used was more significant than reflected in the opaque description of events. In one incident, officers arrested a man because he "tried to physically interfere" with the arrest of another man. While they were arresting him, he began to pull away and grabbed and pushed the officers. According to the arrest reports, one officer "executed a knee strike." But four officers filled out TRRs, indicating that they each used force against him. In describing their actions, one officer checked the boxes for "takedown/emergency handcuffing" and "closed hand strike/punch;" the second checked "open hand strike," "takedown/emergency handcuffing," "closed hand strike/punch," and "kick;" a third officer checked "wristlock," "arm bar," "takedown/emergency handcuffing," "closed hand strike/punch," and "knee strike;" and the fourth officer checked "knee strike." None of the officers reported how many strikes they delivered, where they landed, or why each was necessary. All four officers checked the box indicating that the man was injured, but those injuries were not described anywhere. In the man's booking photo, he has abrasions on his face.

For some files we reviewed, the injuries the victims suffered, rather than the explanations by CPD officers, reveal the level of force that CPD officers actually employed. For example, an officer pushed an 18-year-old female student onto his police car, chipping her tooth, because, as he was walking her to his squad car after breaking up a fight between her and another girl outside of their school, she screamed profanities and flailed her arms. The officer reported that the injury occurred when he performed "an emergency take-down maneuver to regain control." The girl was 5'4" tall and weighed 120 pounds, while the officer was 6'1" and weighed 186 pounds. Without requesting any additional information, supervisors approved this use of force. In the girl's complaint to IPRA, she alleged that when she informed the officer he had chipped her tooth, the officer responded that he did not "give a fuck." IPRA exonerated the officer without interviewing him.

It also appears that officers have been instructed on the language they should use to justify force. We saw many instances where officers justified force based on a boilerplate description of resistance that provides insufficient specificity to understand the force used or resistance encountered. For example, officers frequently reported using force because the person "flailed" his or her arms. Officers used a Taser against a man who appeared to be in crisis when he "stiffened his body, pulled away, and flailed his arms;" drive-stunned a man because, when they went to arrest him, he "began to flail his arms wildly;" deployed a Taser against a man who resisted arrest for theft by "flailing his arms;" and drive-stunned a man because, when they tried to arrest him, he "pulled away and flailed his arms."

The examples above are illustrative of problems we found in the hundreds of files we reviewed. In many of these files, it was nearly impossible for us to understand how much force officers used or whether the level of resistance justified the force used. Further, the design of the form, including that there is so little space for officers to provide a narrative account of the force they used, makes it impossible for officers to provide a complete or useful account of the force incident.

2.   CPD rarely reviews or investigates officers' use of less-lethal force

CPD supervisors consistently violate CPD's force review policy. CPD policy requires supervisors to conduct investigations of every reportable officer use of non-shooting force. When an officer is involved in a use of force requiring completion of a TRR, the officer is to "immediately notify their immediate supervisor that he or she has been involved in a use of force incident." The officer must "submit his or her completed TRR to their immediate supervisor for review." The supervisor is to "respond to the scene when the injury to a subject or member is of the severity to require immediate medical attention," "ensure that all witnesses are identified, interviewed, and that information is recorded in the appropriate report," and request an evidence technician to take photos of subjects who were injured. When an officer uses a Taser, the officer must request that a supervisor respond to the scene, and a supervisor at least one rank higher than the officer must respond. Supervisors must also obtain a copy of the Taser deployment data sheet and are prohibited from approving the TRR until it has been received and reviewed.

In practice, little of this happens. In the hundreds of TRR files we reviewed, we rarely saw evidence that supervisors responded to the scene unless officers shot someone. Canvasses for witnesses rarely occur and even witnesses who are present are rarely interviewed. Even where TRRs make clear that a subject was injured, no photographs are taken of the injuries. In most instances, a "mugshot" is taken of arrestees, and in the files we reviewed we sometimes saw unexplained injuries to the person's face. TRRs are routinely approved without any evidence in the file that a Taser deployment data sheet was obtained or reviewed. Indeed, when we referenced these requirements in interviews with officers in an effort to gain an understanding of the system, officers and supervisors of all ranks seemed surprised to hear that these requirements existed. None asserted that these requirements were adhered to on any regular basis and most struggled to explain what these policies require.

In practice, a supervisor may interview the subject of the use of force if the subject is immediately available to the supervisor. Otherwise, for example if the person has been transported to the hospital, he or she will not be interviewed, which means that supervisors generally do not interview the subjects of the most concerning uses of force. If the person is available and agrees to speak with the supervisor, the supervisor typically documents one or two sentences that summarize the person's statement. Many of the interview summaries we saw suggest the interview centered more on what the subject did to justify the officer taking action at all, rather than the circumstances of the use of force itself. These interviews are not recorded and in none of the files we reviewed did the supervisor document the questions asked of the person.

After the supervisor's force review is complete, the supervisor is supposed to review the TRR "for legibility and completeness and indicate approval of such by signing the appropriate box." In 2014, this requirement was modified to require that the supervisor "review the member's TRR and, if appropriate, approve the report." In practice, sergeants view this role as ministerial. They play no role in reviewing the force itself for appropriateness. Sergeants we spoke to told us their only role is to ensure the form is filled out correctly, and none had ever refused to sign a report based on an evaluation of the force itself. From at least 2002 until 2014, the task of evaluating the force used was assigned to the watch commander, who was to record the subject's statement regarding the use of force and conduct an evaluation to determine whether the force was within CPD policy. In 2014, these tasks were given to lieutenants.

Despite the lack of detail describing most uses of force and the near total lack of additional information collected, supervisors routinely use boilerplate language to approve the TRRs, often only minutes after the officer submits it, even where there is information in the file indicating the officer violated CPD policy or the law. In the files we reviewed, we saw only a handful in which a supervisor referred the incident to IPRA for investigation or requested additional information from the officer.[16] Our interviews with CPD officers were consistent with these findings. One commander told us he could not recall ever calling for further investigation of a use of force. Another said that he has never seen an unreasonable use of force on a TRR. That same commander also said he had never seen any TRR wherein he identified a better tactical decision, even if the force was reasonable.

Illustrative of the inadequacy of supervisory review of force incidents is the troubling incident discussed above in which officers deployed a Taser against an unarmed 65-year-old woman who was in mental health crisis. The TRR file contains only a cursory description of the incident, and without reviewing the Taser data download or requesting any investigation, the sergeant approved this TRR three minutes after the officer submitted it, and the lieutenant approved it less than 25 minutes after that. There is no indication that the lieutenant asked the officers any questions about whether this force was necessary or whether there might have been something they could have done to avoid using force against this woman, such as seeking assistance from a crisis intervention trained officer.

Our investigation also found instances in which CPD officers used canines against children and conducted no investigation to determine whether these uses of force were reasonable or necessary. In one case, officers allowed a canine to bite two unarmed 17-year-old boys who had broken into an elementary school and stolen some items. In another case, officers deployed a canine to locate two boys, ages 12 and 14, who had broken into a school and stolen some candy and basketballs. Fortunately, the canine did not bite them and the boys were uninjured. CPD should have investigated these uses of force to determine whether they were reasonable, yet in both cases supervisors approved the force without an investigation.

F. CPD's New De-escalation Training and Proposed Policy Revisions Should be Expanded and Sustained

In March 2016, CPD began a review of its use-of-force policies in an effort to provide clearer direction for officers on the appropriate use of force. CPD released the draft force policies in October 2016 for public comment. The proposed revisions address core force principles such as the sanctity of life, ethical behavior, objective and proportional use of force, use of deadly force, de-escalation, and force mitigation. CPD is currently reviewing the public feedback and has stated that it will incorporate suggestions and improvements to prepare final versions of the policies. CPD also has begun providing all officers with force-mitigation training designed to better equip officers to de-escalate conflicts safely; recognize the signs of mental illness, trauma, and crisis situations; and respond quickly and appropriately when force is necessary.

We appreciate that CPD has recognized the need to address some of the problems described in this Report. The steps the City has taken are meaningful and important. To be effective, the new approaches to the use of force must be embodied in these polices, and training must be supported by leadership and enforced by supervisors to ensure officers follow them consistently. CPD's past policy rollouts have faced considerable challenges, with policies sometimes issued before officers have been trained on them, leading to confusion and frustration about what is required and why. CPD's Fraternal Order of Police (FOP) union leadership already has expressed concern that the 2016 draft force policies do not adequately address the concerns of officers. CPD must demonstrate more thoughtful planning and commit more resources and time for the training and rollout of force policy revisions so that officers will understand, accept, and be able to safely and effectively implement the new requirements.

Additionally, these revised policies do not improve upon CPD's deficient procedures, discussed above, for reporting and investigating force. In part because of these deficiencies, officers are not held accountable to the current force policies. Until these deficiencies are addressed, revisions to policies and training are unlikely to achieve the necessary changes in how officers use force.

III. CHICAGO'S DEFICIENT ACCOUNTABILITY SYSTEMS CONTRIBUTE TO CPD'S PATTERN OR PRACTICE OF UNCONSTITUTIONAL CONDUCT

❧

A well-functioning accountability system is the keystone to lawful policing. In combination with effective supervision, a robust accountability system is required in order to identify and correct inappropriate uses of force and other kinds of misconduct—with discipline, training, and counseling as appropriate—which in turn helps prevent misconduct. But Chicago seldom holds officers accountable for misconduct. In the five-year period prior to our investigation, Chicago had investigated 409 police shootings and found that just two were unjustified. It is similarly illustrative that the City paid over half a billion dollars to settle or pay judgments in police misconduct cases since 2004 without even conducting disciplinary investigations in over half of those cases, and it recommended discipline in fewer than 4% of those cases it did examine. Our comprehensive investigation of Chicago's accountability structures and systems found clear indications, set forth in detail in this Section, that those structures and systems are broken.

Together with our law enforcement experts, we scrutinized hundreds of misconduct and IPRA force investigations, and closely reviewed related policies and protocols. We looked at the available resources and organizational structure of CPD's accountability components. We talked to scores of current and former IPRA and BIA investigators and supervisors. We also spoke with many line officers, members of CPD leadership, and police union officials about their experiences with and views of CPD's accountability systems. We spoke with members of the public about these same issues.

Our investigation confirmed that CPD's accountability systems are broadly ineffective at deterring or detecting misconduct, and at holding officers accountable when they violate the law or CPD policy. As with most complicated problems that have built up over time and repeatedly been glossed over, we found that many factors contribute to the systemic deficiencies of CPD's accountability system. These are summarized below.

Our investigation revealed that the City fails to conduct any investigation of nearly half of police misconduct complaints and that a number of institutional barriers contribute to this fact. There are provisions in the City's agreements with the unions that impede the investigative process, such as the general requirement that a complainant sign a sworn affidavit and limitations on investigating anonymous complaints and older incidents of misconduct. That said, the union agreements contain override provisions for some of these provisions that the City rarely utilizes. Other barriers have been created solely by the City, such as internal policies allowing investigative agencies to truncate investigations of serious misconduct through mediation, administratively close complaints deemed less serious, and ignore mandatory investigations into uses of force that could identify misconduct or faulty training issues. The City must work to remove these barriers so it can thoroughly investigate all claims of misconduct and uses of force and thus regain community trust.

Our review of files for complaints that *were* investigated revealed consistent patterns of egregious investigative deficiencies that impede the search for the truth. Witnesses and accused officers are frequently not interviewed at all, or not interviewed until long after the incident when memories have faded. When interviews do occur, questioning is often biased in favor of officers, and witness coaching by union attorneys is prevalent and unimpeded—a dynamic neither we nor our law enforcement experts had seen to nearly such an extent in other agencies. Investigators routinely fail to collect probative evidence. The procedures surrounding investigations allow for ample opportunity for collusion among officers and are devoid of any rules prohibiting such coordination. We found that a lack of resources and investigative training contribute to these investigative problems. We also found that investigations foundered because of the pervasive cover-up culture among CPD officers, which the accountability entities accept as an immutable fact rather than something to root out.

In the rare instances when complaints of misconduct are sustained, discipline is inconsistent and unpredictable, and meted out in a way that does little to deter misconduct. Officers are often disciplined for conduct far less serious than the conduct that prompted the investigation, and in many cases, a complaint may be sustained but the officer is not disciplined at all. The police discipline system, including the City's draft disciplinary matrix, fails to provide clear guidance on appropriate, fair, and consistent penalty ranges, thus undermining the legitimacy and deterrent effect of discipline within CPD. And the City's process for finalizing IPRA's and BIA's discipline recommendations further delays and inappropriately influences discipline, and compromises the ability for such discipline to withstand appeal.

We also found deficiencies within Chicago's Police Board that impair its ability to be a fully effective component of CPD's accountability structure. The Board should focus on its function of providing due process to officers and ensuring they are held accountable as appropriate. The Board's current role as conduit for providing community input into CPD's accountability system may be more appropriately handled by the Community Oversight Board that the City has committed to working with the Chicago public to create. We found also that the completeness of Police Board consideration of discipline can be improved by modifying current practices, such as the current rules that bar the officer's "negative" disciplinary history but allow the officer's "complimentary" history, and allowing favorable character evidence by the accused's supervisors to be offered at the liability phase of proceedings.

Throughout the time our investigation has been underway, the City has undertaken positive steps to improve its accountability structure and repair its relationship with the community, and it should be commended for this. But the problems we found are complex and entrenched, and have persisted in part because the City has been unable, and at times has not committed the long-term sustained focus and resources, to eliminate the problem and keep it from coming back.

A. CHICAGO'S SYSTEMS FOR INVESTIGATING POLICE CONDUCT

Chicago's police accountability system is currently divided among three investigative entities: (1) the Independent Police Review Authority (IPRA); (2) CPD's Bureau of Internal Affairs (BIA); and (3) CPD district offices. IPRA was created in 2007 to replace the Office of Professional Standards and is intended to operate as a civilian disciplinary body that is independent from CPD. IPRA serves two main functions: it receives and registers *all* complaints against CPD officers and assigns them to either BIA or itself, depending on the claim; and it investigates specific categories of complaints as well as other non-complaint police incidents and recommends discipline where appropriate.

IPRA investigates four types of complaints: (1) excessive force; (2) domestic violence; (3) coercion; and (4) bias-based verbal abuse. It also conducts mandatory investigations, regardless of alleged misconduct for: (1) officer weapon discharges (including gun, Taser, or pepper spray); and (2) death or serious injury in police custody. Over the last five years, IPRA has received almost 7,000 citizen complaints per year and retained investigative authority over approximately 30% of them as falling within IPRA's jurisdiction. In addition, it receives notification of approximately 800 mandatory investigations a year. IPRA is headed by the Chief IPRA Administrator (currently, Sharon Fairley), who is appointed by Chicago's Mayor and operates with an 80-person civilian staff.

BIA investigates complaints that are outside of IPRA's jurisdiction, which consists of approximately 70% of all police complaints. BIA is an entity within the Police Superintendent's Office, and the BIA Chief reports directly to the Superintendent. BIA is responsible for investigating four types of officer misconduct: (1) criminal misconduct; (2) bribery and other forms of corruption; (3) drug or other substance abuse; and (4) driving under the influence, as well as all operational and other violations of CPD rules. BIA receives approximately 4,500 complaints per year from IPRA and refers approximately 40% of the less serious investigations to the 22 individual police districts for investigation.

Given that many of the same problematic practices are common to both IPRA and BIA investigations, below we discuss those different entities' investigations hand in hand. Where the evidence we found demonstrates that a specific problem is particularly acute in one entity, we have made that clear.

After IPRA and BIA complete their investigations, the investigator issues a finding of "sustained," "not sustained," "unfounded," or "exonerated."[17] If one or more of the allegations of misconduct is sustained, the investigator's supervisor makes a discipline recommendation. While CPD is in the process of changing this, historically, the recommended discipline is not pursuant to any applicable guidelines, but rather is based only upon experience and historical precedence. The investigation concludes with a summary report by the investigator.

Investigators' findings recommendations and discipline recommendations for all sustained cases at either IPRA or BIA are subject to several layers of CPD review before they become final decisions. First, except in cases where discharge is recommended, the recommendations are subject to a Command Channel Review (CCR), in which supervisors in the accused officer's chain of command review and comment on the recommended discipline. Next, recommendations, along with CCR comments, are forwarded to the Superintendent for review. Discharge recommendations skip the CCR review and go directly to the Superintendent. If the Superintendent approves the recommendations, the decision is final, but if not, it is subject to another process before the Chicago Police Board, which is made up of nine private citizens appointed by Chicago's Mayor with the City Council's consent. If the Superintendent disagrees with IPRA's recommendations, the Superintendent has the burden of convincing a three-person panel from the Chicago Police Board that the Superintendent is justified in departing from those recommendations.

The Police Board also acts as a reviewing body by adjudicating CPD decisions recommending discharge, or appeals of suspensions over 30 days for sergeants, lieutenants, and captains. Such reviews consist of a full evidentiary hearing before a Police Board hearing officer who makes a report and recommendation, which is reviewed by the full Police Board before a final decision is made. The Police Board's role in accountability, particularly its role in reviewing disciplinary decisions, is discussed in Section III.H., below.

Other than in discharge cases, which are heard only by the Police Board, officers also can challenge final CPD discipline decisions through arbitration, which can either be a summary disposition on the record or a full evidentiary hearing, depending on the officer's rank and the level of discipline recommended. Decisions of the Police Board and arbitrators are subject to administrative review in the Circuit Court of Cook County and can then be appealed to the Illinois Appellate Court and the Illinois Supreme Court.

In October 2016, the City took steps towards creating the Civilian Office of Police Accountability (COPA). COPA, which under current plans will assume IPRA's responsibilities sometime in 2017, appears to have the potential to be a meaningful improvement over IPRA, but gaps also appear to remain within this entity and through all other components of Chicago's accountability systems. COPA, and its limitations, are discussed at the end of this Section.

B. THE CITY HAS PUT IN PLACE POLICIES AND PRACTICES THAT IMPEDE THE INVESTIGATION OF OFFICER MISCONDUCT

City policies and practices prevent investigation of a substantial portion of CPD misconduct complaints and uses of force, including many it is required by law to conduct. Deficient systems and police culture inhibit many other complaints of police misconduct from ever being filed. These deficiencies keep unconstitutional conduct and practices hidden. We discuss below several of the unnecessary barriers to investigation, including: a formal policy against investigating many complaints about force; referral of verbal abuse complaints to a process in which no discipline can be imposed even if misconduct occurred; a failure to investigate anonymous complaints or complaints without a sworn affidavit; and handling many complaints via a so-called "mediation" process that is in fact antithetical to the tenets and goals of complaint mediation. Collectively, through this patchwork of policies and practices, the City fails to conduct any meaningful investigation of nearly half of the complaints made against officers. This is separate and apart from CPD's failure to investigate most of the Taser and "no-hit" shootings required under local law or to conduct any review of the vast majority of officer uses of force that are discussed in the Force Section of this Report.

While IPRA and the City appeared to have acquiesced to, or developed, many of these restrictions to alleviate a crushing docket, the City's new Police Accountability ordinance has set aside significantly more resources for COPA than IPRA currently has. The City should revisit these restrictions in light of COPA's expanded capacity and ensure that they are removed.

COPA's capacity, in turn, should be increased further if necessary to allow it to investigate the cases that it has previously been unable to because of the restrictions set out below.

1.   The City has unduly narrowed the scope of misconduct allegations that are fully investigated

One way in which the City has acquiesced to narrowing the scope of misconduct complaints it investigates is through the police union contracts' provision requiring a sworn affidavit from the complainant before a claim is investigated. While officers should certainly not be subject to false claims, this affidavit requirement creates a tremendous disincentive to come forward with legitimate claims and keeps hidden serious police misconduct that should be investigated. Until this affidavit requirement can be changed, however, IPRA and BIA should be acting more aggressively to ensure that this requirement does not stand in the way of investigating meritorious, and sometimes egregious, allegations of misconduct.

Most police misconduct complaints begin with a letter, email, or phone call, through which the complainant provides information about a misconduct incident. But in nearly every case, neither IPRA nor BIA will conduct any meaningful investigation of the complaint unless the complainant meets an investigator in person and provides a complete recorded statement of the incident, and submits a sworn statement that all claims are true and correct under penalties provided by law. The City closes about 40% of all complaints (an average of 2,400 complaints a year) because the complainant did not sign an affidavit. A 2015 report showed that between 2011 and 2014, IPRA closed 58% of its total complaints for lack of an affidavit.

There are many understandable reasons why victims of police misconduct may choose not to submit a supporting affidavit. Chicago residents who have lost faith in police accountability altogether have no interest in participating in that very system. Others fear retaliation—that if they proceed with an investigation, they will be targeted by CPD officers. Many more cannot meet the logistical hurdles necessary to file the affidavit, including taking time off of work during a weekday to sit for a lengthy interview. Additionally, civil rights plaintiffs and criminal defendants—both of whom may have potentially valid misconduct complaints—typically follow their attorney's reasonable advice and refrain from providing verified statements pending their criminal and civil litigation. In fact, for most of the lawsuits in which police misconduct victims received significant settlements or verdicts, IPRA's parallel misconduct investigation was closed for lack of an affidavit. In other words, the City routinely *pays large sums* to police misconduct victims who have filed non-verified complaints in civil litigation describing the misconduct in question but fails to *investigate* these same officers for disciplinary purposes because their administrative complaints are not verified. And even criminal defendants who wish to file affidavits so their complaint can be investigated cannot always do so because certain investigators rarely, if ever, go into Cook County Jail or to state correctional institutions to obtain affidavits that would be willingly given.

CPD's unions correctly note that investigators can "override" the requirement for a sworn affidavit, and we agree that IPRA and BIA should make more use of the override option. IPRA investigators we interviewed relayed that overrides are not encouraged, and no training was provided on how to obtain one. Not surprisingly, this override provision was used only 17 times in the last five years. But, there is also no question that the override option is problematic in a number of respects. To obtain an override, BIA or IPRA must obtain an affidavit from the other agency's director, verifying that she has reviewed "objective verifiable evidence" and affirms "that it is necessary and appropriate for the investigation to continue." Not only does this process undermine the independence of IPRA, and create an additional procedural barrier to investigating misconduct, but requiring that objective verifiable evidence exists before an investigation can be undertaken puts the cart before the horse.

Even though the affidavit requirement and the override exception restrict the City's ability to ultimately sustain a complaint, they should not be used as an excuse to avoid a full and fair investigation that begins immediately upon a complaint being made. Currently, investigators conduct no witness interviews until after securing a sworn affidavit. Yet because investigators already have a statement from the complainant describing the basis of the complaint—albeit not "verified"—most times they have sufficient information to conduct their investigation immediately, before witnesses' memories fade and evidence disappears. Additionally, by interviewing witnesses and canvassing for additional evidence, IPRA and BIA would be in a better position to consider an override request. Undertaking such investigative efforts immediately, even without an affidavit, will improve accountability and help demonstrate to the community that IPRA and BIA are not indifferent to complaints of police misconduct.

CPD's and IPRA's failure to investigate anonymous complaints, pursuant to the City's collective bargaining agreement with officers, further impedes the ability to investigate and identify legitimate instances of misconduct. As noted above, given the code of silence within CPD and a potential fear of retaliation, there are valid reasons a complainant may seek to report police misconduct anonymously, particularly if the complainant is a fellow officer. Indeed, it was an anonymous tip that led to the video release of the Laquan McDonald shooting. IPRA and BIA should have greater discretion in investigating tips and complaints from anonymous sources.

Likewise, the CBA contains other provisions that have the effect of impairing investigations of police misconduct. For example, the CBAs mandate disclosure of a complainant's name prior to questioning the accused officer. Like the anonymous complaint prohibition, this provision is problematic because of the significant fear of police retaliation by many complainants. Experts in law enforcement investigations noted that disclosure of the complainant's identity during the investigation has the potential to chill misconduct reporting without providing discernible benefit to the officer. IPRA and BIA already must provide the accused officer with detailed notice of the misconduct charges as well as copies of all relevant police records; this should allow the accused officer to sufficiently prepare before being questioned. Eliminating this identity disclosure requirement, and clearly communicating it to complainants, should encourage more complainants to come forward without fear of retaliation.

Finally, the City has agreed with CPD's police unions to prohibit investigations into older incidents of police misconduct, even where those incidents may include serious misconduct or be probative of a pattern of misconduct. One CBA provision prohibits IPRA or BIA from initiating any disciplinary investigations into incidents over five years old, absent authorization by the Superintendent, and another requires destruction of most disciplinary records older than five years. Yet, CPD's culture and "code of silence" as described elsewhere in these findings may prevent disclosure of serious misconduct in a timely fashion. Moreover, the document destruction provision not only may impair the investigation of older misconduct, but also deprives CPD of important discipline and personnel documentation that will assist in monitoring historical patterns of misconduct.

IPRA and BIA also fail to investigate certain claims of conduct that they cursorily determine are not "serious" enough to warrant a full investigation. Under its "Excessive Force Protocol," IPRA administratively closes, without any investigation, most complaints alleging excessive force in connection with handcuffing, take-downs incidental to arrest, and displays of an officer's gun, because IPRA determines that the force used was "de-minimis." As our expert noted, however, it is relatively easy for officers to gratuitously cause excruciating pain during the handcuffing process merely by overexerting the amount of force used in a trained finger or wrist lock. Such gratuitous punishment is hardly de-minimis, even if it leaves no marks or lasting injury. Similarly, as explained in more detail in above, BIA does not investigate complaints of verbal abuse by an officer, but instead refers them to district supervisors for "non-disciplinary intervention."

It is reasonable for IPRA and BIA to exercise discretion about the resources to assign to certain types of cases. But there is no system in place to ensure that a properly trained investigator is objectively evaluating these force and verbal abuse complaints and performing a sufficiently thorough preliminary investigation to accurately decide whether a full investigation is warranted. Moreover, such information is not properly tracked and maintained to enable IPRA and BIA to determine trends, or ensure that CPD is properly identifying officers who are appropriate candidates for referral to one of CPD's behavioral intervention programs. *See* Report, Section IV.B.

2. The City does not meaningfully investigate certain types of force unless a misconduct complaint is filed

IPRA fails to investigate several types of force despite being formally required to do so. IPRA has long been required by ordinance to undertake investigations of Taser discharges and officer-involved shootings where no one is hit,[18] yet, in practice, it investigates neither. This problematic practice results in a large number of potentially serious policy or constitutional violations going undetected and undeterred. The pattern of unreasonable force our investigation found both reflects this longstanding failure to adequately review officers' use of force and underscores the necessity of doing so to eliminate this pattern of unlawful conduct.

IPRA's failure to meaningfully investigate Taser discharges has had significant implications. In 2009, IPRA reported just under 200 Taser uses, and as required under local ordinance, was investigating each use. A year later, CPD expanded its Taser program, and uses jumped dramatically to almost 900 and have since leveled off at almost 600 a year over the last five years. In 2010, as Taser uses were expanding, IPRA stopped investigating all but a few of the Taser uses—in particular, those accompanied by a citizen complaint or an override. The former IPRA Chief Administrator explained this investigative change was simply due to the fact that IPRA does not have resources to more thoroughly audit every Taser use.

While the number of Taser discharges may have outpaced IPRA's ability to investigate each discharge, this does not excuse the City's failure to ensure that somebody reviewed officers' Taser use. By placing responsibility for investigating Taser discharges in IPRA, and then failing to ensure that IPRA did so, the City created a system in which no one assesses whether Tasers are being used appropriately or effectively. This, in turn, prevents the City and CPD from uncovering the potential need for retraining or additional policy refinement, and of course from deterring future misuse of Tasers by holding officers accountable for abuse. While the City's new Police Accountability Ordinance removes jurisdiction from IPRA for investigating most Taser discharges, it does not create a structure to ensure that Taser discharges or other less-lethal uses of force will be investigated in the future. Such a structure is needed to ensure CPD's pattern or practice of unreasonable force does not continue.

IPRA's longstanding decision not to respond to or investigate officer-involved shootings in which officers miss their intended targets is also problematic. Although "no-hit" shootings raise the same legal, policy, tactical, and ethical issues as "hit" shootings, IPRA essentially ignores the cases unless they generate a misconduct complaint. In most no-hit cases, IPRA merely collects written reports from the involved and witness officers. IPRA does not investigate the shooting scene, does not interview anyone, and does not conduct any analysis of physical evidence. Nor, in cases where officers fire at people who escape, is there any indication that IPRA or anyone else checks with area hospitals in an attempt to confirm that in fact no one was struck. Once it collects the often-sparse documentation of a no-hit shooting, IPRA closes its file with the finding, "administrative closure" without any comment on compliance with the law or CPD policy.

IPRA receives approximately 35 notifications per year for no-hit shootings. Many no-hit shootings we reviewed raised serious questions that warranted investigation, but were ignored simply because the officer missed his intended target. For example, in one case, an off-duty CPD officer fired multiple times at a car, missing the driver, but injuring him with shattered glass. The written reports in the file (there were no recorded interviews) did not address critical questions, such as where the officer stood in relation to the car, where his bullets struck, or the car's direction of travel. Notwithstanding these glaring omissions and CPD's policy generally prohibiting officers from shooting at vehicles, IPRA closed the file.

The difference between a hit and a no-hit shooting case may only be a matter of bad aim; investigation of no-hit cases is thus vital to uncovering deficiencies in policies, procedures, tactics, equipment, and training that could prevent unnecessary or inappropriate shootings in the future.

In nearly all Taser and no-hit shooting cases, no complainant comes forward. This reluctance, even in questionable shootings, is understandable both because of retaliation fears described above and because of the possibility that such individuals may have been involved in criminal conduct. Nevertheless, the officer may have intentionally or unintentionally engaged in unreasonable force in the incident, or otherwise violated policy. It is thus essential that investigations in these cases occur even in the absence of an underlying complaint.

3. <u>Attempts to expedite investigations through so-called "mediation" allow officers to circumvent punishment for serious misconduct</u>

Many serious misconduct complaints that avoid the investigative barriers described above are not fully investigated but instead are resolved through what IPRA calls "mediation." However, this program is not true police-complaint mediation where parties meet to arrive at a mutually agreeable resolution of their dispute and, often, gain a better understanding of each other's perspective along the way. Such programs, like the one that has been implemented in conjunction with our consent decree regarding the New Orleans Police Department, provide an opportunity for dialogue and understanding between victims of police misconduct and the officers who are the subject of their complaints in the presence of a neutral third party. "Mediation" at CPD, however, is a euphemism for a plea bargain, and is used in a way that often inappropriately, albeit quickly, disposes of serious misconduct claims in exchange for modest discipline, while misleading the public into thinking that accountability has been achieved.

"Mediation" is used by IPRA to resolve an allegation of misconduct, usually by having the officer agree to a sustained finding in exchange for reduced punishment. Mediation is always used before investigations are complete, including before the accused officer is ever interviewed. This premature use of mediation deprives investigators of important information they could use to better determine the severity and breadth of the misconduct.

The complainant is generally excluded from the process altogether, further separating the "mediation" process used by Chicago from the typical mediation used in other departments. Persons who complain of police misconduct are afforded no opportunity to meet with the officers who are the subject of their grievances or provide input into the resolution of their complaints if disciplinary action is taken. At the end of this process, complainants receive a letter that even IPRA leadership admits can be misleading, because it advises that the complaint was sustained but never discloses the precise charge that was sustained or the discipline imposed.

These flaws are particularly concerning given how often IPRA uses mediation. From 2013 through 2015, mediations accounted for approximately 65% of all sustained cases. The investigators we spoke to stated that by December 2012, a year after the pilot program began, they were told to attempt mediation in *every* case. So instead of using mediation only in a limited number of appropriate circumstances, such as allegations where the facts are undisputed and there is no victim, IPRA mediates a wide range of complaints despite the seriousness of the allegations. This includes cases that are facially inappropriate for mediation, such as allegations of excessive force and domestic violence by officers.[19] Approximately 50% of the mediations from 2013–2015 were for domestic violence or a full range of excessive force claims.

Moreover, because IPRA is intentionally lenient in exchange for an officer agreeing to mediation, the discipline imposed for misconduct violations resolved through mediation is often far lighter than the allegation facts merit. We reviewed one complaint where an officer fractured his girlfriend's nose during a domestic dispute. In this case, investigators recognized the seriousness of the allegations and requested an affidavit override after they could not secure the victim's agreement to participate in the investigation because the victim feared retaliation from the officer and his friends within CPD. It is laudable that the investigators recognized the seriousness of the offense and pursued the investigation without the victim's agreement to participate in the investigation. Yet, in the end, the investigators still sent the case to mediation, and the officer received only a five-day suspension. Another officer received a one-day suspension for admitting that he had shoved his baton into a victim's side. And in over half of these excessive force and domestic violence cases, there was no real discipline at all, but simply a "violation noted" in the officer's record, such as the case in which a CPD officer who participated in mediation received only a "violation noted" after being accused of verbally and physically abusing his wife in public, where there were witnesses to the event.

In addition to mediation often leading to lesser disciplinary penalties, agreeing to mediate a misconduct complaint also allows officers to accept a sustained finding on a less serious charge in exchange for the IPRA investigator dropping more serious charges from the complaint file. For example, one investigative summary publicly available on IPRA's website describes an officer who was accused of verbally abusing her mother and brother, striking her brother in the head, scratching his face and neck, stealing her mother's Social Security check, and charging unauthorized items on her mother's credit card. The accused officer was ultimately arrested for domestic battery. Yet, IPRA allowed the complaint to proceed to mediation, and after admitting to the lesser violation of scratching her brother's face and neck, this officer was given only a two-day suspension.

During the course of our investigation, the City and current IPRA leadership recognized that mediation is currently misused. IPRA officials also admitted that mediation is used to reduce caseloads and preserve resources. While this practice may have saved resources, IPRA staff admitted, and we confirmed, that mediation, as it is currently used, is both inappropriate and a significant impediment to true accountability.

Some, but not enough, of the problems described above were addressed in the new ordinance creating COPA. The ordinance prohibits COPA from using mediation for "complaints alleging the use of excessive force that result in death or serious bodily injury and cases of domestic violence involving physical abuse or threats of physical abuse." The ordinance, however, does not provide sufficient guidance on other circumstances where mediation should not be used as a means to negotiate a plea bargain.

C. INVESTIGATIONS THAT CPD DOES CONDUCT ARE NEITHER COMPLETE NOR FAIR

Our review of hundreds of investigative files revealed that IPRA and BIA investigations, with rare exception, suffer from entrenched investigative deficiencies and biased techniques. These investigative flaws cover not only all complaint-driven investigations conducted by both BIA and IPRA, but also the mandatory investigations into officer-involved shootings handled by IPRA.

Our review of investigative procedures, interviews of current and former investigative personnel, and careful analysis of 400 IPRA and BIA investigations revealed a consistent unwillingness to probe or challenge officers' accounts of the incident, even when these accounts were inconsistent with physical evidence, credible eyewitness statements, or common sense.

Investigators have permitted union representatives and attorneys to coach officers in the middle of recorded interviews—with official protocols actually prohibiting investigators from preventing this, or even referring to it on tape. Investigators frequently failed to collect basic evidence needed for the investigations by failing to interview important witnesses—including the accused officer—and failing to collect information from other court proceedings involving the same incident. These deficient practices, set forth in detail below, undermine accountability.

1. CPD's initial response to officer-involved shootings

While IPRA is vested with the authority to investigate officer-involved shootings, the initial evidence gathering and reporting on the scene of an officer-involved shooting is largely in the hands of CPD. Understanding the circumstances surrounding the early stages of an officer-involved shooting investigation is important to appreciating how IPRA officer-involved shooting investigations are compromised—and far from independent of CPD—from the outset.

Under CPD rules, all firearms discharges must immediately be reported to CPD supervisors, and if the shot hits a civilian, it triggers two separate but overlapping investigations: a criminal investigation conducted by CPD's Detective Division to evaluate possible criminal conduct by civilians involved in the shooting; and (2) a mandatory administrative investigation conducted by IPRA to determine whether the shooting officer was unjustified. IPRA does not investigate an officer-involved shooting where no one is hit, as explained previously.

Upon notification of a shooting, IPRA sends investigators to the officer-involved shooting scene, where they must wait outside the taped area until a CPD commander in charge of the scene completes the preliminary assessment, which consists of a walk-through of the area and evidence, as well as individual interviews with the officers and civilians present. At the same time the commander is conducting this preliminary review, many other non-IPRA personnel are allowed within the taped area to also interview witnesses and view evidence, including supervising sergeants, detectives, and union representatives. All of these interviews are conducted outside the presence of IPRA investigators and none are recorded. During these communications and particularly before CPD supervisors arrive on-site, there is no prohibition against officers talking with each other about the shooting, and there is no requirement that they remain separate from each other.

After the commander completes his preliminary investigation, he or she allows IPRA inside the taped area and leads the investigators in a walk-through of the scene and provides a narrative of the incident. Generally, IPRA does not speak directly to witnesses until they convene later at the area headquarters, where, again, CPD controls the flow of information and people. While officers complete police reports and review video, CPD supervisors, detectives, union representatives (often accompanied by union counsel), and sometimes prosecutors from the State's Attorney's Office (SAO) conduct additional, unrecorded private interviews with officers and civilians in one area of the station while IPRA investigators are quarantined in a separate room. Union representatives and attorneys not only interview the involved officers but also may assist in completing police reports concerning the incident.

IPRA is the last in line to interview civilian witnesses and officers. After CPD and SAO interviews are finished and after providing the officer with the two-hour notice required under the collective bargaining agreement (CBA), IPRA is then able to conduct recorded interviews of the non-shooting officers at the station. IPRA is sometimes unable to interview civilians at the station, as it depends on the witnesses' willingness to remain at the station after CPD and SAO interviews, as well as cooperation from CPD detectives who are controlling the station scene. Under applicable CBA provisions, the earliest time IPRA can interview the shooting officer is 24 hours after the incident. However, if IPRA makes a preliminary determination that the shooting is unjustified, it will typically refer the matter to the SAO to consider for criminal charges, and defer the interview until it receives a declination letter from the SAO.

These procedures are highly troubling. Allowing involved officers to engage in private, unrecorded conversations with the commander, supervising sergeants, detectives, and union staff before ever speaking with IPRA allows for the inadvertent or intentional conflating of recollections, or the appearance thereof, and greatly impairs IPRA's investigative abilities. If false or mistaken narratives justifying shootings are created during these private conversations and advanced in reports and officer statements, it is exceedingly difficult for even well-trained and diligent investigators to accurately evaluate whether the shooting was justified. We appreciate that officers have a right to counsel, but there are numerous precautions that can be taken to protect the integrity of the investigation without impinging on this right.

The possibility of officer collusion in this setting is more than theoretical. The release of police cruiser video from the 2014 Laquan McDonald shooting led CPD to fire seven officers for falsifying their reports about the shooting. The officers' written reports generally read the same, stating that the teenager was advancing on officers and threatening officers with a knife. The video of the shooting appears to undercut those seven officers' accounts. Additionally, the release of body-worn camera videos from the July 2016 Paul O'Neal shooting shows officers involved in the shooting speaking to each other about the incident moments after the shooting occurred. Officers can be heard discussing the facts of the incident, including confirming they all had the same perception of events. As concerning, CPD officials condone this behavior, and encourage them to have the conversations without making a record of what was said. One video depicts a CPD command official telling officers who are speaking about the shooting to "talk about that stuff afterwards." The same video captures the official informing one involved officer not to say anything until the administrative process has started, and advising other officers that if they have on a body-worn camera, they should not go near the involved officer until the administrative process has completed.

Notwithstanding these most recent scandals and the many others that preceded it, CPD has not amended its policies to address the risk of officer collusion or inadvertent witness contamination. No CPD policy requires involved or witness officers to separate themselves and avoid speaking to each other about a deadly force incident. This is out of step with accepted practice in many agencies, which follow a protocol similar to this one used by the Los Angeles Police Department:

> After all public safety concerns have been addressed, the [on-scene] commander shall ensure that involved officers and witness officers are transported from the scene, physically separated unless logistical problems (e.g., the number of involved officers and/or supervisors) preclude individual separation, and monitored to eliminate the possibility of contaminating their statements prior to their interview by [Force Investigation Division] personnel.

The on-scene commander must be permitted to communicate with officers and witnesses in addressing public safety concerns (e.g., tasks and communications necessary to preserve evidence, secure the scene, address medical needs, determine whether suspects are at large), of course. Once this is done, however,

CPD rules should at a minimum prohibit officers from discussing the incident (other than with counsel) outside of IPRA's presence, and this rule should be stringently enforced with significant penalties imposed for violations.

To the extent these restrictions conflict with CBA notice provisions, such as the provision requiring that IPRA provide witness officers with two-hour notice and accused officers with 24-hour notice before interviews, then these provisions should be renegotiated or, alternatively, all witness discussions with CPD must likewise be delayed until IPRA can participate.

We realize that IPRA is now entitled to more control over an officer-involved shooting scene in the wake of the recent passage of the Illinois Police and Community Relations Improvement Act, 50 ILCS 727, but remain concerned that absent proper oversight and guidance, this law will not, by itself, correct the current organizational and control deficiencies that impact accountability for officer-involved shooting scenes.

Additionally, IPRA should interview the shooting officer as soon as possible after the incident, and should not delay it due to a possible criminal investigation. Neither constitutional rights under *Garrity* nor any other valid investigative principle requires delaying such an interview, and CPD's history indicates that an immediate administrative interview is warranted. If a compelled statement must be taken and a criminal investigation subsequently ensues, IPRA should either assign a "clean" and a "screen" investigative team for the parallel investigations, or it should refrain altogether from performing criminal investigative tasks on behalf of the SAO. Indeed, severing the current relationship where IPRA acts as the criminal

investigative arm for the SAO in excessive force cases not only will provide more independence from the SAO but will better ensure that IPRA resources are spent aggressively pursuing administrative investigations rather than serving and acquiescing to the needs and motives of SAO. Finally, the CBA-imposed 24-hour rule should be eliminated for these same reasons, but until this is done, CPD and IPRA should arrive at creative and enforceable ways to ensure that both the shooting officers' well-being and Chicago's broader accountability goals are satisfied.

2.   Interviews of officers and civilian witnesses

We identified many cases where investigators failed to take reasonable steps to contact and interview identified civilian eyewitnesses to the incident. For example, in one incident an off-duty officer shot and wounded a burglary suspect who apparently attempted to wrest the officer's weapon from him. During the struggle, the suspect was shot in the chest and abdomen. However, the suspect also sustained a third gunshot wound to his back—an injury not explained by the officer. A witness canvass report identified two residents who reported two loud bangs, a pause, and a final bang. The report plainly raised the question of whether the officer fired the final shot—perhaps the unexplained shot to the back—after the threat was neutralized. Yet IPRA did not interview these two witnesses and instead accepted the officer's account and deemed all three shots justified. Similarly, in one investigation of a complaint of misconduct, an IPRA investigator interviewed an 8-year-old girl who complained that a CPD officer working secondary employment in a school grabbed the girl by her hair, swung her around, and choked her while breaking up a fight in a school hallway.[20] IPRA did not interview the identified student witnesses and entered a non-sustained finding based primarily on the accused officer's written statement.

Moreover, in numerous files we reviewed, *officer* witnesses and even the *accused officers* in misconduct cases were never interviewed. In one misconduct case involving an allegation that officers broke into a home and beat two men, IPRA interviewed a mother and her two children who witnessed the incident and testified in support of the claim. IPRA identified but never interviewed any of the officers involved, discounted the mother's testimony and ignored the children's testimony because of their ages, and made a "not sustained" finding. In another case, a man alleged two officers stopped him on the street and slammed him against a car, requiring hospitalization. Although the hospital records supported the injury described and IPRA identified the officers involved, IPRA never interviewed the officers and instead deemed the allegation "unfounded" because the medical records indicated that the complainant was intoxicated.

Where investigators do seek to interview officers, they frequently do so by sending what is known as a "to/from" memo requesting that the officer provide written answers to general questions about the complaint. One high-ranking IPRA staff member admitted during our interview with him that he believed inadequate staffing caused investigators to rely too heavily on "to/from" statements from officers instead of conducting live interviews. This practice is not as effective as a live interview; it allows for collusion and for answers to be drafted or influenced by others, whereas hearing the officer directly during an interview allows for more spontaneous responses, more probative follow-up questions, and more well-informed credibility determinations.

Finally, in BIA investigations, interviews are not electronically recorded and transcribed. Instead, the BIA investigator types up the questions and answers provided during the interview, and then tenders the final printed version for witness signature. In the context of the other systemic deficiencies noted herein, this practice further undermines the quality of the interview because it prevents an auditor from meaningfully reviewing or evaluating an interview.

3. <u>Officer collusion and witness contamination</u>

Our review of officer-involved shooting and misconduct investigations revealed that IPRA investigators exhibit little interest in whether CPD officers have colluded with each other or have otherwise been subject to contamination. For example, in one case involving an officer who had shot an unarmed man in the back, IPRA reviewed and obtained a copy of video footage from the officer's patrol car that appeared inconsistent with the account the officer had related to CPD detectives immediately after the shooting. IPRA postponed its officer interviews for nearly a year while the State's Attorney's Office reviewed the matter for possible prosecution.[21] Although the incident had become well-known throughout the Department and the community, IPRA did not ask the officers if they had seen the video or ask them to relate what they had read, seen, or heard about the incident.

We found this problem in virtually all officer-involved shootings we reviewed, where IPRA investigators very rarely made any effort to explore the possibility that involved officers and witness officers were lining up their stories or had been influenced by outside information such as video footage or press reports. Instead, officers were given free rein to provide apparently rehearsed accounts, with no follow-up questions aimed at ferreting out collusion or contamination. This was true even when the officers used very similar language or otherwise exhibited signs of coordinating their stories. For example, in one case, two officers involved in an officer-involved shooting separately related the incident in nearly identical terms, and even included the same digressions at the same point in the narrative. The IPRA investigator never inquired whether the officers had spoken to each other prior to their investigative interview or asked them to identify all persons with whom they had discussed the incident.

Investigators in misconduct complaint investigations demonstrated this same indifference to witness contamination. They frequently use "to/from" memos or unnecessarily delay interviews of accused and witness officers for extended periods, with some case files containing explicit assertions from investigators that an interview delay of months or years is based on the investigator's heavy caseload. And similar to shooting cases, when interviews do occur, investigators in misconduct complaint cases rarely explore whether the officer consulted with other officers prior to the interview.

Investigators' routine failure to explore the possibility of officer collusion or other forms of witness contamination contributes to a culture in which officers have felt free to compare their accounts before meeting with investigators. Although investigators generally cannot ask officers to disclose confidential communications with their attorneys or union representatives, they can and should routinely ask officers to identify all other persons with whom they had discussed the incident. This is routine practice in many other agencies.

4. Hidden witness coaching during officer interviews

IPRA itself undermines the integrity of its investigations by actively enabling officers to receive coaching during the course of an investigative interview. IPRA's investigation procedures manual expressly *requires* investigators to permit legal representatives to consult with officers about questions and their answers *during* a recorded interview.[22] In addition, these procedures *require* investigators to hide the extent of this consulting by turning off the tape recorder whenever officers or their representatives request—even if (and often because) a critical question is pending. The procedures likewise *require* investigators not to state on the record who is requesting a pause in the recording, why the request was made, how long the parties were off-tape, and not to mention anything that occurred while off-tape. In striking contrast, IPRA's procedures for civilian interviews *require* that time on and off tape be recorded.

Although these procedures are limited by their own terms to misconduct investigations—i.e., cases where the officer is accused of specific offenses that may lead to discipline—IPRA applies them in practice to officer-involved shooting investigations as well, despite the fact that in virtually all cases, the officer has not been accused of any particular offense.

The important protections provided by the right to counsel do not explain or justify these practices. We have not identified any other agency that permits witness coaching to occur in the very presence of investigators, much less requires those investigators to cooperate with others in the room to conceal such efforts from the tape recorder and omit any mention of them in the investigative file. At CPD, however, the practice is institutionalized, with IPRA investigators often starting their interviews by inviting officers to use a hand signal if they want the investigator to turn off the tape recorder.

We found these coordinated, coach-and-conceal efforts reflected in many of the investigations we reviewed. Moreover, we found that it was not uncommon for officers to change the course of the narrative or walk back statements they had made after their legal representatives whispered a few words. Consider, for example, this exchange in an interview of a witness officer:

Investigator: Okay. Do you remember hearing anything that your partner might've said during this whole incident? After you exited the uh squad car and you positioned yourselves, do you remember hearing your partner saying anything either commands to the offender or comments to you or anything like that?

Officer:	I remember hearing my partner say police as he announced his office. Investigator: Okay. Was that before or after he fired shots?
Officer:	Before.
Investigator:	Okay. All right. (pause)
Union Attny:	(whispers to client)
Officer:	My partner also uh stated he has a gun.
Investigator:	Okay. Do you remember when he said that, when your partner said that?
Officer:	Inside the dumpster pen.
Investigator:	Okay.
Union Attny:	(whispers to client)
Officer:	Uh as I ordered the offender to put his hands up is when I heard my partner say that, he, he's gotta gun.

These practices are particularly troubling given that witness and subject officers almost invariably share the same attorney and union representative. Under such circumstances, where the representative is coaching witnesses, the legal representatives are in a position to (1) take careful note of what a witness officer states in one IPRA interview and (2) share that information with the next witness or involved officer to be interviewed. Because communications between officers and their legal representatives are generally privileged, IPRA lacks the means to determine the extent to which such information-sharing occurs.

5. <u>Use of leading and otherwise inappropriate questions</u>

IPRA investigators not only routinely facilitated witness coaching by officers' legal representatives, but at times directly sought to influence officers' statements—in the officer's favor—by asking unnecessary leading questions during investigative interviews. For example:

Investigator:	Was [the victim] given a sufficient number of verbal commands to drop his weapon before an exchange of fire ensued?

Another example similarly illustrates this practice:

Investigator:	Okay. Was there time available or a split-second decision to fire your weapon?
Officer:	It was a split-second decision.

We found essentially the same exchange in other cases, such as this one:

Investigator:	Okay. Was there time available or a split-second decision to fire your weapon?
Officer:	Yes. Investigator: Which one?
Officer:	It, oh it was a split second.

In other instances, the investigator asked leading questions evidently aimed at eliciting from officers a statement that they feared for their lives when they used deadly force. This line of questioning of an officer who shot an unarmed teenager is illustrative:

Officer:	Then he stumbled to the ground, and then he came up. That's what I'm saying—he—how he jumped the fence, he stumbled to the ground, came up with his hands still in his waistband. That's when I left one round.
Investigator:	And when he came up, he was facing you?
Officer:	Yes.
Investigator:	Okay, so he—as he's standing back up again, he still had his hands in his waistband?
Officer:	Correct.
Investigator:	And you felt like he had something in his—in his hands?
Officer:	Correct.
Investigator:	And you—you were in danger?
Officer:	Yes, I was—I was in fear—I was in fear of my life.
Investigator:	You were in fear for your life so you fired how many times? Officer: Once.

IPRA reviewers also routinely asked officers leading questions about whether they experience "tunnel vision" or "auditory exclusion" that might impair their ability to provide a completely accurate account. We were told that such questions are asked because stress can impair sense perception. However, strikingly IPRA does not pose the same leading questions to civilians—not even civilians such as crime victims wounded by gunfire. Similarly, it bears noting that neither Illinois law nor CPD policy provides for any "cooling off period" before investigators may interview civilians. Instead, stated concerns about the impact of stress on perception and memory appear strictly confined to police officers.

IPRA investigators also pose leading questions that assume the truth of matters in significant dispute. For example, in one case involving a man shot in the buttocks as he fled officers, the IPRA investigator asked a CPD officer, "And uh could you tell which hand let's see, yeah, which hand the [fleeing man] held the weapon in?" Prior to that question, the officer had not said anything to the investigator about seeing a weapon. In another case, also involving a fleeing suspect shot in the back, an officer had told the IPRA investigator that the suspect had not offered any physical resistance other than running away. The IPRA investigator then stated, "Right. Okay. And he was reachin', he had the hand on his weapon." The officer then replied, "Correct." Another case, involving shots fired at a vehicle, included this exchange:

Investigator: As [the vehicle] turns I guess that's what you're seein' is the window rolled down?
Officer: Yes.
Investigator: And you think they're about to start shootin'?
Officer: I think the driver is about to start, yes.

6. Failure to probe officer accounts, even when inconsistent with other evidence

Investigators rarely asked officers probing questions about their accounts of officer-involved shootings or the alleged misconduct. This reluctance to ask probing questions was particularly evident in cases where the physical evidence—often gunshots to the rear of a subject, or a lack of a weapon recovered at the scene—appeared inconsistent with the officer's story.

For example, in one case, an officer claimed that as he struggled to extract a suspect from a car, the suspect pointed a gun at him, leading him to shoot the suspect in the abdomen. However, the seated suspect somehow had sustained one of his gunshot wounds to the buttocks. IPRA did not pursue the apparent conflict. In another case, an officer fatally shot a man in the back during a foot pursuit. The officer claimed that he fired because the man faced him while pointing a gun. However, IPRA learned the night of the shooting that the man had been shot in the back. IPRA did not pursue the apparent inconsistency or press the officer for details about his position or that of the shooting victim. In a third case, an officer reported shooting a fleeing suspect in the back after he had allegedly turned to point an object the officer thought was a gun. However, video footage of the incident showed the suspect running away when the officer fired. IPRA never pursued the discrepancy or asked the officers present about what was depicted on the video. This failure to probe officer accounts of incidents even in the face of apparently inconsistent other evidence undermines accountability.

7. Failure to adequately address physical evidence

Our review of IPRA's investigative files identified other deficiencies and irregularities that related to the collection, analysis, and reporting of physical evidence. Although the IPRA procedure manual states that "physical evidence is crucial to any case," and "investigators should pay close attention to physical evidence," we found IPRA files lacking in key respects. CPD routinely swabs recovered weapons and suspects' hands for DNA and gunshot residue (GSR) so it may determine whether an individual held or fired a weapon. Most officer-involved shooting files we reviewed noted the collection of DNA or GSR evidence. Rarely did the files contain the lab results of DNA tests or an explanation for why they were missing. More frequently, we saw lab results for GSR tests, but in most cases, IPRA only mentioned the results in the rationale for their finding when the results corroborated the officers' accounts.

This outcome is troubling, especially in cases where there were sharp disputes between officer and civilian witnesses. For example, in one case, an officer shot a man in the elbow following a foot chase. According to the officer, he saw the man turn and point a gun at him. The officer reportedly told the man, "Drop the gun," and then fired when the man continued pointing the weapon. The officer then claimed the wounded man threw the gun over a fence as he was falling to the ground. Two other officers, located further away, provided a similar account. However, a nearby resident told IPRA she had seen the conclusion of the foot pursuit but had not seen any gun, and instead saw the man begin to raise both hands after an officer shouted, "Show me your hands." A second witness reported hearing the same command followed almost immediately by gunfire. Under the circumstances, analysis of the recovered weapon bore special importance, especially because the gun lacked any recoverable fingerprints. Still, IPRA's final report, which accepted the officers' version, did not mention the outcome of DNA or GSR tests or state whether they were still pending.

We found IPRA files lacking in other critical respects relating to the collection and analysis of physical evidence. First, virtually none of the files included a copy of crime-scene logs or any other documentation identifying who entered or exited the crime scene or when they did so. Second, many files lacked a report regarding crime-scene measurements or even a scaled diagram of the crime scene that identified the location of key evidence such as expended shell casings, bullet fragments, and the like. Third, few files reflected even a rudimentary effort to analyze bullet trajectories. Fourth, nearly every file lacked any photographs depicting the point of view of any civilian eyewitnesses IPRA interviewed, making it difficult to evaluate the reliability of their accounts.

8.   Lack of appropriate use of evidence from civil and criminal proceedings

Some police misconduct allegations are the subject of a criminal prosecution or private civil litigation. IPRA and BIA investigators do not properly review these cases, or, where appropriate, incorporate evidence from these proceedings, in order to inform or strengthen administrative investigations. Additionally, in other cases—particularly within BIA, where the same investigators handle both the criminal and administrative investigations—investigators improperly rely on the outcome of a parallel criminal investigation when deciding whether to substantiate administrative charges based on the same conduct, even though the standards for civil and criminal violations are very different. Both practices result in investigators not using the information at their disposal to properly conduct and resolve administrative complaints.

a. Ignoring evidence from civil and criminal proceedings

The failure of IPRA and BIA to collect information from parallel criminal prosecutions or civil litigation involving the same alleged police misconduct represents a missed opportunity. Some misconduct cases are also the subject of a parallel criminal investigation. Motions to suppress in these criminal cases, as well as the underlying criminal trial, may yield important information that allows BIA or IPRA investigators to discover additional evidence or witnesses, or that assists in credibility determinations of officer witnesses. Yet there is no system that requires investigators to review parallel criminal proceedings, and no such periodic review of such criminal proceedings is done.

Similarly, in excessive force cases, it is not uncommon for the same conduct that IPRA or BIA has jurisdiction to investigate to be litigated in a Section 1983 civil rights lawsuit. Where there is an open IPRA or BIA investigation that is also the subject of a parallel civil case, investigators do not appropriately review and incorporate information from that parallel case into their administrative investigation. Moreover, there is no dependable procedure in which new civil lawsuits alleging police misconduct trigger investigations by IPRA or BIA. Indeed, many such complaints never make it to BIA or IPRA for consideration, and even when they do, no disciplinary investigation is automatically opened since a lawsuit is not deemed to satisfy the complainant affidavit requirement described above. Though IPRA has the authority to override the affidavit requirement, it rarely exercises it in these circumstances.

However, once a police misconduct lawsuit is settled or judgment is entered in favor of a plaintiff, a City ordinance requires IPRA to review the case in question for a possible disciplinary investigation. But IPRA has no timely systematic review process to comply with the ordinance, and often such settled lawsuits will sit on IPRA shelves for months or years before being reviewed at all. And when reviewed, many of these lawsuits—even though settled—still fail to clear the complainant affidavit requirement, and thus no investigation is ever conducted.

And for those settlements that are substantively reviewed and investigated by IPRA—i.e., because they include a supporting affidavit—the complaints almost never result in a sustained finding, despite the fact that the City judged the case worthy of paying large amounts of money to the complainant. During our investigation we discovered that of the hundreds of misconduct settlements IPRA reviewed over the seven-year period from 2009–2015, it recommended discipline in less than 4% of them.

The City should review settlements and judgments on a broader scale to spot for trends, identify officers most frequently sued, and determine ways to reduce both the cost of the cases and the underlying officer misconduct. The City's Office of Inspector General (OIG) recently issued an advisory report criticizing the City's risk management systems as a whole. In particular, the OIG found that because the City does not analyze trends, including trends in police misconduct, or take action on the basis of such analysis, the City "spends tens of millions of dollars annually to pay claims." In response to OIG requests for information, the City's Department of Finance (DOF) admitted that the City "has no comprehensive program in place to examine claims against the City (including small claims, settlements, and judgments)," and that the limited analysis DOF does specifically excludes police misconduct claims. The City responded that a "risk management working group" is being convened, but that police misconduct claims will not be a part of that review, citing the pending conclusion of this investigation. This response should be corrected now that this Report has been issued.

b.   *Erroneously closing administrative investigations when investigators are unable to prove criminal charges*

We also reviewed BIA *administrative* investigations that appear to have been closed simply because there was not enough evidence to hold the officer *criminally* liable. Unlike criminal investigations, in which findings are based on a "beyond a reasonable doubt" standard, findings in administrative investigations are based on the significantly lower "preponderance of the evidence" standard. This standard is appropriate because, if it is more likely than not that an officer has committed misconduct, the Department must take action to ensure it does not continue. In addition, even where officers' conduct may not have violated any criminal code, it may have violated numerous CPD policies. However, in cases we reviewed that were investigated by BIA, it appeared that BIA did not pursue or sustain administrative charges because criminal prosecution was declined, notwithstanding the possibility of policy violations.

In one case, the BIA investigator documented that he was not sustaining any violations in the administrative investigation because the elements of two crimes the officer had initially been charged with, criminal sexual abuse and unlawful restraint, were not met. That case involved an allegation that a CPD officer attempted to rape a woman at a party. Numerous witness accounts of what took place before and after the attempted rape were consistent, including that the victim reported the assault to the witnesses. The file also contains evidence of numerous text messages sent by the accused officer following the incident, including one in which the officer joked with his friend, "I thought she was an easy lay." The officer was later arrested, and the victim identified him in a lineup. Prosecutors originally classified the criminal allegations against the officer as potential felonies, but eventually dropped the case. The administrative investigation in the file mirrors the criminal investigation, indicating that BIA did no additional work in the administrative case other than talking to the victim again. In the investigator's summary of the administrative investigation, the investigator finds the victim's allegations unfounded, stating "the criminal charge of criminal sexual abuse was Nolle Prosequi by the Cook County State's Attorney office because the elements of this offense were not met. In addition, the elements of criminal sexual abuse were not met in the administrative investigation."

9. <u>Superficial investigation documentation and investigative bias in favor of officers</u>

We also identified numerous shortcomings in IPRA and BIA's final reports concerning officer-involved shootings and other misconduct complaint investigations. For example, the reports typically do not discuss or even cross-reference inconsistencies between officer statements and physical evidence or civilian eyewitness accounts. Similarly, very few point out inconsistencies between officers' written reports and their interview statements. They often gloss over or simply fail to mention conflicts between officer accounts of the incident. For example, in one case, two officers were running next to each other as they pursued a man carrying a gun. One officer told IPRA the man had turned toward his partner, so he fired repeatedly. However, the partner contradicted this claim. He told IPRA the man had not turned toward him and had not raised his arm. IPRA chose not to mention these conflicting statements or otherwise indicate that the two officers' stories appeared to be at odds with each other.

In another case, an officer shot a teenager in the back, claiming the boy had turned toward him and pointed a weapon. A firearm was located nearby, but on the other side of a tall hedge. During his IPRA interview, the officer was unusually vague when asked how the gun ended up where it did. First, the officer stated that as the boy fell to the ground, "the gun went over the hedge." Next, he said the gun "just went over" the hedge, and finally said the boy "*apparently* threw it over" the tall hedge (emphasis added). IPRA did not pursue the matter further with that officer. A second officer, who stood nearby, denied seeing the teenager with a gun. Each interview lasted less than 15 minutes, and the IPRA report failed to include the second officer's denials or otherwise indicate that the second officer's account appeared to be in substantial tension with the first officer's.

IPRA reports sometimes omitted mention of crucial physical evidence that appeared to undermine officer accounts. One of the most troubling cases in this respect involved an officer who shot an unarmed suspect in the back at close range. The officer had reported to arriving CPD detectives that the man had pointed an object she mistook for a gun and opened fire. Those detectives briefed IPRA on this statement when it arrived at the scene. However, less than 24 hours later, IPRA had obtained police video footage that showed the confrontation. Far from supporting the officer's story, the police video, recorded at close range, showed the suspect running away from the officer. Nonetheless, IPRA issued a report that accepted the officer's story at face value. The report did not even acknowledge the police video.

We found other IPRA reports that either exaggerated or misstated evidence in a manner favorable to the officer. In one case, for example, officers shot a man in the leg after he reportedly pointed a gun at them. IPRA accepted the officers' accounts, though they were disputed by a civilian witness at the scene. In finding the shooting justified, the IPRA report stated that the shooting victim had admitted to treating physicians that he had pointed his gun at the police. However, the medical records referenced by IPRA in support of this conclusion actually reflect that the claim about pointing the gun was made by a CPD officer, not the shooting victim.

Finally, in sexual assault and domestic violence cases, we also found that investigators were quick to credit officers' versions of events despite the availability or potential availability of additional evidence. For example, in one case, a CPD officer's wife called the police to report that her husband had pointed his gun at her during an argument. The investigation revealed that the officer had a 19-year history of physically abusing her. The victim's son told investigators that he had pulled out a barbeque fork during the incident to protect himself and his mother. The officer admitted to pulling out his gun during the argument but said he did so because his son had come at him with the fork, and had punched him. The IPRA investigator's summary report noted that there were "conflicting descriptions" of the physical altercation, and that the officer "denied committing the alleged act." The investigator also noted that "although it is undisputed that [the officer] pointed his weapon at [the victim's son], the described sequence of events is in conflict, and the appropriate finding is not sustained." Throughout the case summary report, the investigator credited the officer's version of events and said, despite two contrary witnesses and the officer's history of domestic abuse, that because the officer claimed the alleged events did not occur, there was not enough evidence to sustain any of the allegations of misconduct.

10. Racial and ethnic disparities in the City's handling of misconduct complaints

IPRA and BIA sustained only 1.4% of all closed complaints from January 2011 through March 2016. It is not surprising, given the deficiencies discussed above, that so few filed complaints were sustained. What these deficiencies do not explain are the racial and ethnic disparities in sustaining complaints of CPD misconduct, particularly complaints of excessive force.

Our analyses show that, overall, complaints filed by white individuals were two-and-a-half times more likely to be sustained than complaints filed by black individuals, and nearly two times as likely to be sustained than complaints filed by Latinos: 1% of misconduct complaints filed by black residents, and 1.4% of complaints filed by Latino residents, resulted in at least one allegation being sustained, compared with 2.7% of the complaints filed by whites.[23] A closer analysis revealed that the disparity in sustained rates based on the race or ethnicity of the complainant was even greater at the individual allegation level. Black complainants had 2.4% of their individual allegations sustained; Latinos had 3.2% of their individual allegations sustained; and whites had 8.9% of their individual allegations sustained. In other words, for each allegation contained in a complaint, a white complainant is three-and-a-half-times more likely to have the allegation sustained—and the officer held accountable for his or her misconduct—than a black complainant, and twice as likely to have the allegation sustained than a Latino complainant.

Disparities in how IPRA resolves allegations of excessive force are even starker. 2% of all allegations of excessive force involving black complainants and only 1% of such allegations against Latino complainants were sustained, as compared to 6% of allegations of excessive force involving white complainants. In other words, whites were three times more likely than black complainants to have CPD uphold their allegations of excessive force, and six times more likely than Latino complainants to have their excessive force allegations sustained.

This does not necessarily indicate that the complaint process is biased, as these numbers do not say anything about the quality of the complaint. While our investigation did not determine why these disparities exist, these disparities are significant and should thus prompt IPRA and BIA to take a close look at their practices to ensure that they are not discounting complaints based on the race or ethnicity of the complainant. Such a practice would itself be a disservice to Chicago's black and Latino residents, and would send the message to CPD officers that CPD and the City have a higher tolerance for misconduct against black and Latino complainants, which could in turn lead to disproportionate abuse of individuals within these groups and undermine community trust in CPD. It is thus imperative that the City work to better understand the reasons behind these disparities and eliminate them to the extent they have no race-neutral, legitimate basis.

11. Inadequate training of investigators

The investigative problems we found are in part attributable to the lack of training investigators receive both at the start of their work as investigators and throughout their career. Like the deficiencies in CPD's training more broadly, *see* Report, Section IV.A., the City does not provide investigators with sufficient training to do their jobs competently and effectively. Investigators we spoke with stated that they do not receive adequate formal training, and they learned how to do their jobs from observing supervisors and co workers.

As with the lack of general training for investigators, we found that the lack of specific training in how to investigate domestic violence and sexual assault allegations appeared to further undermine BIA's and IPRA's ability to conduct these investigations effectively. Victims of sexual assault and domestic violence may be more likely than other complainants to be reluctant to participate in the investigation beyond reporting due to feelings of shame, however unwarranted. For sexual misconduct in particular, victims may be reluctant to participate in the investigation because the nature of the misconduct and of investigations means that victims may have to retell intimate and embarrassing details numerous times to complete strangers. Domestic violence victims may be particularly unwilling to continue participation in an investigation when the perpetrator is a police officer, given the potential impact of a sustained domestic violence finding on an officer's career.

Investigations we reviewed indicate that investigators handling these cases may not understand these dynamics, including how to interact with victims in a manner that encourages their participation in the investigation. One investigator told us that it was "up to [the survivors of domestic violence] if they wanted to talk," and admitted that he had not received any training on how to get domestic violence victims to trust him and provide information about their assault. An IPRA investigator we spoke to admitted that many of the investigators handling domestic violence cases believe that an incident does not qualify as domestic violence unless it is "a punch in the face," and that, as a result, many allegations of abuse that do not meet this threshold are not investigated. These misconceptions impact the intensity with which IPRA investigates these claims. For example, in one complaint, the girlfriend of a CPD officer alleged that he pushed her to the ground and hit her on the head with an object, injuring her, and that the officer had assaulted her on four different occasions in the past. Two days after the initiation of the complaint, the victim told the investigator that she did not want to pursue the case further because the officer agreed to seek anger management counseling, and because the two had decided to "work on their relationship." In light of the considerations in domestic violence cases described above, the investigator in this case should have attempted to gain her trust and cooperation to enable the investigation to move forward. Instead, IPRA closed this case.

The City recognizes that investigators need more training, and IPRA is beginning to substantially revamp and increase training for all staff, especially investigators. As part of the newly formed COPA, the City plans to create new trainings for all staff, including a one-week "on-boarding program" for all COPA employees and a new investigator/legal staff academy. IPRA's current Chief Administrator informed us that the academy will last five to six weeks, and will cover topics such as investigative policies and procedures, case management practices, crime scene management, external investigative resources, and investigative skill building. The creation of these new training programs is an important step towards improving the quality of misconduct investigations and changing the culture to one that is more determined to resolve investigations and reliably determine whether an officer committed misconduct. CPD has not informed us of similar plans for BIA investigators, although such training is necessary for those investigators as well.

In addition to the new general training plans described above, the City should also improve allegation-specific training to ensure investigators are equipped to properly handle the nuances and complexities of more complicated allegations. Although IPRA's Chief Administrator informed us that the new training program will cover investigative subject areas, including training in each of the areas under IPRA's/COPA's jurisdiction, the depth and breadth of that training is unclear.

D. INSUFFICIENT STAFFING CONTRIBUTES TO IPRA'S INVESTIGATIVE DEFICIENCIES

Although lack of resources cannot account for all of the investigative deficiencies we found during our investigation, it is clear that the City has given IPRA a tremendous responsibility without providing sufficient resources to accomplish the mission effectively. Many of the troubling shortcuts we found in individual investigations, as well as the policy decisions that prevent cases from being meaningfully investigated, have the hallmarks of an overwhelmed agency working in a constant state of triage. The City has recently committed to providing more funding to IPRA when it becomes COPA, and the agency has already begun to hire additional staff. But COPA's range of responsibilities will also be much broader than IPRA's, and there has not been sufficient analysis to determine whether COPA will have the capacity to do any better than IPRA. The City should be mindful of the concerns discussed below and ensure that it provides resources to COPA adequate for it to succeed.

IPRA's historically high caseload was in part due to the sheer size of CPD and in part due to the large volume of cases it inherited from OPS. When IPRA replaced OPS in 2007, it took on a tremendous backlog of cases, which continued to grow for several years, causing some investigators to carry as many as 60 investigative files. Operating with fewer than 90 total staff, IPRA struggled to work through this backlog while keeping up with new complaints filed against CPD's 12,000-plus sworn members. Although no comprehensive staffing study has been done to determine how many investigators are needed at CPD, IPRA's current staff is too small by any estimate. As described by a former high level IPRA official, "IPRA was never given the resources for the volume it was expected to handle."

In addition to causing the investigative delays described below, IPRA's burdensome workload has negatively impacted its investigatory methods and even its findings. IPRA investigators and supervisors agreed that the resource issue incentivizes investigators to reach not-sustained findings. They explained that it is easy and less work to develop a case enough to justify a not-sustained finding, but that it takes a lot more work to push the case to either a sustained or unfounded finding. Investigators are also inclined towards not-sustained findings because they know the case will not need approval beyond their immediate supervisor. Our review of investigative files indicates that this admission might plausibly explain many instances in which IPRA's findings appeared at odds with the facts.

Insufficient resources also incentivize IPRA investigators to close cases prematurely.

Investigators told us that high caseloads led supervisors and IPRA leadership to implement new procedures designed to close cases more quickly, even though they represent poor investigative practice. IPRA staff reported the following examples of such problematic procedures, each of which is discussed elsewhere in this Section, that in their view are directly attributable to inadequate staffing:

- The development of the Excessive Force Protocol that allows for administrative closure, without investigation, of force complaints deemed to be minor, even though proper investigation of such complaints might reveal more serious misconduct.

- Declining to investigate officer firearm discharges where the officer did not hit a subject (either intentionally or unintentionally, e.g., because the officer had bad aim), even though IPRA supervisors agreed that such investigations would reveal deficiencies in training or policy in need of correction.
- Referral of many cases to "mediation," because it eliminates the need to interview the officer or write a summary report (and the investigator does not need to attend the mediation), even though mediation may be inappropriate given the conduct alleged.
- Administratively closing investigations of Taser use, even though such investigations are mandatory.
- Relying too heavily on "to/from" statements from officers instead of demanding live interviews, even though live interviews would, among other things, allow investigators to probe behind officers' statements and make vital credibility determinations.
- Reducing the number of people who review investigative summary reports, regardless of the finding.

All of these procedures sacrifice accountability because they preclude IPRA's ability to conduct meaningful misconduct investigations in all circumstances.

Lack of resources also means that investigators are not engaging in other important oversight and accountability tasks that would benefit CPD, the City, and the community as a whole. For example, as noted elsewhere in this Report, IPRA is supposed to review settlements entered into by the City in civil rights lawsuits filed against police officers. IPRA staff admitted that these mandatory investigations of settled cases sometimes sat piled up on a shelf for years because such reviews were too time consuming to tackle given their current caseloads.

Moreover, although IPRA staff acknowledged that ideally they would be tracking and collecting valuable investigative information from parallel police misconduct lawsuits that are ongoing, they reported being unable to do so due to large workloads. IPRA recognizes that beyond investigating individual allegations of misconduct, with proper resources, the agency could also proactively engage CPD in efforts aimed at preventing future misconduct, such as providing policy and training recommendations to CPD; performing broad-based trend analysis based on its investigations; and monitoring individual officers who are subject to a high number of complaints. Unfortunately, insufficient staffing has prevented IPRA from undertaking these important tasks.

IPRA leadership is enthusiastic about again taking on these tasks and more under the new accountability ordinance once COPA is in place. But it is far from clear whether COPA's increased funding will sufficiently cover its new expanded responsibilities. Without a meaningful evaluation of needs, and a steadfast commitment to meeting those needs, there is little doubt that high caseloads, with the profound impact this has on the quality and timeliness of IPRA's investigations, will remain.

E. INVESTIGATIONS LACK TIMELY RESOLUTIONS, UNDERMINING THE QUALITY OF INVESTIGATIONS AND CREDIBILITY OF THE PROCESS

IPRA expects, and its enabling ordinance requires, that it will complete investigations within six months. However, this is rarely accomplished. In cases where IPRA sustains the allegations in a complaint, it takes an average of two-and-a-half *years* to complete the investigation. Members of the Department and the public alike are frustrated with how long it takes CPD and IPRA to complete these investigations.

1. Structural deficiencies cause investigative delays

Structural deficiencies within Chicago's investigative entities allow complaints of officer misconduct to go unresolved for unreasonable amounts of time. Investigations are often delayed at the outset because of the affidavit requirement, as discussed above. IPRA and BIA often take weeks and months before securing an affidavit. Not only does this delay the preservation of evidence through witness interviews, but the more time investigators spend chasing complainants for affidavits, the less time they spend trying to complete other investigations, thus causing additional delays.

And after an affidavit is secured, the investigative agencies do not appear to follow strict deadlines for the completion of various steps or the investigation as a whole. While IPRA gives its investigators some guidance on how long it should take to complete some investigative steps, these do not appear to be firm deadlines, nor do there appear to be repercussions for when investigators fail to meet them. Nor are there deadlines for supervisory review, resulting in reviews taking anywhere from one week to six months. While internal deadlines are sometimes easier set than kept, providing clear guidance about important investigative deadlines and prioritizing tasks helps promote timely investigations. Some investigations are inherently more complex than others, and adherence to tight deadlines will be difficult, if not impossible. However, without any firm deadlines for investigative activities, these investigations have strung out for years, often transferring between several investigators before even basic steps are complete.

Another policy causing delay is the unwillingness of IPRA and BIA to pursue administrative charges against an officer while criminal charges are contemplated or pending in court. The Chief of BIA stated that BIA will never conduct parallel investigations, and will always wait for a declination of charges from the State's Attorney's Office before continuing an administrative investigation. IPRA investigators acknowledged following the same practice. This means that administrative investigations remain open for months, if not years, awaiting the resolution of a criminal case that, in nearly every instance, is not prosecuted.

Most investigators interviewed believed incorrectly that such practice is required under *Garrity v. New Jersey*, 385 U.S. 493, 500 (1967) (holding that an officer cannot be compelled to make a statement against his will for the purposes of an administrative investigation that will then later be used against him in a criminal investigation). However, parallel administrative and criminal investigations can and do occur as long as precautions are taken to not taint the criminal investigation with any evidence from compelled interviews in the administrative investigation. Given that both IPRA and BIA investigators generally provide investigative assistance to prosecutors in criminal investigations, pursuing parallel investigations may require additional resources, and in some cases, a valid reason may exist for deferring administrative investigations pending the outcome of a criminal investigation. However, when at all possible, IPRA and BIA should pursue the administrative misconduct investigation notwithstanding parallel criminal investigation, even if this requires staffing a "clean" and a "screen" investigative team for purposes of *Garrity*.

Finally, although we are not able to quantify it, our investigation found that another factor contributing to delayed investigations is the lack of resources described above. In many investigations not involving parallel criminal proceedings, important witness interviews did not take place for months or years after the incident, and the investigators admitted in the file that such delays were due to burdensome demands in other investigations."

2. <u>Investigative delays undermine investigative outcomes and reduce public and officer confidence</u>

The consequences of delayed resolutions of investigations are severe. Most importantly, lengthy delays can make it impossible for investigators to uncover the truth: memories fade, evidence is lost, and investigators may not be able to locate those crucial witnesses needed to determine whether misconduct has occurred. Our review of investigative files shows that many witnesses, and particularly the accused, are not interviewed for months or years after the incident. A Chicago Tribune report reflected consistent results, showing an average four-month delay in officer-involved shooting cases before the shooter was interviewed, and in 15 cases the interview occurred over a year after the shooting.

Delayed investigations also compromise CPD's ability to make discipline recommendations withstand appeal. Not only do protracted investigations enable the accused officer to argue the case should be dismissed on due process or statute of limitations grounds, but it greatly compromises the City's ability to present a strong case during the layers of appeal afforded to officers. CPD's discipline case typically relies on civilian witnesses who may not be available years after the incident or may not be cooperative or invested in the case since they have little to gain and much to lose by testifying openly about police misconduct in front of the accused officer.

Apart from the negative impact on outcomes, investigative delays also undermine the message that the City takes these complaints seriously. It disheartens complainants to learn that an officer they know to be abusive remains on the force for years after being the subject of a credible complaint of serious misconduct. These delays are unwelcome to officers as well: CPD and IPRA delays in completing misconduct and force investigations were one of the first and most frequent complaints we heard from officers from the outset of this investigation. Accused officers who have not engaged in misconduct are burdened with the scrutiny of being under investigation, and may be stuck doing "desk duty" for years while investigations languish.

During our investigation, we heard from many officers who described understandable frustration with having their careers put on hold, sometimes for years, while the investigation creeps forward.

F. CPD AND THE CITY DO NOT TAKE SUFFICIENT STEPS TO PREVENT OFFICERS FROM DELIBERATELY CONCEALING MISCONDUCT

When officers—at any rank—conceal misconduct, it thwarts, often insurmountably, efforts to investigate and hold officers accountable. IPRA and BIA treat such efforts to hide evidence as ancillary and unexceptional misconduct, and often do not even investigate it.

1.   Code of silence

One way to cover up police misconduct is when officers affirmatively lie about it or intentionally omit material facts. The Mayor has acknowledged that a "code of silence" exists within CPD, and his opinion is shared by current officers and former high-level CPD officials interviewed during our investigation. Indeed, in an interview made public in December 2016, the President of the police officer's union admitted to such a code of silence within CPD, saying "there's a code of silence everywhere, everybody has it . . . so why would the [Chicago Police] be any different." One CPD sergeant told us that, "if someone comes forward as a whistleblower in the Department, they are dead on the street."

When officers falsify reports and affirmatively lie in interviews and testimony, this goes well beyond any passive code of silence; it constitutes a deliberate, fundamental, and corrosive violation of CPD policy that must be dealt with independently and without reservation if the City and CPD are genuine in their efforts to have a functioning system of accountability that vindicates the rights of individuals who are abused by CPD officers.

We cannot determine the exact contours of this culture of covering up misconduct, nor do we know its precise impact on specific cases. What is clear from our investigation, however, is that a code of silence exists, and officers and community members know it. This code is apparently strong enough to incite officers to lie even when they have little to lose by telling the truth. In one such instance, an officer opted to lie and risk his career when he accidentally discharged his pepper spray while dining in a restaurant—a violation that otherwise merits minor discipline. Even more telling are the many examples where officers who simply witness misconduct and face no discipline by telling the truth choose instead to risk their careers to lie for another officer. We similarly found instances of supervisors lying to prevent IPRA from even investigating misconduct, such as the case discussed elsewhere in this Report in which a lieutenant provided a video to IPRA but recommended that the case be handled with non-disciplinary intervention rather than investigated, describing the video as only depicting the use of "foul language" and affirmatively denying that it contained any inflammatory language or that the victim made any complaints —both patently false statements as demonstrated by the video. High ranking police officials and rank-and-file members told us that these seemingly irrational decisions occur in part because officers do not believe there is much to lose by lying.

Rather than aggressively enforcing and seeking discharge for violations of CPD's Rule 14, which prohibits making false statements, enforcement in this area is rarely taken seriously and is largely ignored. The IPRA enabling ordinance makes it discretionary for IPRA to initiate Rule 14 investigations incidental to one of its delegated mandatory investigations. Investigators rarely exercise this discretion, and it is so little used that there is much confusion even over whether BIA or IPRA would have jurisdiction over such a Rule 14 investigation. Provisions in the CBA add to the obstacles facing Rule 14 enforcement. Under the FOP contract, investigators cannot base Rule 14 charges on a video unless the officer is first allowed to view the video and correct prior false statements, regardless of their materiality.

Not only are Rule 14 investigations not encouraged, but past IPRA leadership prohibited investigators from initiating such Rule 14 investigations without obtaining approval from the IPRA Chief Administrator, sending a strong message to investigators not to expand their investigations into collateral Rule 14 charges. Such Rule 14 requests required a *de facto* higher standard of proof and were rarely approved. One IPRA supervisor told us that while investigating an incident involving an off-duty officer in a bar, she discovered the officer lied in a police report but was denied permission to bring Rule 14 charges. In another case, an investigator sustained a Rule 14 charge for making false statements in his interview, but IPRA leadership rejected this recommendation and directed the report be changed to exonerated.

The former IPRA Chief Administrator explained his reluctance to authorize Rule 14 charges: "we don't make Rule 14 allegations in a cavalier way, because we realize how significant it is and how devastating it can be to a police officer's career . . . it impacts their credibility as a witness, and in so many instances can be a career killer." Of course, no legitimate investigative body should make *any* misconduct allegations in a cavalier way. But the reason for not doing so should be based upon a firm commitment to act only based on the evidence, not undue concern about an officer's career. After all, officers who lie cannot be effective officers, should not be testifying in court proceedings, cannot instill confidence in the community, and discredit and demoralize the many honest officers on the force.

In practice, IPRA rarely asserts Rule 14 charges when officers make false exculpatory statements or denials in interviews about alleged misconduct, even when the investigation results in a sustained finding as to the underlying misconduct. This is true even in some cases we reviewed in which video shows the accused officer lied about the underlying misconduct or tried to cover up evidence. One case we reviewed included witnesses statements and a video showing the accused officer lied in a police report about the basis for arresting the complainant, but no Rule 14 charges were made and the officer received a two-day suspension following mediation. In another case, the video shows an officer punch a handcuffed woman in a massage parlor and then shows the officer looking for the video recorder he realized had captured the abuse. IPRA failed to discipline the officer for the obvious cover-up attempt and settled the physical abuse claim in mediation for an 8-day suspension.

Nor do investigators hold witness officers responsible for covering up misconduct of others. Investigators do not diligently review the investigative records to determine whether witness officers have lied in police reports or whether supervisors have blindly approved reports without attempting to determine whether the reports are fabricated. In one case we reviewed, the complainant alleged an officer punched him while handcuffed in a hospital, which was denied by both the accused officer and his partner. A video later surfaced showing that both officers lied, but Rule 14 charges were never brought against the *witness* officer. Indeed, our investigation revealed that there were only 98 Rule 14 charges sustained over the last five years. Only one of these sustained cases was initiated by IPRA against an officer *witness* who IPRA discovered lied to cover up misconduct of another. Moreover, in many of the cases where Rule 14 charges were brought and sustained against accused officers for lying, the discipline imposed was less than discharge. Almost one-third of all the sustained Rule 14 cases had a recommended punishment of 25-day suspension or less, and some of the discharge recommendations were reduced or overturned on appeal.

Furthermore, even in the rare case where a Rule 14 charge is made and results in a sustained finding, officers face little risk that such finding will impact their ability to testify in criminal cases in support of the prosecution. We learned in our investigation that there is no system in place to ensure that all officer disciplinary findings bearing on credibility, including Rule 14 findings, are supplied to the State's Attorney's Office and criminal defendants, even though this is required under *Giglio v. United States*, 405 U.S. 150 (1972).

The Laquan McDonald case demonstrates that Rule 14 violations are ignored by IPRA. Neither the IPRA investigators nor the IPRA Chief Administrator considered pursuing Rule 14 charges against any of the officers who witnessed the shooting and completed reports that seem inconsistent with the video footage, nor against the supervisors who approved such reports. Not until Chicago's Office of Inspector General took over the case were Rule 14 investigations opened and sustained findings made. The point here is not to prejudge whether such Rule 14 charges arising out of the McDonald shooting should have been sustained or will survive challenge, but rather to highlight by example the reluctance of IPRA investigators to even initiate a Rule 14 investigation. IPRA's unwillingness to open Rule 14 investigations or bring Rule 14 charges, even when there is evidence that officers attempted to conceal misconduct, only perpetuates the code of silence. It is critically important that IPRA change its historical practice and pursue Rule 14 charges against officers, including witness officers, whenever there is evidence of deceit, concealment or cover up.

Finally, IPRA and BIA investigators must not just sit back and wait for a testimony-impeaching video to appear. Instead, they should be collecting all available information and assessing whether officer's stories match the evidence. A valuable source of such information includes judicial proceedings where judges occasionally make affirmative findings that an officer's testimony is not credible. This information should be critical not only to police officials who supervise those testifying officers, but also to IPRA and BIA to better evaluate credibility in pending and future investigations involving those officers. More importantly, they should be evaluating whether the circumstances surrounding a judicial credibility finding would support a sustained Rule 14 investigation. For example, in investigating the many administrative charges against one CPD officer, including a fatal officer-involved shooting, it would have been helpful for IPRA investigators to know that a judge had found this officer to have lied in court testimony in 2011. Yet prior to our investigation, there was no system in place for CPD or IPRA to collect such judicial information. Not surprisingly, none of the Rule 14 charges brought against officers in the last five years was based on false testimony in court. This indifference to judicial proceedings involving officer credibility is particularly troubling in the criminal context where IPRA and BIA should have already had a system in place to evaluate whether suppression hearings should trigger administrative investigations into 4th Amendment violations.[24]

2. Tampering with video and audio

Real-time audio and video footage of alleged misconduct is one of the most effective tools in overcoming the code of silence and making credibility determinations. Such evidence provides direct insight into what actually took place, has been shown to deter unfounded misconduct complaints, and minimizes the risk that witnesses will later give false statements about the incident, increasing accountability and the public's confidence in the accountability system. Yet, CPD has done very little until recently to ensure that police conduct is captured on audio and video.[25]

Not until the public release of the McDonald shooting video—captured on only two of the five car cameras and excluding all related audio—has CPD made much effort to ensure that cameras and microphones entrusted to officers are working properly and are not tampered with. A January 2016 CPD report following the McDonald video release found that the audio capability of 80% of the Department's dash-cams was either not working or had been tampered with. The report stated that officers had routinely removed microphone batteries, destroyed antennae, and stashed mics in the glove compartment boxes of their squad cars.

CPD's law enforcement partners have similarly expressed frustration with the Department's failure to capture officer conduct, despite having video and audio recorders. Former Cook County State's Attorney Anita Alvarez, for example, called the lack of audio in police dash- and body-cam videos was "frustrating" and "something . . . the Police Department has to address." Similarly, our investigation revealed that officers consistently failed to check or sync their dash-cam mics with the in-car system, rendering them useless. Yet IPRA and BIA have rarely investigated whether these instances were deliberate attempts to tamper with video or audio recordings, and, if so, taken any disciplinary action.

Shortly after our investigation began, the CPD Superintendent warned beat officers that they would be disciplined for failure to follow proper dash-cam protocol. The reminder that officers should follow this policy was probably needed: prior to the McDonald case, it is hard to find any inquiry into the suspicious failure of most of CPD vehicles' dash-cams.

In the aftermath of the release of the McDonald video, the Department pledged to expand its body-worn-camera initiative, announcing in September 2016 that all CPD patrol officers will have body-cams by the end of 2018. However, in a December 2016 press release, CPD announced that the initiative was being fast-tracked and that all officers in the 22 police districts will have body-cams by the end of 2017, a year ahead of schedule. This is a positive accountability reform. But body-cams will not be any more successful than dash-cams unless CPD works with police unions and community groups on policies and protocols for body camera usage and develops better accountability measures. Currently, the CPD policy on the use of such cameras is insufficient, and in many instances directives are vague or confusing. There is no policy directing supervisors as to when or whether they regularly review recordings to ensure proper use of the cameras and identify officer training opportunities or conduct concerns. Further, current policy does not explicitly provide that an officer who deliberately fails to use his or her assigned body-cam properly will face discipline. It should therefore come as no surprise that a recent high-profile use-of-force incident in a July 2016 shooting of an unarmed teenager by an officer wearing a body camera was inexplicably not captured on audio or video. It appears that officers have become used to ignoring CPD rules requiring them to use dash- or body-cams because such behavior was not being investigated or punished. It will take committed effort for CPD and IPRA to undo this attitude.

Transparency tools like dash- and body-cameras have perhaps unmatched potential to simultaneously confront the Department's recognized code of silence and make the City safer for both officers and civilians. They can do neither, however, if they are not used. We are encouraged by the City's respect for and focus on the powerful accountability tools of audio and video. Strong foundational policies and long-term oversight is necessary to ensure their potential is realized.

3. <u>Complainant and witness intimidation</u>

We identified a significant number of incidents where the evidence supports concluding that CPD officers intimidated potential complainants or witnesses from filing or testifying regarding misconduct complaints.

We heard from numerous advocates and individual victims of police abuse that officers who engaged in force against a civilian routinely file baseless police assault and battery charges against the victim and other witnesses to the misconduct. In 2006, a patron in a restaurant claimed that after being beaten up by several off-duty officers, he and witnesses to that incident were falsely arrested for battery to cover up the incident. In another case in 2009, the City settled for $100,000 a lawsuit alleging a CPD lieutenant falsely arrested him for battery to cover up the officer's abuse of the plaintiff. In 2014, the City settled another lawsuit for $30,000 where a driver alleged an off-duty officer aimed his gun at him and then filed false battery charges to cover it up when other officers arrived on the scene.

Filing false assault charges not only constitutes an independent civil rights violation, but is powerful discouragement to potential complainants and witnesses regarding police misconduct. Criminal assault charges against witnesses also undermine their credibility when testifying about the misconduct, as we know from the 2006 restaurant incident mentioned above.

Failure to investigate and discipline for witness and complainant intimidation not only prevents CPD from resolving allegations of misconduct, but undermines the integrity of the system as a whole. Moreover, using complainant non-cooperation as a rationale for closing cases where the complainant explicitly alleges intimidation sends the message to CPD officers that witness intimidation can be an effective tactic. In one illustrative case in which a woman alleged that an officer had raped her, she refused to provide BIA the officer's name, and refused to sign an affidavit, telling the investigator that the officer had told her that he had "bigger power" over her and would "fuck her up" if she went to the hospital or the police. The woman alleged that the officer had also threatened her girlfriend, a possible witness to the rape. Despite providing a detailed account of the alleged rape—on two separate occasions—to the investigator, the investigator did not follow up on the results of the rape kit, did not attempt to interview a known witness, and did not canvass for witnesses at the location where the victim and the officer reportedly met. Nor does the investigator appear to have sought an affidavit override. The BIA investigator instead closed the investigation, "based on the victim's refusal to cooperate any further."

G. The City's Discipline System Lacks Integrity and Does Not Effectively Deter Misconduct

On the rare occasions when an allegation of misconduct is sustained, and the even rarer occasions when the sustained finding results in true discipline, CPD initiates a convoluted, lengthy process of determining, and revisiting, the appropriate discipline through several layers. The lack of guidance for determining the initial disciplinary penalty; the many opportunities for second-guessing and undermining the penalty; and the amount of time this process takes, has made CPD's disciplinary policy illegitimate in the eyes of officers and the public alike, and rendered it ineffective at deterring misconduct and contributing to a culture of integrity.

1. Discipline system

Once an IPRA or BIA investigator determines that an allegation against an officer should be sustained, the investigator and/or the investigator's supervisor recommends discipline. The discipline that an investigator can recommend ranges widely. Despite the sustained finding, sometimes no discipline is actually imposed, or the only discipline that is imposed is that a violation is noted on the officer's record. A "violation noted" penalty is only slightly less meaningless than a "no discipline imposed" resolution, as it will only remain on an officer's disciplinary history for one year. During the January 2011 through March 2016 time period we reviewed, 28.4% of sustained findings resulted in "no discipline imposed" or only a "violation noted." Investigators can also recommend that the officer receive a "verbal reprimand," which amounts to a supervisor addressing the officer's wrongful conduct verbally, but nothing more. Sustained findings were resolved with "verbal reprimand" in 24.8% of the closed cases we reviewed. Investigators can also recommend suspension from one to 365 days, and in certain circumstances, discharge from CPD. CPD officers received suspensions in 45.6% of sustained cases we reviewed, with an average recommended suspension of 7.8 days. However, the average is inflated by a small number of cases that resulted in lengthy suspensions. The most frequent suspension length was one day; the median suspension length was three days. Discharge occurred in nine cases, or 1.1% of the cases during the time period we reviewed. The investigator's recommendation to sustain an allegation and impose discipline is subject to review within IPRA, including review by IPRA's general counsel and the chief administrator, prior to the recommendation leaving IPRA. While CPD is currently developing a matrix of disciplinary penalties to guide this decision-making process, CPD's unions have not signed off on it, and it has significant deficiencies, as discussed below.

After the recommended discipline is finalized at either IPRA or BIA, there are many layers—up to seven—of review before it is final and can be imposed. First, except in cases where discharge is recommended, the recommendation is subject to a Command Channel Review (CCR), in which supervisors in the accused officer's chain of command review and comment on the recommended discipline. Next, the recommendation, along with CCR comments, is forwarded to the Superintendent for review. Discharge recommendations skip the CCR review and go directly to the Superintendent. The Chief of BIA makes a final disciplinary decision that is forwarded to the Superintendent for review after the BIA investigator's recommendation has gone through the CCR process.

The Superintendent has 90 days to respond to discipline recommendations by IPRA, or the discipline is deemed accepted. There is no time limit for Superintendent review of BIA disciplinary recommendations. At any point along this path, the command channel can essentially start the process over again by sending the case back to the investigative unit and asking for more investigation.

Once a disciplinary recommendation reaches the Superintendent he can approve it or, if he disagrees with it, he must meet with IPRA's Chief Administrator to attempt to resolve the dispute. If they cannot agree, a three-person panel of the Chicago Police Board will resolve the disagreement. *See* Section IV.H. The Superintendent can also ask for more investigation to be done, possibly restarting the review process, or even overturning the sustained finding. Once the Superintendent has approved a disciplinary recommendation, it is "final" unless it must be submitted to the Police Board for a full hearing. *See* Section IV.G. In these instances, discipline is not final until approved by the Board, a process which generally takes additional years.

CPD officers can and frequently do challenge the "final" disciplinary decision. If the recommended discipline is suspension of 10 days or less, the officer can go through a binding "summary opinion" process. If the recommended discipline is suspension for a period between 11 and 30 days, the officer may also challenge the discipline by filing a grievance, which will be decided through arbitration. Finally, if the recommended discipline is suspension between 31 and 365 days, the officer may appeal the decision to the Police Board or an arbitrator, at the officer's election. Under the grievance procedures, if the parties are unable to settle during the initial negotiations with the officer's commanding officer or in mediation, the officer is entitled to a full evidentiary hearing before a neutral arbitrator. Decisions of an arbitrator through the grievance proceedings as well as appeal decisions by the Police Board are subject to administrative review in the Circuit Court of Cook County and can then be appealed to the Illinois Appellate Court and the Illinois Supreme Court. Pursuing the grievance procedure adds an average of three extra years to the disciplinary process.

Only after these steps are completed can discipline actually be imposed on an officer. And, when a suspension finally is imposed, an officer can serve the suspension by using paid vacation or furlough days, resulting in no loss of income to the officer.

2. CPD's disciplinary system is ineffective

The outcomes of officer-conduct investigations are critical to holding officers accountable for misconduct and deterring future misconduct. *See McLin by and through Harvey City of Chicago*, 742 F. Supp. 994, 1001 (N. D. Ill. 1990 ("A failure to discipline officers, resulting in increased abusive behavior by police officers, has been recognized to be a policy for which municipal liability may attach."); *Sassak v. City of Park Ridge*, 431 F. Supp. 2d 810, 816 (N.D. Ill. 2006) (noting that failure to discipline allegations often support a finding of municipal liability because "a policy of condoning abuse may embolden a municipal employee and facilitate further abusive acts."). CPD's system for imposing discipline on officers who it has determined have committed misconduct suffers from systemic deficiencies that undermine its fairness, consistency, and effectiveness.

a. CPD's disciplinary process takes too long and needlessly introduces opportunities to undermine accountability

Having individuals at all levels weigh in on disciplinary recommendations, and even send cases back for more investigation, creates needless opportunity to undermine accountability. Additionally, these multiple layers of review make discipline unduly slow to be imposed. The City's current process thus leaves both victims and officers unclear how, when, or if an officer will be held accountable for misconduct the officer committed, sometimes for years after a finding has been sustained. On top of the delays that occur while an investigation is still with BIA or IPRA, once an investigative finding is made, the additional layers of review by the CCR, Superintendent, or Police Board can result in *years* of additional delay from the time when an allegation is sustained until discipline is actually imposed and served.

The City should take measures to reduce delays in this process, but should ensure that in doing so it does not introduce new problems. One example of this complicated dynamic involves the City's use of "summary opinions." An officer's right under his collective bargaining agreement to challenge imposed discipline can result in even further delays. The most recent FOP collective bargaining agreement created the "summary opinion" process, which was intended to resolve discipline grievances more quickly. This option has allowed for more speedy resolution of these matters. The Police Accountability Task Force found that, when summary opinion was used, the average time from the misconduct to the issuance of the arbitrator's opinion was 447 days, as compared to 1,049 days under the older system that did not allow for summary opinion.

In addition to these delays, CCR undermines accountability more directly. While the accused officer's supervisory chain should certainly receive notice of the disciplinary decision, which would allow them to better supervise their officers, little value is gained and much is lost in the current process. As the Mayor's Police Accountability Task Force recently stated, "Command Channel Review (CCR) provides a platform for members who are potentially sympathetic to the accused officer to advocate to reduce or eliminate discipline." The Task Force also found that arbitration decisions overturning discipline quote reviewers who not only disagreed with the discipline but opined that the allegation should not have been sustained at all. The Task Force's conclusions are consistent with our findings on this point. Indeed, we recommended to the City during the course of this investigation that it modify the CCR process, and instead have discipline decided at a disciplinary conference headed by a single individual whose decision is reviewed directly by the Superintendent. We further recommended that investigators should never recommend discipline following a sustained finding. The disciplinary conference process we recommended is used in law enforcement agencies across the country to improve accountability systems. With the latest version of the draft disciplinary matrix, discussed below, the City appears to have rejected our suggestions and decided to leave this broken process in place with only superficial changes.

By eliminating unnecessary layers of review, and holding necessary reviewers to strict deadlines, the City would be able to decrease how long it takes for a complaint to reach final resolution, and better ensure that discipline is not overturned. This, in turn, would enhance certainty and speed, increasing officer and public confidence that the complaint adjudication system is fair and efficient, and giving it far greater deterrent value.

b. *Lack of appropriate guidance for determining discipline results in too much discretion and inconsistencies in how discipline is decided*

A lack of clear guidance on appropriate penalty ranges undermines the legitimacy and deterrent effect of discipline within CPD.

Prior to the start of our investigation, investigators' disciplinary recommendations were not guided by any formal standards. Instead, the discipline recommended following a finding of misconduct was entirely up to the discretion of the investigator and his or her supervisor. This resulted in disparities in discipline recommended both across incidents involving the same offense, and even within a single incident as it proceeds through various layers of review. For example, we reviewed one incident where investigators recommended a 150-day suspension for various misconduct violations; command channel reviewers disagreed, and recommended between six and eight days for those same violations; and the IPRA administrator finally recommended a 60-day suspension. This case is currently pending before the Police Board, and the ultimate discipline that will be imposed (for an incident that occurred in January of 2011—six years ago) is still unknown.

In recent months the City has been developing a "disciplinary matrix" that outlines presumptive penalties for misconduct violations by offense type. There are three categories of penalties for each offense type: mitigated, presumptive, and aggravated. In other words, for each offense type, there is a presumptive penalty range, but also a "mitigated" range that can be imposed if certain mitigating circumstances are presented, or a heightened "aggravated" range if there are aggravating circumstances present. The City also created a "guidelines" document to explain what each offense category encompasses, and how to use the disciplinary matrix, including the factors to consider when imposing discipline and mitigating down or aggravating up from the presumptive penalty.

During this investigation, we reviewed and provided feedback on the first draft matrix and guidelines. The City incorporated some of the changes we suggested, but did not incorporate some of the more difficult but critical modifications that we believe are necessary to ensure the disciplinary system will be fair, impartial, and transparent. For example, the current versions still remain unnecessarily vague. There are several "miscellaneous" categories that do not provide sufficient direction for what offenses are included in those categories. Another category, "failure to ensure civil rights," is described as a violation where the "member fails to ensure that a person's civil rights are not violated." Because these categories are so sweeping, it is unlikely that they will be applied consistently and fairly.

The current draft matrix also still prescribes unusually low punishments for conduct that is inconsistent with constitutional, respectful policing, and allows for mitigation in circumstances where doing so would be inappropriate. For example, the latest version of the matrix allows a mitigating range for the offense of "verbal abuse-racial/ethnic," meaning the use of language that is racially or ethnically derogatory.

Moreover, although the guidelines reference how second and third offenses should be considered, the matrix itself does not account for progressive punishment for subsequent offenses. The language in the guidance suggests only that third offenses result in a penalty "at or near the top end of the Aggravated Penalty Range . . . except in extraordinary circumstances." Those circumstances are not defined, leaving decision makers unclear when a subsequent offense merits harsher discipline. Without clear, well-defined guidelines for how subsequent offenses will be punished, the matrix system does not ensure sufficient accountability for repeat offenders.

Other disciplinary ranges in the matrix are so large that they provide no useful guidance. For example, for "Crime Misconduct" categories such as

"Conspiracy to Commit a Crime," "Other Misdemeanor Arrest," and "Sex Offense, Other" the discipline range is 31 to 365 days. If the offense is "aggravated," separation is permitted. Yet, it is difficult to imagine conduct that is serious enough to warrant discipline on the upper end of the presumptive range, yet not serious enough to warrant separation. Moreover, it is unclear why the City believes that an officer found to have engaged in some of these offenses should remain on the police force at all. In any event, the ranges provided for these types of offenses allow for too much variation and discretion, which may result in unfair disparities.

Finally, adherence to the draft disciplinary matrix is not mandatory. As currently drafted, the guidelines state that "the CR Matrix is to be used as a *set of guiding principles* in the administration of discipline. It does not prohibit the [decision-maker] from assessing a different penalty where unique and exceptional circumstances may warrant." (emphasis added). "Unique and exceptional circumstances" is not defined, and CPD does not provide even a single example of such circumstances, or illustrate how they fairly factor into discipline. At best, this lack of specificity leaves well-meaning individuals to guess whether a given set of circumstances is unique or exceptional. At worst, this language leaves the door open for less well-disposed individuals to favor or disfavor officers according to whim. In both instances, it would be difficult to hold anyone accountable for poor decisions.

The creation of the disciplinary matrix and guidelines is an important step towards providing greater consistency and clarity in discipline for officer misconduct, but the deficiencies described above still allow for too much discretion and the imposition of discipline that is incongruent with the offense.

H. CHICAGO'S POLICE BOARD

The Police Board has a long history of overturning the Superintendent's misconduct findings and proposed discipline, but this trend has changed over the past year. While this change is welcome and appropriate, our investigation indicated that there are structural challenges to the Board's process that, unless addressed, may prevent this change from taking hold long term. We found also that the Police Board's effectiveness is undermined by the same investigative deficiencies that render CPD's accountability ineffective more generally. Below we discuss these challenges to assist Chicago's efforts to ensure that the Board continues to become, and remains, a stronger component of CPD's accountability structure.

1. Background of Chicago's Police Board

Created in the wake of a crisis (the Summerdale Scandal of 1959), Chicago's nine-member Police Board was expected by many Chicagoans to function primarily as an independent accountability check on CPD. But the Police Board arguably has undermined accountability by routinely overturning or reducing the Superintendent's disciplinary decisions, often overturning sustained findings altogether, even in instances where Board members may believe the officer in fact committed misconduct. This misconduct includes the unreasonable use of deadly force and other violations for which the Superintendent and IPRA recommended termination.

To understand why the Police Board is perceived as an ineffective accountability mechanism, despite the best efforts of many of its members, it is important to recognize the Board's built-in structural conflict. Through a combination of policy and practice, the Board has evolved into an amalgam of at least three, typically separate, types of police/civilian entities.

It appears clear that, at least when it was formed, the Board was meant to serve some of the functions that *police commissions* serve in some other large cities (such as Los Angeles). That is, by its authorizing municipal ordinance, the Board is tasked with adopting "rules and regulations for the governance of the police department of the city," and with influencing the selection of Police Superintendent by nominating the names of three candidates to the Mayor, from which the Mayor is to select. As confirmed by several Board officials during our conversations with them, the Board has "never" really fulfilled its duty of adopting CPD rules and regulations.

The Police Board has instead evolved into a combination of civil service protection panel and independent-oversight backstop, but without sufficient guidance as to how to effectively navigate this difficult dual role. The Police Board in some respects acts as a *civil service commission*, part of a system meant to "protect efficient public employees from partisan political control." *See Glenn v. City of Chicago*, 628 N.E. 2d 844, 850 (Ill. App. 3d 1993). In this role, the Board has viewed itself as focused on ensuring procedural due process for any officer subject to discipline. The Board officials we spoke with emphasized, for example, the Board's role in giving the officer a robust opportunity to "confront the evidence" against him or her, and to ensure that the officer receives "due process."

The Board also appears to see itself, however, as serving the role of an *independent oversight agency*, having a responsibility to the broader Chicago community to ensure that the values and views of the public are reflected in the Department's misconduct findings and imposition of discipline. Board officials thus emphasized their role ensuring that the hearing process is "transparent," and that "ordinary citizens" have input into discipline, and that they are "not all lawyers" and that they represent people who live both in Chicago's "wealthy" and "poor" areas. Similarly, the Board's website lists "holding monthly public meetings that provide an opportunity for all members of the public to present questions and comments to the Board, the Superintendent of Police and the Chief Administrator of [IPRA]" as one of its "primary" powers and responsibilities.

There is no inherent conflict between ensuring that officers' procedural rights are protected and that the Chicago public has insight into how the police officers who serve them are held accountable for misconduct. However, as Chicago's Police Board demonstrates, it is difficult for one entity to serve as both an arbiter of appropriate discipline and a conduit for public-police discourse, and impossible without a clear mandate and a set of balanced protocols. The Police Board lacks such a mandate or protocols, so rather than balancing these two roles effectively, has seemed to vacillate between them. The public, police officers, and Board members alike are frustrated with public meetings during which the Board does not engage with the public and has no authority to address the concerns raised by the public, and at which the Superintendent and IPRA leadership may or may not show up to address public concerns and report on what they have done to address previously raised concerns. It appears clear that the Board's civilian outreach functions would be better placed in another entity, like the Community Oversight Board that the City reports it has committed to implementing within the next six to nine months.

Moving these civilian outreach functions to another entity would allow the Police Board to focus its efforts on where its greatest focus already lies and where it has its greatest potential impact: deciding CPD disciplinary matters in which the Superintendent is recommending discharge or lengthy suspensions.[26]

2. The Police Board's role in deciding disciplinary cases

The Police Board is required to decide disciplinary cases in which the Superintendent has recommended termination of an officer, or suspension over one year, or suspension of a supervisor (rank of sergeant or above) for over 30 days. At the officer's election, the Board also reviews officer suspensions that are between 31 days and one year.[27] The Board's decision is *not* subject to Superintendent approval or veto, and may not be challenged via arbitration.[28]

a. Past trends in Police Board discipline decisions

The Police Board has long been known for reversing many of the Superintendent's findings of misconduct, including most of the cases in which the Superintendent proposes discharging an officer. According to the Police Board's 2014 Annual Report (the most recent available), of the 16 discharge cases the Board decided, it upheld the Superintendent's discharge in only six, or 37%. It found "not guilty" in another six cases, thus going beyond refusing to discharge to wiping the slate entirely clean in another 37% of the cases in which the Superintendent had sought to discharge an officer. In another four cases, the Board reduced the Superintendent's recommendation of discharge to a suspension or reprimand.[29] Similarly, of the 27 cases the Board decided in 2013, the Board upheld the Superintendent's recommendation of termination in only 11, about 40%, and overturned the sustained finding in an additional two. This trend was longstanding: a 2009 study by the Chicago Justice Organization found that the Board upheld the recommended discipline for a sworn officer in only 37% of the cases it heard.[30]

This historically high rate of overturning the Superintendent's misconduct and disciplinary determination would not have been concerning if it reflected the Board's accurate determination that the Superintendent had erred in finding misconduct or in levying heavy discipline. And certainly there appear to have been many instances where this was the case and the Board served its important function of ensuring that police officers are not unfairly or unduly harshly punished. But our investigation, including our conversations with past and current Board officials, makes clear that it too often has been the case that Board officials have overturned the Superintendent's findings of misconduct and/or the level of proposed discipline—including in cases where they firmly believe that the officer committed the alleged misconduct.

The statistics set out above, alongside a review of the type of misconduct and discipline the Board has overturned over the years, makes clear that this dynamic has had a negative impact on officer accountability and police legitimacy in Chicago. The Board has, for example, reduced a case that resulted in an in-custody death (and a $1.3 million dollar settlement) from discharge to reprimand, and reinstated an officer, despite a criminal conviction, for falsifying a field sobriety test that led to the arrest of a citizen. The City has paid out nearly $400,000 in five lawsuits related to this officer's DUI stops.

b. Recent changes in Police Board discipline decisions

The Board's trend of overturning the Superintendent's recommendation to discharge an officer is changing. Over the past year, the Board tended to uphold the Superintendent's discharge recommendations far more frequently. In 2016, the Board sided with the Superintendent in the eight cases in which he recommended discharge. Additionally, in two discharge cases where the Board had previously found the officer not guilty, the City appealed the Board's decision and, upon remand, the Board imposed a 31-day suspension in one case and discharge in another. In another case on remand, given instructions to impose a penalty less than discharge in a case in which it had previously agreed with the Superintendent's proposed discharge, the Board imposed a suspension of five years. The Board reduced the Superintendent's recommended discharge, to an 18-month suspension, in only one case. In the one suspension case the Board decided, it affirmed the Superintendent's 60-day suspension. In seven other cases, the officer resigned after the Superintendent filed charges with the Board.

In 2014, the Board took the unique step of increasing and officer's discipline. It ordered an officer's discharge in a case in which the Superintendent had recommended a 60-day suspension. The Appellate Court found this to be a legitimate exercise of the Board's authority. *See Lesner v. Police Bd.*, 2016 Ill. App. (1st) 150545. This is potentially an important step forward in allowing the Board to serve a valuable, unique role in ensuring appropriate officer accountability in Chicago.

c. Challenges to effective Police Board review

As discussed below, there are numerous changes the City can and should make to ensure that the Board, as an institution, garners and retains greater confidence among CPD officers and the broader public.

It is worth noting at the outset that even if the Board corrected these structural challenges, many members of the public in Chicago might still find the Board a disappointment and even question its utility. This is because the Police Board only reviews cases where IPRA *and* the Superintendent have *already* determined that the officer committed misconduct. The Police Board does not provide independent civilian input into whether officers who were *not* found to have committed misconduct should have been.[31] Nor does the Board have any authority or ability to ensure that IPRA completes investigations more quickly or more competently, or that an officer be recommended for discharge if neither IPRA nor the Superintendent have done so. The Police Board thus does not, and was not meant to, address the broad concern in Chicago—a concern that our investigation finds to be well-founded—that the Superintendent and IPRA sustain far too few allegations of misconduct, and propose discipline that is too low in the cases they do sustain.

Nonetheless, even as the Police Board cannot make up for problems in other components of the City's accountability processes, in the past it has done great harm by exacerbating the City's accountability failings through unnecessarily overturning so many of the very few cases that the City has managed to sustain. While this trend appears to have reversed itself in the past year, the discussion below is meant to help the City ensure this remains the case.

i. Description of Board hearing process

The Board conducts hearings pursuant to Rules of Procedure, most recently amended in April 2015. These Rules provide the framework for a quasi-trial process, with pre-hearing motions practice and hearings, which can last several days, in which the rules of evidence do not apply, although hearsay evidence is not admissible. At these hearings, the City has the burden of demonstrating, through the presentation of documentary evidence and live testimony, that the Superintendent's sustained finding is supported by a preponderance of the evidence. The officer has the right to cross-examine all witnesses and otherwise challenge the testimony, and offer evidence in defense and mitigation. Should the City prevail at the "liability" phase, the trial proceeds to a "penalty" phase. Contract attorneys called hearing officers, of which there are three, have sole authority over the hearing itself. These hearing officers are attorneys from private practice and the only requirement is that they have five years' experience as an attorney. Their main functions, according to the Board officials with whom we spoke, is to create a good record for the Board's consideration; to present the case impartially to the Board; and to write up the Board's decision. Board members are provided with transcripts and video recordings of the hearing and meet privately to confer. The Board's final vote on each case is made at a public meeting. In 2012, these Rules were amended to require all Board decisions to be supported by written findings. These written decisions are posted on the Police Board's website.

Our investigation indicated that there are several elements of the Board's hearing process, and the City's accountability processes more generally, that contribute to officers avoiding accountability when they appear before the Police Board.

ii. Information available to Board unfairly skewed in officers' favor

The hearing officer and Board do not have full access to the officer's complaint and disciplinary file: due to restrictions in the collective bargaining agreement, even sustained findings of misconduct are available to the Board only if they occurred within the past five years. Nor does the Board know the officer's disciplinary or lawsuit history at the "liability" phase, even where that history could provide powerful probative evidence of whether the officer has a history of dishonesty, or whether the officer's current alleged misconduct is consistent with misconduct the officer has repeatedly been accused of, or even found to have committed, in the past. Even as the Board is denied access to this potentially critical information, it is given the officer's complete "complimentary" history—spanning the entirety of an officer's career.

In addition, the officer is permitted to have other officers, including commanders, testify as character witnesses for the officer, *at the liability phase* of proceedings, even where the charges do not place the officer's character at issue, notwithstanding the fact that the Superintendent is recommending discipline, often termination, for the officer. While this is styled as "character witness" testimony in support of "evidence in mitigation," its inclusion at the liability phase belies this label, as do the statements of some Police Board officials that the testimony of CPD supporting officers and commanders "means a lot" and that they "give their testimony more weight" (although other Police Board officials told us they give this testimony "no weight"). The Superintendent recently filed a motion to keep this information under seal or move it to a separate post-liability hearing. Board officials told us the Board denied this motion because it would extend the proceedings one month.

The format of the Board's hearing process may also undermine the effectiveness of the Board because it deprives the Board of the ability to directly assess the evidence. Because the Board reviews transcripts and video recordings of the hearing after it is completed, it is unable to ask clarifying questions or otherwise direct the proceedings to ensure the Board, as fact-finder, gets the information it needs to make a decision. Instead, it must rely entirely on the hearing officer. The precise extent to which the Board relies upon these hearing officers is unclear. One Board official told us that the hearing officer is "not allowed" to make credibility determinations; another Board official told us that the Board will in fact ask the hearing officer for credibility determinations. Regardless, it is clear that the quality of the hearing officer impacts the Board's ability to make a decision. In one case, the Board reported it had to send the case back because the hearing officer had done such a poor job creating a record, "we couldn't make sense of it."

iii. City has in the past not effectively advocated for accountability

The relative inexperience of the attorneys representing the City and Superintendent, compared to the attorneys representing the officers, has undermined accountability, although this is reportedly improving. The Board told us that they feel compelled to let off officers they are sure committed the misconduct, because "the City messed up on the evidence." Board members and others report that attorneys for the officers, all former state's attorneys, have extensive trial experience and, in the words of one Police Board member, "make the Superintendent have to work." At the same time, according to Police Board members, the City's attorneys have little trial experience, and, in the past, have had to handle the trial on their own. In the words of one Board official, there is a "big disparity in experience and effectiveness" between City and officer attorneys. Still other advocates point to the potential for conflict: the City is advocating to discharge the officer even as it may be defending the City in civil litigation stemming from the same incident. One long term observer of the Police Board and Corp Counsel's office asserts that this problem is exacerbated because the "firewall in the Corp Counsel's office has not been honest or effective." The City reportedly has recently begun to outsource representation of the City at some Board hearings, and sending better prepared attorneys (and more than one attorney) to others. Board members report that the quality of the City's representation has increased in recent months "dramatically" as a result. The City should continue to build on these efforts.

iv. Board members and hearing officers lack training

The Board's own lack of training regarding adjudicating police misconduct further undermines its effectiveness. Board members are generally not lawyers and have no background in policing or accountability. One Board member told us of voting against a Superintendent's sustained finding of an unlawful search, even though the Board member agreed the search was unlawful, because of the amount of drugs the officers found during this "clearly" illegal search. Hearing officers can be similarly inexperienced, with a "wide variance in quality," and problems creating a clear record for the Board's consideration.

For at least the past 20 years, there has been no set or required training for either group. The training as described by one Board member consists of little more than a binder of materials; a tutorial on the burden of proof; the opportunity to watch an academy class on use of force; and an offer to go on a ride-along. The Board's Executive Director conceded that "this is one area that needs improvement." One former Board member pointed out that Board members should have a respect for policing, but that the Board would also do well to "put [Board members] in the homes of people on the West or South Side for a day and see what they go through."

That the lack of training impacts Board decisions appears evident from some of the decisions themselves, described above, as well as in the disagreements we heard directly from Board members about proper application of the rules, such as when an officer should be discharged for lying, or whether officers should ever be found guilty for using profanity. Poor decisions may have been avoided with better training for both hearing officers and Board members.

v. Lack of investigative timeliness and quality undermines accountability

Board consideration of the Superintendent's recommendations is unquestionably compromised by the poor quality and lack of timeliness of IPRA and BIA investigations discussed elsewhere in this Report. According to Board officials, among cases decided since 2010, the median time from the date of the incident to charges being filed is four years for IPRA cases and over two years for BIA cases, and our conversation with Board members and a review of Board decisions makes clear charges are sometimes filed much longer than this after the date of the incident. In one case we reviewed, charges were filed in 2014 for incidents that took place sometime between 1999 and 2003. In other cases, the Board is unable to affirm the Superintendent's charges of excessive force because the charges were brought more than five years after the incident, in violation of Illinois' statute of limitations on excessive force charges brought against officers.[32] In one such case, the Appellate Court upholding the Board's decision not to affirm the Superintendent's findings based on this lack of timeliness, stated:

> [W]e find it necessary to express our dismay with the unreasonable length of time the Superintendent took bringing charges in this case . . . . The Superintendent brought charges more than six years after the incident, without any explanation other than a "mix-up" occurred. A delay of this magnitude does nothing to foster the public's interest in effective oversight and supervision of police officers nor does it foster the protection of a police officer's right to due process in defending serious disciplinary charges. The passage of an unreasonable amount of time adversely affects witness availability and recollection and the officer's ability to present a meaningful and effective defense to unjustified charges.[33]

Board members and accountability advocates expressed similar concerns about the impact of delays on Board hearings. As one former Board member stated, the cases before it were "so old and so stale" that it was "unfair to the police officers; unfair to the witnesses; unfair to the victims." This lack of quality and timeliness has ramifications much broader than undermining the Police Board's ability to hold officers accountable, but this impact is particularly harmful given the severe nature of the misconduct that the Board often considers.[34]

vi   The Police Board's lack of transparency

The Police Board's process provides a greater window into officer discipline than is available in many police disciplinary processes; in this respect the Police Board represents an advance over accountability systems that rely solely upon opaque internal processes and arbitration. But the Board also provides less transparency than is available through most police civilian oversight entities, and less than it professes it should. The City and Board have both asserted that the Board is intended to provide transparency as an "essential value" to "increase the public's and police officers' confidence in the process for handling allegations of police misconduct." It is thus incumbent upon the City and Board to make reasonable efforts to be as transparent as possible.

There are several steps that the Police Board can and should take to be more transparent and increase confidence in its process. First, the Board could post all materials related to its hearings on its website, including transcripts and videos. Currently, members of the public must request hearing transcripts through public records requests, and the City does not release videos of the hearings.[35]

The Board could also increase transparency by tracking and publishing more detailed case-specific and aggregate data about its decisions, and making this information available in a timely manner. Currently, the Board provides only vague anonymized data in untimely annual reports (the most recent one was in 2014). Even the Board's monthly reports to the Superintendent containing complaint statistics must be requested through public records requests. Some groups have requested materials and attempted to analyze and publicly report on Board statistics. But CPD officers and the public should not have to rely upon the voluntary efforts of a third party to have access to data about the Board's work, and this system leaves the public guessing about whether publicly available data is accurate or complete.

I. THE CITY'S POLICE ACCOUNTABILITY ORDINANCE AND SIMILAR EFFORTS TO CORRECT THE PROBLEMS OUR INVESTIGATION IDENTIFIED

As discussed above, the City's Police Accountability Ordinance created COPA, which will replace IPRA as the independent agency responsible for investigating serious police misconduct. Besides the name change, COPA's main differences with its predecessor include (1) expanded investigative authority, (2) a guaranteed budget floor, (3) authority to hire independent counsel, (4) a five-year ban on former police officers serving as investigators, and (5) a modified mediation program. These changes and other recent IPRA-initiated reforms are positive steps to enhance police accountability.

But the reforms do not directly address the many problems we identified with IPRA's deeply flawed investigative system. For example, as discussed above, it is not clear that COPA's increased budget will be enough to satisfy both its existing investigative duties conveyed from IPRA as well as COPA's expanded investigative obligations. And while the new law attempts to correct IPRA's inappropriate use of mediation, it can still be used for many serious cases not appropriate for mediation and defers until later the precise policies under which the new mediation program will operate. Allowing for independent counsel and limiting new employees with police backgrounds will enhance independence, but may not be sufficient. Finally, if none of these changes fixes the defective investigative practices identified in the Accountability Section under IPRA, then COPA's expanded investigative authority simply exacerbates these investigative problems.

The City believes that IPRA's newly published operational rules will increase investigative oversight, facilitate coordination with the Law Department, and improve processes for affidavit overrides and officer-involved shootings. The test will be in how well these new rules are implemented. The City likewise highlights its plans for new investigator training, as discussed above, and new information technology. These plans are a positive first step. COPA is just beginning to engage consultants, who will help diagnose the training and IT problems and only then will set out to develop a plan.

COPA's success in the public eye will depend on how well it addresses the credibility crisis that IPRA faced for most of its existence. The City understands this, which in large part drove its decision to change IPRA's name to COPA. Indeed, all of new changes contained in the COPA ordinance as well as the recent programmatic reforms could have been accomplished without creating COPA. However, the City believed that IPRA's reputation in the community was so badly damaged that it needed a new name. But the City must do more than a name change to repair the broken trust that surrounds this investigative agency, particularly since most residents remember the last time the City employed this same rebranding strategy eight years ago when it replaced OPS with IPRA.

Finally, COPA's companion ordinance creates a new deputy inspector general for public safety who will be charged with initiating reviews and audits of CPD, COPA, and the Police Board. These are welcome changes from an accountability standpoint, and certainly the Inspector General's Office has a level of community support and respect that surpasses the other agencies in Chicago's police accountability network. The description of how these new duties will be interpreted and implemented has yet to be decided, and will impact this position's effectiveness. Moreover, while this new deputy inspector general has authority to make recommendations to COPA and CPD that may impact misconduct investigations, it has no enforcement power. The City has made important strides in improving accountability, but the systemic and entrenched nature of the deficiencies we identified cannot be remedied by these reforms alone.

IV. CPD DOES NOT PROVIDE OFFICERS WITH SUFFICIENT DIRECTION, SUPERVISION, OR SUPPORT TO ENSURE LAWFUL AND EFFECTIVE POLICING

༄༅

A. TRAINING

Our investigation revealed engrained deficiencies in the systems CPD uses to provide officers with supervision and training. CPD's inattention to training needs, including a longstanding failure to invest in the resources, facilities, staffing, and planning required to train a department of approximately 12,000 members, leaves officers underprepared to police effectively and lawfully. Officer errors and misconceptions that result from lack of training are not corrected in the field, because CPD has neither structured supervision in a way that will adequately support officers, nor invested in programs and systems that will detect when officers are in need of help or exhibiting behavior that must be corrected. Officers' ability to stay safe, protect public safety, and police within constitutional standards suffers as a result.

To set and maintain a culture of policing safely, effectively and constitutionally, a law enforcement agency must provide its officers strong training both at the outset and throughout their careers. Proper training gives officers the confidence and knowledge to police safely and effectively. Training at all levels—pre-service, in-service, and in the field—should foster communication, problem-solving, and analytical skills; facilitate acceptance of community policing principles and tactics; and encourage creative thinking. Training also shows officers how effective policing is not only consistent with, but bolstered by, police tactics that abide by the law and build stakeholder trust. Effective training is delivered through meaningful content, not just hours sitting in a classroom. A solid foundation of recruit training, field training for new officers, and ongoing in-service training ensures a culture of respectful and lawful policing that is active and effective. Through the course of their careers, police officers confront stressors, discouragements, and shifting legal and policy ground. Effective training helps them navigate those challenges, and is crucial not only for the safety of the public, but also for the safety of the officers themselves.

CPD and the City of Chicago have not provided such training to CPD officers for many years, to the disservice not only of those officers but to the public they serve. CPD's Academy training and post-Academy field training program do not sufficiently prepare new CPD officers for their jobs, and the absence of meaningful, regular in-service training prevents officers from reinforcing previously-learned material and gaining knowledge of current policy, legal issues, tactical developments, and police operations.

Officers at all ranks—from new recruits to the Superintendent—agree that CPD's training is inadequate. The City has announced steps that, if properly resourced and effectively staffed, could represent critical improvements to the way that officers are trained throughout their police careers. These announcements are welcomed, but cannot be allowed to languish or to be handled in a quick, reactive manner, which is how officers characterized prior trainings that were only provided in response to a crisis of the moment. As the City's training consultant stated, "implementation will be complicated and will be a long term process." It also will be costly and involve difficult decisions. Our investigation makes clear both that this effort is well worth it, and that the City must sustain focus on its ambitious set of reforms.[36]

1. <u>CPD Academy training does not instill in new recruits a culture of service towards all Chicago communities or the tenets of constitutional policing</u>

Academy training is foundational to building the knowledge and skills needed to protect public safety and earn community trust. Effective Academy training not only teaches recruits of their obligations under law, policy, and widely accepted law enforcement standards; it is also the first opportunity to acculturate new officers with the Department's values and priorities.

Academy training should therefore instill recruits with the ethos that protecting all facets of the Chicago community, especially those that are most beleaguered by crime, is their core function and primary responsibility. This ethos is sometimes framed as a "guardian" mindset, as opposed to an inordinately fear-based "warrior" mentality.[37]

Unfortunately, CPD's Academy does not meet these objectives. Instead, it has, for many years, suffered from severe deficiencies that impede recruits' preparedness to police constitutionally and safely. CPD's Academy provides recruits with approximately 1,000 hours of training on a variety of topics, including firearms, use of force/control tactics, gangs, vehicle stops, law enforcement driving, and report writing. However, there has been insufficient attention to whether training content matches recruit training needs; the validity of training materials; and to whether this content is effectively delivered. The Academy program relies on outdated materials that fail to account for updates in legal standards, widely accepted law enforcement standards, and departmental policies.

As just one example, a class we observed on deadly force involved officers viewing a video made roughly 35 years ago, prior to key Supreme Court decisions that altered the standards used to evaluate the reasonableness of use of force. The tactics depicted in the video were clearly out of date with commonly accepted police standards of today. Following the video, the instructor spoke for approximately thirty minutes, but did not give detailed information on justified versus unjustified use of deadly force or the standard of objective reasonableness—all essential topics for deadly force training. The training itself was inconsistent with CPD's force policies, further undermining its utility in teaching recruits their obligations under Department policy and constitutional law. Several recruits were not paying attention, one appeared to be sleeping, and there was minimal attempt made to engage the students in the lesson. In fact, the instructor arrived to the class ten minutes late and dismissed students twenty minutes early from this critical class on how CPD officers should use deadly force. The impact of this poor training was apparent. At the academy and during ride-alongs, our retained training law enforcement expert asked several PPOs to articulate when use of force would be justified in the field; only one PPO out of six came close to properly articulating the legal standard for use of force.

We observed over 60 hours of training at the CPD Academy, and found that poor delivery of Academy training was pervasive. Rather than pursue widely accepted teaching methods centered on adult learning principles, in particular scenario-based training and encouraging hands-on skills, CPD continues to employ ineffective strategies to train its new recruits. CPD's Academy curriculum is over-reliant on the PowerPoint/lecture model of classroom instruction, broadly acknowledged as one of the least effective ways to train new recruits. One CPD training supervisor referred to this type of training as "check-the-box" training, meaning that the emphasis is on making a record of having provided the training as opposed to actually providing effective instruction. As discussed further below, these problems with training content and delivery are compounded by significant inadequacies in staffing and facilities.

In observing one of the scenario-based trainings that was offered, we found that Academy staff seemed unfamiliar with how to properly run or evaluate role-play exercises. As part of this training, recruits were "dispatched" to a call for service inside of the training building, and all staff instructors were inside the building role-playing in the scenario. No staff instructors were on the outside of the building to watch and evaluate the approach of the recruits, nor were any instructors assigned as evaluators. If they had been outside the building, the instructors would have noticed the recruits parking in front of the location of the call—a practice that exposes them to unknown dangers and places them at a tactical disadvantage. After observing this, our expert concluded that "trainings such as this instill bad tactics and often, bad tactics lead officers into a situation that requires a use of force that could otherwise have been avoided." Our discussion in the Force Section of this Report confirms that this training may well have instilled bad tactics that have led to avoidable force.

To be sure, we did observe some scenario-based training that seemed well-done, particularly during the newly developed Force Mitigation/Mental Health training, as well as in other contexts at the Academy. We observed one instructor during a scenario give proper instruction on handcuffing and cautioning that a subject may react if he is in pain, noting the importance of not jumping to an unwarranted conclusion that the subject is resisting. The instructor conducted a solid de-brief following the exercise and ensured the students understood the material. However, we did not observe this quality of instruction in many other trainings we observed.

Many of the Department members we spoke with during ride-alongs, district tours, interviews, and small-group meetings confirmed the inadequacies described above. One officer said that Academy instructors are unable to go "off script" and deviate from the PowerPoint lectures, and that at least one Academy instructor was teaching an outdated procedure that had not been used in years. Speaking about instruction at the Academy more generally, another officer told us that "[CPD's] training was fast, sloppy, and it's getting people in trouble." A training official lamented that "CPD is using litigation to measure training effectiveness," i.e., the lack of quality training is resulting in civil lawsuits. Another officer put it more starkly, stating simply, "our co-workers are going to die because of no training."

Because training and the evaluation of its impact on new recruits is so deficient, CPD cannot properly identify which recruits need further training or even dismissal, resulting in new recruits policing Chicago communities who, despite their best intentions, from the outset are ill-equipped and perhaps incapable of policing effectively and constitutionally. Indeed, while precise figures regarding Academy attrition rates are difficult to obtain, CPD officials expressed that the attrition rate is "very close to zero" and thus well below normal levels present in police academies across the country. CPD recognizes that changes are needed. In the last few months, CPD began to plan for potential changes to the Academy training program, including, among other things, forming a "Recruit Curriculum Working Group" to review the current curriculum and suggest changes; searching for new instructors; and creating "feedback loops" to identify trends and deficiencies where training must be improved. As stated earlier, CPD and the City's recognition of these issues is laudable, but must be accompanied by concrete plans to implement these changes, including through additional resources and staffing.

2. CPD's Field Training Program undermines effective and lawful policing

Similar to the Academy, CPD's post-Academy Field Training Program is poorly structured and operates in a manner that actively undermines, rather than reinforces, constitutional policing. In a functioning field training program, once recruits graduate from the Academy, they are paired, one-on-one, with an experienced Field Training Officer (FTO) for hands-on mentorship, training and evaluation. A strong field training program is essential for reinforcing the policies and practices recruits learn at the Academy. When done correctly, FTOs serve a vital role in engraining within probationary police officers (PPOs) an ethic of effective and constitutional policing that will guide them throughout their carriers. Conversely, a weak FTO program can blunt even the most effective Academy training program.

CPD's FTO program suffers from longstanding systemic deficiencies that have disabled the program's ability to serve this function. One high-ranking official in CPD's Education and Training Division repeatedly referred to the Field Training Program as a "hot mess;" another official described the program simply as "terrible." A third supervisor told us that FTOs are simply "warm butts in a seat" and that is all that matters to CPD. CPD officials also told our retained law enforcement training expert that it was common knowledge that anyone entering the field training program would make it through, meaning that, much like the Academy, the FTO program is not set up to distinguish capable recruits from ill-suited ones. Significant changes to the Field Training Program are necessary to ensure PPOs are adequately prepared to police constitutionally and safely.

CPD does not currently deploy a sufficient number of qualified FTOs to meet the field training demands of the Department. During our tours and ride-alongs in various CPD districts, we consistently observed FTOs responsible for two PPOs at a time, and were told by CPD officers that FTOs can even supervise three PPOs at a time. Three PPOs per FTO is bad practice, and even two per FTO may undermine the effectiveness of the program. When FTOs are assigned more than one PPO, they are not able to develop the rapport conducive to the sometimes difficult redirection new recruits need. Nor is the FTO able to adequately observe and provide instruction.

One reason CPD's Field Training Program remains unsuccessful is that the selection process knowingly discourages many of the most-qualified officers from serving as FTOs and allows problematic police officers to continue acting as FTOs. CPD officers wishing to serve as FTOs must meet certain minimum qualifications to be considered. Interested officers apply in response to a vacancy announcement and sit for an exam. Officers' leadership, mentorship, or instructional skills are not necessarily considered in selecting new FTOs.

An officer's disciplinary record bears on his or her eligibility to serve as an FTO only where the officer has sustained misconduct investigations that resulted in suspensions of more than seven days in the last twelve months, or three or more sustained investigations resulting in suspensions of any length in the last five years. Another reason for the failures of the program is that officers working as FTOs must be willing to relinquish control of their district and shift assignments. This dis-incentivizes officers with significant experience, who because of their years of service qualify via CPD's assignment system for coveted posts and shifts, from applying for FTO positions. Additionally, being an FTO is not viewed by CPD officers as a prestigious position because unlike other departments in which serving as an FTO is a stepping stone to promotion, CPD FTOs receive no such benefit. Working as an FTO comes with a pay increase, but the amount is viewed by officers we spoke with as negligible–only a little more than $3,000 per year. As one supervising training official described it, serving as an FTO is a "road to nowhere."

The Department has done little to make this crucial training position more attractive, despite the fact that these problems with CPD's FTO program are not new. In 1997, the mayoral Commission on Police Integrity noted that "the FTO program is currently understaffed and in need of a complete overhaul." More specifically, the Commission recommended that the "number of FTOs should be expanded from its current level of 67 officers to at least 200 officers." The Commission also recommended increasing the FTO salary to attract a larger number of officers to the position and "to ensure that good patrol officers want the job." By 2014, CPD had added some, but not many, new FTOs, and committed to building the program to at least 150 FTOs. Yet, years later, CPD has not met even this limited goal, or heeded decades of recommendations that the FTO program be substantially expanded. FTO pay was never significantly increased, and the program was never adequately expanded. Currently, there are only around 107 FTOs for the entire Department. The Deputy Chief in charge of Training estimates that the number of FTOs actually available, due to furloughs and medical absences, is closer to 60 to 75.

Further, because the City does not consider the limited number of FTOs when hiring new recruit classes, recently-graduated PPOs are often forced to wait for Field Training Program spots to become available before being assigned to an FTO. In the past, PPOs awaiting placement in the Field Training Program were assigned to "hot zones" around the city–areas of high crime – to increase police visibility. This practice, referred to by some officers as "Operation Impact Zone," placed PPOs on foot patrol in locations where they do not have the experience or training necessary to deal with situations that may arise. Although the PPOs are just there to provide presence, and are not supposed to take any action in response to criminal activity, this type of assignment can still negatively impact PPOs' views of their job; they are justifiably unprepared and overwhelmed by these assignments, which impacts their acceptance of community policing principles, decreases their confidence, and clouds their perception of those communities. Placement of inexperienced officers as a show of force also negatively impacts those communities' views of CPD. Such placements could last up to three months while the PPO awaits placement with an FTO. Although we were told that "Operation Impact Zone" has ceased, we understand that PPOs may still be assigned to foot patrols downtown or on parade routes, without adequate supervision, while awaiting openings in the Field Training Program. No matter where they are assigned, placement of PPOs on patrols without an FTO prior to completion of the Field Training Program is dangerous, and demonstrates CPD's disregard of the training necessary for new officers to do their jobs safely, effectively, and lawfully.

When recruits are able to enter the FTO program, they do not receive sufficient supervision and guidance. In addition to supervising too many PPOs at one time, we observed that FTOs do not operate according to any uniform protocols. One more experienced FTO we spoke with reported receiving no training prior to becoming an FTO. Although there is now a five-week FTO training program in place, more senior FTOs may have not received any training at all. Even with a five-week training, we observed that there is no consistency in how FTOs teach and mentor their PPOs, meaning that the quality and content of instruction varies significantly Department-wide. Our retained law enforcement training expert observed FTOs and PPOs interacting and found that the FTOs did not provide proper redirection. For example, our expert observed a PPO driving erratically and making rude and disrespectful comments about the community in the presence of the FTO, but the FTO did not correct this behavior. And further demonstrating how problematic CPD's poor FTO instruction and overall training program can be, CPD's FTOs frequently tell PPOs to "throw out" what they learned in the Academy because the FTOs will show them how to "be the police." The quality of the supervision and training a PPO receives from his or her FTO directly impacts whether the PPO's policing will reflect the Department's values. FTOs' unwillingness to reinforce Academy training, whether because they accurately judge it to be inadequate or because they do not respect CPD's core values, sends a perilous message to recruits and undermines any improved polices or procedures intended to inculcate a culture of respectful and constitutional policing.

Finally, CPD does not evaluate the effectiveness of the FTOs or the FTO program as a whole. Although, pursuant to the hiring criteria for FTOs, an FTO may be relieved of FTO responsibilities if he or she demonstrates a lack of knowledge, skills, or abilities for the assignment, training academy personnel confirmed that FTOs are never actually evaluated in this regard. FTOs are under the command of the Bureau of Patrol, and therefore despite serving a critical role in the training of new officers, they are not evaluated or held accountable by the Education and Training Division. Neither the Bureau of Patrol nor the Education and Training Division engages in regular auditing of the Program or solicits feedback to determine areas for improvement, and the City's proposed reforms make no mention of how any of its proposed changes will address this need.

As with other aspects of CPD's training program, CPD recognizes that the FTO program is in need of a significant overhaul. CPD has acknowledged that several changes are needed, including hiring more FTOs, identifying ways to incentivize more qualified officers to apply for FTO positions, "upgrading the supervisory structure" for the FTO program so that there are supervisors in the districts who oversee the program, and putting systems in place to ensure that the FTO program is more closely coordinated with the Academy. The City also is planning on "upgrading the system for evaluating FTOs" and PPOs. These reforms, however, like the proposed reforms to CPD's Academy, are in the very initial stages, and CPD has no concrete plan for how, or by when, these goals will be accomplished.

3.   CPD provides only sporadic in-service training

Once a CPD officer leaves the Academy, he or she is not required to participate in any live, regular annual training for the remainder of his or her career. Instead, CPD's mandatory in-service training consists of last-minute reactive trainings, as described below; videos played at roll call; and "e-learning" courses provided online. One officer summarized CPD's entire post-Academy training program as "Watch a Video."

The impact of the lack of in-service training cannot be overstated. Without regular, mandatory training, CPD officers do not receive ongoing instruction on critically important topics, such as proper use of force, responding to persons in mental health crisis, handling domestic violence calls, or updates in the law regarding stops and searches. This prevents officers from accepting and emulating a culture of constitutional and fair policing. It also inhibits officer confidence that they know how to do their jobs safely and effectively.

CPD also does not provide regular refresher trainings on important basic skills that can help reduce the need for the use of force, including deadly force. These include proper handcuffing techniques and pursuit tactics. At a minimum, generally accepted police practices dictate at least 40 hours of continuing education per year, which usually includes roughly 24 hours of force-refresher skills. Several CPD officers reported to us that, once they left the Academy, they were not required to retrain on any basic skills. CPD officers must qualify on their firearms annually, but qualification is not training. As discussed in the Force Section of this Report, our review of CPD force, including hundreds of force incidents and several video-recorded incidents of CPD uses of force, revealed CPD officers engaging in dangerous tactics that indicate they do not remember or were never taught basic police skills. This results in officers approaching suspect vehicles in a manner that puts officers and civilians in jeopardy; firing at fleeing vehicles in inappropriate circumstances; using force unreasonably; and failing to render aid to suspects who have been shot. Consistent with our review, interviewees were unanimous in their belief that the lack of continuing training has a direct connection to the improper use of force in patrol and other field assignments.

In-service training also is necessary to teach officers about changes in law, technology, community expectations, and developments in national police practices and for presenting changes to Department policy. CPD does not use regular in-service training to meet either of these important objectives. Instead, officers reported that they do not receive sufficient training when policies change, and they worry that they will be criticized for not adhering to a policy that was never explained to them. By not providing regular in-service trainings, CPD makes it unnecessarily difficult for officers to remain aware of changes to law and policy and how to operationalize those changes.

In lieu of actual in-service training, CPD disseminates new information to Department members through roll call, using techniques that are not effective for adult learning and often not appropriate for the complexity of the material being presented. In-service training comes primarily through videos or announcements by supervisors at roll call, or videos available through e-learning modules. Supervisors acknowledge that officers do not pay attention to these trainings. CPD also more generally recognizes that this is an ineffective way to provide new material or refresh previously learned lessons, as roll-call trainings and e-learning videos do not teach skills, and it is difficult to measure learning.

CPD recognizes that providing real in-service training is necessary to build a more effective and qualified police force, and is just beginning to develop plans to institute a comprehensive in-service program. CPD informed us that, going forward, it would like to provide 40 hours of mandatory in-service training for all Department members through a combination of Academy-based and district-based training. CPD still needs to do an assessment of what courses are needed most; create a process for developing, vetting, and reviewing those courses; and identify how and when that training could be delivered. CPD has also not considered whether additional in-service training may be necessary up front, given that there has not been any regular in-service training for years. Once again, CPD's plans for in-service training, while ambitious and potentially beneficial to the Department, are very preliminary, and it remains to be seen whether CPD's stated commitment to more in-service training will actually translate into the sustainable, effective provision of such training in the months and years to come.

4. CPD does not provide training that is proactive, organized, and tailored to Department needs

Until a few weeks ago, CPD did not have a committee tasked with identifying the Department's training needs and establishing priorities, or making sure that training is delivered efficiently, timely, and effectively. The training committee is in the first stages of developing a training plan.[38] The previous absence of a committee and plan has prevented CPD from providing training that is proactive and comprehensive. Currently, although most training is coordinated through the Training and Education Division, there are no protocols for the development, coordination, or delivery of training. Proper planning in this area would help CPD allocate its resources to meet the greatest departmental needs and deliver a cohesive message to Department members about the vision, mission, and culture of the agency. Developing a comprehensive training plan will help in developing trainings that give officers the ability to connect policy to practice, which, in turn, will increase officer confidence that their training as a whole has taught them how to police safely, lawfully, and effectively.

In particular, CPD has not attempted to ascertain the training needs of experienced officers or where additional training might benefit particular units or the Department as a whole. CPD does not actively solicit suggestions from Department members for future trainings, or follow through on requests from officers for training on particular topics. And, as noted elsewhere in this Report, CPD does not use data to evaluate trends of problems within the Department, including patterns of excessive force or other misconduct. CPD has recognized this failure and reports that it plans to develop "feedback loops" from various stakeholders to inform training. This prospective reform is critical; the historic failure to proactively evaluate trends has blinded CPD to understanding where additional trainings could both improve performance and community relations, and decrease harmful incidents and CPD's exposure to liability.

CPD's overall lack of planning results in training that is ad hoc, disorganized, and reactive to the most recent crisis, rather than thoughtful, proactive, and demonstrably responsive to officers' training needs. Because there is no regular, mandatory in-service training, post-Academy training is offered primarily in response to crises, such as high-profile officer-involved shootings or other uses of force. City leadership is, and should be, responsive to the legitimate concerns of its constituents; but at the same time, CPD should be given time, space and resources to develop thoughtful and effective training that is sustainable.

Instead, training staff are told to "get it done" and "make it work" quickly. Such trainings are often scheduled with only a few days of notice. As a result, the Education and Training Division is not given sufficient time to identify or develop an appropriate curriculum or secure trainers with subject matter expertise. Similarly, although the Academy has a set curriculum, recruit classes often begin on short notice, leaving Division staff little time to secure qualified subject matter experts to train on the various topics. As a result, trainers are often ill-equipped to present the material they are scheduled to teach, decreasing the potential impact of the training.

This haphazard approach to training also hinders officer buy-in that the training being provided is important and valuable for their jobs. Officers feel that CPD trains only in response to crises, rather than pursuant to measured, thoughtful consideration of officers' training needs and desires.

CPD's recent experience introducing Investigatory Stop Reports (ISRs) underscores the consequences of CPD's approach. ISRs require officers to document their stops and searches more systematically than they had done previously. Although instituted in CPD to resolve an ACLU lawsuit,[39] documenting stops and searches in the manner captured by ISRs is a practice that has been in place for many years in other large-city police departments. In Chicago, the new ISR forms were quickly rolled out without a thoughtful, comprehensive training plan that took into account officers' predictable concerns and the broader context. Instead of taking the opportunity to instruct officers about how to conduct lawful and safe stops and searches, the ISR training focused only on how to fill out the new form. The training failed to anticipate or address officers' fears that filling out these forms would subject them to individual liability. Supervisors did not receive training before their subordinates did, and were therefore unprepared to provide guidance; officers found the forms onerous and confusing, and did not understand why the changes were instituted. When officers belatedly received training, they found it inconsistent and contradictory. CPD's failure to plan or deliver this training properly increased officers' frustration and fear that this change was being driven by the need for political-cover instead of as an integral part of policing the community safely and effectively. As a consequence, many officers do not support the reforms or understand how to implement them effectively. This reaction likely could have been minimized if CPD had appropriately planned this training, and delivered it in the context of a robust in-service training program that addresses connected issues, such as constitutional policing and CPD policies on stops, searches, and arrests.

Similarly, in response to the release of the Laquan MacDonald video in November 2015, the City mandated that all CPD officers be trained on Taser use by June 1, 2016. Effective training on this skill requires small class sizes so that officers have the opportunity to practice using the device in various scenarios, and engage with the instructor to ensure they understand the concepts, including when and how it is appropriate to use a Taser. It also requires a thoughtful curriculum that provides officers with direction on how to avoid the need to use force, while giving them confidence in using the weapon where necessary. CPD, however, quickly cycled large numbers of officers through poorly designed training. As a result, officers were not effectively taught how or when to use the Taser as a less-lethal force option. Many CPD officers told us the training they received did not adequately prepare them to use Tasers in the field. One officer told us that officers had been requesting Taser training for years, but those requests went unfulfilled until the City suddenly changed course. As he put it, "the City's lack of preparation is now our emergency."

This crisis-driven approach to in-service training does a disservice to both CPD officers and the public. Advanced planning and organization is necessary to ensure that trainings are effective in positively impacting officer safety and teaching officers the skills they need to do their jobs.

5. <u>CPD's Education and Training Division lacks the resources it needs to provide training that is coordinated, forward-thinking, and effective</u>

   a. *CPD has insufficient and inexperienced training staff*

CPD's Education and Training Division, which runs the Academy, specialized trainings, and the FTO program, is perennially understaffed and staffed with individuals who are not sufficiently trained or prepared to teach the subject matters they are assigned. We found that many instructors are not properly prepared to teach the materials they are assigned, and are not chosen for their qualifications or abilities, but rather only on how they score on a written test.

We also found that Academy curriculum is not vetted in any manner by experts in curriculum design and/or instruction, resulting in gaping omissions and gross misapplications of materials developed. We found that the person tasked with developing and teaching the instructor's training course (where teachers are trained on how to teach) was well qualified and had expertise, but the course itself does not use sufficient evaluation instruments for CPD to determine whether, following the training, the trainees are sufficiently prepared to teach.

CPD now recognizes the need for additional training staff, but leadership must be committed—for the long term—to providing the resources necessary to ensure a sufficient number of competent, well-qualified trainers. CPD must invest in recruiting and hiring trainers and curriculum development staff who will develop and deliver progressive, effective training programs, and re-train or replace existing staff to ensure these roles are carried out successfully.

b. CPD has inadequate training space

CPD's training facilities are in disrepair. CPD has made few physical upgrades to its main training facility since it was built in 1976. Training equipment is old and frequently breaks down. This makes conducting trainings difficult, and potentially dangerous. Poor upkeep of CPD's training facilities also signals to those who work there, those who train there, and to the public, that training is not valued by CPD.

The current facilities used by CPD are also insufficient to meet the training needs of a department as large as CPD. The spaces CPD currently uses for outdoor drills and exercises are not secure. Features typically used to support recruit training are non-existent. CPD lacks, among other facilities, an outdoor shooting range, a driver training area, marching/drill grounds, and mock buildings for scenario-based training. Storage for firearms at the training facilities is not secure. Our expert found CPD's shooting range at the Academy to be "exceptionally substandard." Indeed, firearm training is provided indoors in a building with ventilation so inadequate that it is unhealthy for participants.

One of CPD's scenario training buildings, which houses the Training and Tactics Unit, is dangerous, both because of the dilapidated, inadequate facility, and the lack of adequate safety protocols. When we visited, this facility did not have locked main doors. The armory room—a former school office—was unlocked with loaded guns left in open, unlocked cubbies in a room left unattended. Training guns and ammunition were stored close to guns loaded with live rounds. The close proximity of these materials, without adequate controls or labels, created a serious risk that the real guns would be mistaken for training ones, or that the guns and ammunition could go missing or be stolen.[40]

CPD leadership recognizes that the training facilities are inadequate. However, CPD has not dedicated adequate resources to remedying these conditions, significantly impacting the quality and breadth of trainings CPD is able to provide. The need to allocate additional resources to the Education and Training Division is especially urgent in light of the City's stated plans to hire nearly 1,000 new officers. This hiring would require the Education and Training Division to run huge classes through the Academy each month—while completing recently mandated specialized training, such as the force mitigation/de-escalation training, for the approximately 12,500 current officers. The Division does not have sufficient personnel, equipment, or space to meet these demands.

6. <u>CPD's current plans for reform</u>

CPD recognizes that whole-scale changes are needed to its training program, and that these changes should be guided by a comprehensive training committee and plan. CPD told us of an ambitious dashboard of changes to its Academy, in-service, pre-service, and FTO training. Currently these plans amount to verbal commitments with uncertain dates for completion. These plans should be committed to writing. Some of the changes CPD would like to make—such as limiting Academy instructor tenure, or adding new incentives to encourage quality officers to serve as FTOs—may impact the City's collective bargaining agreements. Moreover, CPD must identify the resources necessary to make these changes or obtain commitments from the City to provide what is needed. CPD should be empowered with the resources and support it needs to make changes in the best interest of the officers and the public they serve.

We commend CPD for conducting a review of its training program using an expert consultant, and for recognizing and accepting the longstanding deficiencies with the training program that this expert identified. CPD's willingness to identify these problems and work towards solutions is an important first step in bringing CPD's training program in line with national standards. However, as CPD's own expert put it, "the devil is in the details." With many of the recommendations CPD reportedly embraced, CPD has not yet worked out whether these reforms are possible given CPD's current infrastructure, resources, and personnel, and if the reforms *are* possible, precisely how they will be accomplished, and by when. As noted by CPD's consultant, significant external pressures are necessary for any organization to follow through with plans as ambitious as these.

B. SUPERVISION

Instead of encouraging the chain of command to instill proper policing tactics and respect for constitutional policing in CPD officers, CPD provides little incentive, or even opportunity, for supervisors to meaningfully guide and direct CPD officers. CPD provides even less incentive for supervisors to hold officers accountable when they deviate from CPD policy and the law.

The City has long known that CPD's direct supervision of officers is inadequate, including through the fact that multiple reports in the last two decades have highlighted deficiencies in CPD's supervisory practices. Yet, City and CPD leadership have not made the necessary reforms to CPD's supervision structure and processes, and community and officer safety suffer as a result. Providing robust, meaningful supervision would better prevent officer misconduct and would significantly help CPD police safely and effectively.

Our conversations with rank-and-file Department members, and our observations throughout each of CPD's 22 districts, illuminated the breadth and depth of CPD's failure to provide proper supervision. Our overarching impression of supervisors from officers is that, with notable exceptions, supervisors do not lead. We were told on several occasions that sergeants are "not there to ruffle any feathers." Rather than ensuring that officers under their watch are policing constitutionally, many sergeants instead focus on keeping their subordinates out of trouble when there may be reason for discipline. Supervisors do not review the personnel records of the officers they are supervising, either because they do not know how, they do not have access to the information, or they do not see the value in doing so. *See* Report, Section IV.D. Consistent with this broad sense among officers, supervisors told us they are wary of intervening to correct rule or tactical errors, because "no one wants to be the bad guy." As one commander framed the problem, "supervisors lack courage to hold officers accountable." We also heard from several Department members that supervisors, particularly sergeants and lieutenants, are more concerned with being "friends" with their subordinates than providing adequate supervision. As one deputy chief told us, "we have a culture where we [the supervisors] are people's friends rather than supervisors." Another deputy chief stated that supervisors stay "too close" to their former peers after being promoted, which is why "many of them do not step up to the task" of adequately supervising and holding accountable those under their command.

It has long been recognized that first-level supervisors, through their action or inaction, profoundly affect the performance of the officers under their command.[41] In the patrol setting, sergeants are most directly involved in setting the tone of policing on the street. Sergeants who take a lax approach to supervision foster an environment in which mediocrity and misconduct flourish. As one former police manager observed,

> Police officers are extremely sensitive and attuned to what fellow officers do and do not do. Officers know who files false injury claims, who the second car is on a "man with a gun" call, who steps over the line with excessive force, and who is likely to get lost for a full tour of duty. When officers in the middle of the bell curve see that these people are not dealt with, they sometimes begin to imitate their behavior. Similarly, when those in the middle of the bell curve see fellow officers take extra calls, quickly respond as backup, and testify clearly and honestly, they begin to imitate them as well.[42]

It is readily apparent that there is a critical failure of leadership at the first line of supervision within CPD. Officers provide little documentation of their activities—particularly with respect to use of force—and sergeants consistently take a hands-off approach to the means by which officers take enforcement actions. As discussed in the Force Section of this Report, supervisors provide very little supervision of officers' use of force. With the exception of officer-involved shootings, officers are not required to provide details of the incidents in which force was used, and little is done to investigate whether the force used was reasonable, and/or whether policies, training, or equipment should be modified to improve force outcomes in the future. Sergeants informed us that, in reviewing a use of force, their role simply is to ensure the form is filled out correctly. Our review of files confirmed this—in most of the Tactical Response Report (TRR) files we reviewed, we saw no evidence that sergeants took steps to determine what force officers had used and whether it was appropriate, lawful, or safe.

Supervisors do not hold officers accountable for the force they use, and supervisors are themselves not held accountable for failing to investigate whether force used by officers under their command was proper. This failure to provide first line supervision of officers' use of force contributed to the pattern or practice of unconstitutional force we found. CPD has not taken the necessary steps to transform supervision within CPD. As discussed further below, CPD does not provide sufficient training for supervisors. CPD also fails to hold supervisors accountable when they do not hold officers accountable or do not provide the oversight and direction that might prevent officers from committing misconduct or policing poorly. As discussed below, supervisors who do not report the misconduct of their subordinates—or worse, supervisors who cover up that misconduct—are rarely held accountable, with exceptions in a few high-profile cases. At the same time, CPD does not properly incentivize or reward the courageous and diligent supervisors who swim against this tide to provide close and effective supervision to officers, including through holding officers accountable for violations.

These practices, in combination, send a clear message to all ranks within CPD that close, meaningful supervision is neither valued nor rewarded, which in turn has predictably led to a lack of effective supervision throughout the Department.

1. CPD's supervisory structures and responsibilities do not provide for meaningful supervision of all officers

CPD does not demand that supervisors perform fundamental supervisory tasks, such as direct observation and meaningful evaluation of officer performance, including the quality of arrests or uses of force, or mentoring officers. Many supervisors we spoke with are committed to effective, safe, and constitutional policing within their districts; yet, systemic flaws in what CPD expects of them and the priorities that CPD sets prevent line supervisors from meeting those goals.

> a. *CPD requires that first-line supervisors spend too much time doing non-supervisory tasks, at the expense of providing officers supervision*

CPD first-line supervisors do not engage in the supervisory tasks typically expected of their positions. Most CPD supervisors with whom we spoke appeared uncertain or reluctant about the role they can and should play in identifying and addressing positive *or* negative police behavior. Although there are many well-meaning supervisors within CPD's ranks, a large number do not make sufficient efforts to communicate with, observe, instruct, or mentor their subordinates. This results in missed opportunities for subordinates' learning and job improvement, and allows both lackadaisical policing and inappropriately aggressive policing to go unaddressed.

CPD sergeants generally spend their shifts on administrative tasks rather than interacting with and guiding their officers. One officer told us that in general, he would not see a sergeant after roll call. When sergeants do go into the field, too often their supervision is tentative and formalistic. One sergeant told us when he goes into the field, he spends his time "logging" his officers, that is, driving around and laying eyes on each car twice per shift. This means that the sergeant checks boxes and does administrative work instead of providing meaningful oversight or analysis of officer activity.

The lack of true supervision is in part due to the failure of supervisors to see these tasks as part of their role. It is also attributable to the myriad duties placed on supervisors that could, and should, be done by other entities. Sergeants, for example, are bogged down with tasks that would be more appropriately assigned to civilian administrative assistants. CPD employs fewer civilian employees than other large police departments, leaving supervisors to take on administrative tasks that do not involve police work. CPD leadership recognizes that the low number of civilian employees working for CPD results in officers and supervisors spending too much time doing administrative and other tasks, and that additional efforts to change this are needed to bring CPD "up to industry standards." In the last year, the City began a push towards "civilianizing" certain jobs, that is, hiring civilian staff to do work now being done by officers and supervisors. However, during the course of our investigation, we found that the administrative demands on sergeants serve to shift much of the supervision responsibility to lieutenants, even though they too are overburdened with administrative work.

> b. *A too-broad span of control and lack of unity of command prevents supervisors from performing critical supervisory functions*

Even if sergeants and lieutenants understood their role as supervisors and were able to dedicate their entire shift to supervision-related tasks, CPD deploys far too few patrol supervisors to ensure adequate supervision of all officers. The number of officers under a supervisor's watch, often referred to as the "span of control," must be narrow enough for supervisors to be able to interact with the officers, observe their performance, and assist when needed. Prior consultants to the City recommended no more than 10 officers assigned to each sergeant on every watch at each district. Experience in Chicago and elsewhere, however, makes clear that the ratio may need to be even smaller than this in some circumstances. A span of control of seven officers to one sergeant is a generally accepted industry standard, although the appropriate ratio will depend in part on the dynamics of the particular district and assignment. CPD frequently operates under a span of control far greater than this recommended limit, even in the busiest districts. One captain told us that sergeants *should* only supervise 8 officers at a time, and at least one sergeant told us he supervises 12 cars at a time—meaning, potentially, 24 officers, assuming two officers per car. Another officer told us that he has seen 2 supervisors in charge of 70 officers at a time. Yet another officer relayed to us an example where a single sergeant was responsible for an entire district during the day shift. The district included 25 officers on patrol, plus 14 officers stationed in 7 different high schools throughout the district. This left one sergeant in charge of nearly 40 officers spread out over a wide geographic area. In each of these examples, CPD's span of control far exceeds industry standards, which prevents sergeants from providing adequate supervision and jeopardizes the safety of the community and the officers themselves.

CPD's rotational system of scheduling also prevents supervisors from maintaining "unity of command," meaning that officers are not consistently scheduled to be supervised by the same sergeants or lieutenants, or assigned to the same beat. Currently, CPD patrol officers work pursuant to a rotational schedule, where they rotate the days off that they have each week. Officers are not assigned the same days off as their supervisors, meaning that they do not consistently interact with the same supervisor on every shift. This prevents supervisors from establishing mentoring relationships with officers and providing guidance targeted to the particular needs of each individual officer. The lack of consistency also inhibits supervisors from identifying changes in an officer's behavior that may indicate the officer is in need of assistance or disciplinary intervention. Officers complained that this prevents them from getting to know their beat well and doing their job effectively.

These issues are not new. The 2014 study of CPD's supervision and accountability structures conducted for the Safer Report, which the City commissioned, recommended changes to staffing and operational patterns to increase monitoring of officer behavior. In particular, the Safer Report strongly recommended switching from the current rotational system to a "patrol squad system," wherein each patrol sergeant is responsible for developing and monitoring a designated group of officers. It noted that the current system "limit[s] the sergeants' ability to develop officers under their command and creat[es] inconsistencies in management styles and expectations." The Safer Report also warned CPD that its current ratio of sergeants to police officers and lieutenants to sergeants is low, and that "maintaining a healthy ratio of supervisors to subordinates is critical to ensuring proper supervision of each officer." CPD did not adopt the Safer Report's recommendation and made no changes to either span of control or unity of command.

CPD leadership recently publicly recognized that reduction in span of control is needed to allow for "more hands-on guidance and direction in difficult situations." As part of the City's recent efforts, in late September 2016, the Superintendent announced plans to hire 112 sergeants and 50 lieutenants over the next two years to "provide valuable guidance to officers on the street." We agree that more supervisors are needed. However, promoting additional officers alone will not resolve the span of control problems that have plagued CPD for years, especially if the City does not deploy officers and supervisors pursuant to a comprehensive staffing analysis. Notably, CPD recently pledged to develop a "fair, transparent, and objective methodology" to determine where to assign new officers and supervisors. CPD noted that the new study will be more "in-depth" than a previous 2010 study by the same group that analyzed the number of patrol officers needed each shift in each district, because it will consider more variables than just calls for service.

The City must not only plan for the effective deployment of new supervisors, but also address the more deeply entrenched problems in supervision that have previously evaded reform. CPD must actively engage in reforming its culture, the structure and scope of supervisory responsibilities, and its adherence to a rotational schedule that does not consistently place supervisors with the same subordinates. Adding additional supervisors alone will not solve the lack of meaningful supervision within CPD.

2. <u>Supervisors are not trained to provide meaningful supervision</u>

CPD does not adequately train its sergeants and lieutenants to provide meaningful supervision. This failure to train both reflects and contributes to CPD's culture of lax supervision.

Out of the 165 hours of pre-service sergeant training, only 7 hours are dedicated to instruction on leadership, when most new sergeants do not have any previous experience as supervisors. For the May 2015 lieutenant training, out of 134 hours of training, there were no courses dedicated to leadership and supervision skills. Nor do the course schedules for either the sergeant or lieutenant trainings reflect courses in professional development, interpersonal relationships, or other important managerial topics.

The insufficiency of CPD's leadership training is not a recent revelation. The Safer Report recommended adding an informal mentorship program for newly minted sergeants to provide "on-the-job" training designed to teach them how to supervise and monitor other officers for the first time. This suggestion was not adopted. The Safer Report also suggested that supervisors be given more courses in leadership, including courses in "Progressive Coaching," and that CPD should offer these courses on a regular basis rather than only at the Academy. However, in-service training remains as irregular for supervisors as it does for other CPD officers. CPD recently informed us that it will be "upgrading" its supervisory training to provide more training on issues relevant to supervisors, but, like other recently proposed reforms, there is no actual plan in place yet, nor information on the tangible changes CPD envisions or how those changes will be achieved.

1. <u>Supervisors are not held accountable for failing to report misconduct</u>

The supervision failures described above are perhaps most acute when it comes to CPD supervisors' unwillingness to step in to correct their officers' problematic behavior. Under CPD policy, supervisors are obligated to report information regarding misconduct by subordinate officers. Yet, CPD culture discourages supervisors from reporting the misconduct of subordinates.

As one captain told us, sergeants in particular are disinclined to report misconduct because they have to work with their officers every day, and they want to avoid conflict. A lieutenant told us that supervisors are concerned about branding a subordinate officer with a negative employment record by formally reporting their misconduct. A deputy chief told us that CPD operates under a culture "where we are people's friends rather than supervisors," and that "no one wants to be the bad guy." And another deputy chief stated that the widespread supervisory failure to hold officers accountable has caused accountability to become CPD's biggest problem.

This failure to report is particularly strong where the officer committing misconduct is regarded as having impunity because of that officer's connections within the Department. CPD officers we spoke to referred to this as someone who "has a phone call," meaning the officer has the protection of a powerful person in the Department who can influence assignments, promotion, and discipline. Supervisors decline to discipline these officers because any such efforts would not only be futile, but could be counterproductive to their own careers. In turn, these CPD members reportedly are able to engage in misconduct with impunity.

Moreover, IPRA and BIA fail to hold supervisors accountable consistently for their failure to report officer misconduct. Rather, one investigator indicated to us that he uses potential "failure to report" charges against a supervisor as a bargaining chip to get accused officers to mediate their misconduct complaints. In other words, if an investigator wants to encourage an officer to mediate a misconduct complaint, the investigator may tell the officer that if he or she rejects mediation, the investigator will launch a separate investigation against the officer's supervisor for failing to report the alleged misconduct. Investigators told us that this practice was effective in resolving misconduct complaints quickly through mediation.

This failure of supervisors to report misconduct also includes the failure to accept and report complaints of officer misconduct that community members make at the districts. CPD policy requires supervisors to accept, record, and forward such complaints to IPRA, yet supervisors often do not do so. An IPRA investigator told us that individuals who call 911 or a district police station to ask for a CPD supervisor to report officer misconduct are told that their complaint will not be documented by CPD, and that they should call IPRA instead. In another example, two teenage boys and their mothers complained to a supervising sergeant at a CPD district that an officer slammed one of the boys to the ground, cuffed him, shoved a gun in his face, and threatened to blow up the boy's house. The sergeant refused to report the complaint to IPRA as required. The mothers filed a complaint directly with IPRA, and the officer involved in the misconduct was eventually disciplined; IPRA did not, however, sustain allegations against the sergeant for failing to report the officer's misconduct. In another IPRA investigation, a complainant said that she asked a desk sergeant how she could file a complaint of officer abuse and was told to "get the fuck out of the station." This allegation in her complaint was never investigated by IPRA. In yet another file we reviewed, the complainant stated that CPD officers pulled him over, abused him, and stole his car keys, leaving him stranded. The complainant told IPRA that he went to a district to file his complaint, but the sergeant he spoke with refused to take it down.

This evidence and the statements from officers at all ranks within CPD are consistent with the findings of the 2014 Safer Report, which noted that "discovering and addressing misconduct is too often viewed as the responsibility of IPRA and BIA, and not of the offending officer's immediate supervisor and chain of command . . . this attitude is misguided and must be changed." The Mayor's Police Accountability Task Force (PATF) report two years later found the same, explaining that "CPD has fostered a culture in which supervisors turn a blind eye to misconduct and do not provide sufficient oversight to ensure that officers perform their duties with integrity." The City's recently proposed changes to CPD's accountability system do not adequately address this important facet of CPD's culture and supervision structure. More changes are necessary to ensure that supervisors hold their subordinates accountable for misconduct, and if they fail to do so, that they will be held accountable themselves.

4. CPD's "early intervention system" exists in name only and does not assist supervisors in identifying or correcting problematic behavior

Compounding CPD's supervision problems, the Department does not use long-available supervisory tools, such as a comprehensive early intervention system (EIS), to identify patterns of concerning officer behavior and prevent patterns of misconduct and poor policing from developing or persisting. A well-designed EIS would allow CPD to track officer conduct, proactively assess risk for future problematic behavior, and intervene when necessary to improve behavior through non-disciplinary corrective action, such as additional training, counseling, or other supportive programs. Currently, despite having spent significant time and resources building an EIS, CPD does not have a functioning system. Instead, there are several semi-connected data-collection, intervention, and counseling programs, each of which suffers from inefficiencies that render them essentially useless. In a positive development, the City recently began an initiative to revamp and revise its EIS once again. However, for this initiative to have the best chance of success, the City and police unions must negotiate collective bargaining agreements that enable an EIS that is accurate, complete, and that allows for meaningful support of officers by redirecting problematic behavior.

a. *Performance Recognition System*

One CPD system, an electronic "dashboard" referred to as the Performance Recognition System (PRS), is a computer data-tracking program designed to "assist[] Department Supervisors in recognizing exceptional or adverse behavior related to job performance of members under their command." Data is entered into the system by Human Resources, and supervisors are obligated by policy to "monitor and track, on a continual basis," the information contained in the PRS dashboard.

During conversations with district command staff, we learned that CPD supervisors do not understand how the PRS works or how to use the information it presents. In particular, supervisors do not understand what they are supposed to do when the dashboard shows that "early performance indicators" are present for an officer assigned to their district. For each officer, the various indicators are marked in the dashboard as green, yellow, or red. These indicators include data points such as the number of Summary Punishment Action Reports (SPARs) and complaints filed against the officer; the officer's arrest and TRR numbers; the officer's use of medical leave; and more. The dashboard also provides two ratios: the ratio of complaints to arrests, and the ratio of TRRs to arrests. The thresholds used to determine if an indicator is green versus yellow or red is apparently set by CPD's Human Resources Office. For the TRR ratio, for example, officers with more than a certain percentage of arrests involving force are marked in red. However, at least one commander responsible for using the dashboard did not know the threshold that would turn a TRR ratio from green to yellow or red, including whether the threshold is static or relational (i.e., whether it varies, depending upon, for example, officer assignment). He opined that a straight comparison of number of arrests to number of arrests involving force would be problematic, in that it would mark in red an officer who was involved in only one arrest, but that arrest happened to involve force. Indeed, the commander showed us one officer's record in the PRS dashboard that marked the officer in red; the officer had been involved in two arrests, one of which involved force, meaning that the officer had used force in 50% of his arrests. The commander agreed that the ratio was artificially high because the officer had been involved in so few arrests, and intervention in that case was probably inappropriate. Yet, he noted that there is no meaningful guidance given to supervisors about when "red" indicators should trigger a response. Nor does policy dictate what that response should be. Instead, the PRS policy gives examples of potential supervisory responses to "early performance indicators" in vague terms, such as "coaching," "counseling," "reviewing Department training tools," and "field monitoring," and provides little to no guidance regarding the circumstances in which each different form of response should be adopted.

The dashboard is also underused. The command staff we spoke with reported that they rarely use the PRS. Supervisors also question whether data that they enter into the PRS is actually saved. Although supervisors are supposed to review the system regularly, most do not, and CPD does not audit supervisor adherence to this or any other aspect of the PRS policy. The problems with the PRS become cyclical: supervisors do not use it because it is inaccurate, and it is inaccurate because CPD does not use it properly or consistently. As we were told by one supervisor, "the info in the PRS is not accurate[;] . . . you got garbage going in so you got garbage going out."

b. *Non-disciplinary intervention, Behavioral Intervention System, and Personnel Concerns Program*

CPD also offers three separate intervention programs to which officers can be referred on the basis of certain behavioral criteria, but each of these programs suffers from shortcomings that prevent appropriate enrollment and undermine effectiveness.

First, officers may be subject to "non-disciplinary interventions" when they engage in less-serious transgressions, such as using foul language or being disrespectful. This program triggers intervention by a supervisor after multiple incidents, and the interventions available are limited. They include, among other things, speaking with the officer, reminding the officer of available counseling programs, and instructing the officer to review training videos on courtesy and demeanor. Subsequent incidents trigger increasing interventions, including additional conversations and involvement of rank further up the chain of command.

If there are four or more incidents that would otherwise qualify for non-disciplinary intervention, or if the officer is involved in more serious allegations of misconduct, CPD can refer the officer to the Behavioral Intervention System (BIS) or Personnel Concerns Program (PCP). By policy, Human Resources recommends enrollment in BIS based on the existence of several "performance data," including sustained misconduct charges, low performance grade, or a pre-set number of instances of other misbehaviors such as tardiness, being absent without permission, or medical roll misuse. The ultimate decision of whether to enroll a member in BIS generally rests with the member's commander, although Human Resources may override a commander's decision not to enroll his or her subordinate. Employees enrolled in BIS undergo a physical examination, including drug testing, but are not required to undergo a psychological evaluation. Once placed in BIS, CPD may give employees counseling services or an individual performance plan.

The final option available is the PCP. CPD places Department members into PCP when they are involved in more serious transgressions, such as sustained excessive force charges, domestic violence, or five or more sustained misconduct investigations in the last five years.

CPD members who fail to comply with an individualized performance plan under BIS can also be placed in PCP. PCP is essentially the "last stop" for officers exhibiting problematic behavior to correct that behavior and remain on the force.

The BIS and PCP programs are ineffective methods for identifying and remedying patterns of negative behavior. First, policy and officers' collective bargaining agreements prevent these systems from considering the full range of behaviors that could be indicative of a problem. Policy prohibits maintaining misconduct allegations older than five years in PRS, or in some circumstances, considering them at all. With one exception, investigations of misconduct complaints that result in a "not sustained" finding are not considered, no matter how recent, even though a finding of "not sustained" indicates that the incident could neither be proven *nor* disproven.[43] Given the historical failures of CPD and IPRA to properly investigate and sustain allegations of misconduct, the universe of complaint and disciplinary data entered into PRS is egregiously incomplete.

In addition to the fact that policy restrictively limits eligibility for intervention, CPD also does not consistently refer for intervention the individuals who *are* identified as eligible. Pursuant to CPD policy, an officer's chain of command, BIA, or IPRA may refer the officer for BIS. However, there are no quality checks to ensure that the appropriate officers are actually being referred. A high-level official in Human Resources told us that, "if a recommendation [for intervention] is not made up the chain to HR, it falls through the cracks" and an otherwise eligible officer will never be enrolled. Another official told us that the BIS program is not getting the appropriate amount of referrals. Leadership at CPD does not enforce the BIS and PCP policies; consequently, BIA, IPRA, and the chain of command do not take seriously their obligation to identify and refer problematic officers.

Our review of CPD's data confirms that the Department enrolls very few officers in its interventional programs, especially for a department of its size. Between January 2010 and July 2016, CPD enrolled only 38 officers in BIS. An additional 60 members were referred for enrollment, but never enrolled. Notably, 56 of those members were referred to BIS because of their alleged involvement in a domestic incident. An additional nine officers were flagged as eligible for BIS, but their command staff declined to recommend them. 28 officers were referred for enrollment, but removed from the program; the data that CPD provided us did not explain why. Finally, between March and June 2016, after the start of our investigation, CPD identified an additional 50 officers as eligible for the program, but as of mid-July, their status in the program was still listed as "pending." In 2015, only seven officers were enrolled in BIS all year, most for having too many SPARs in a single year.

Review of CPD's complaint data compared to the BIS enrollment program also confirms that there are a significant number of Department members with lengthy complaint histories who were never referred to or enrolled in BIS. Between January 1, 2010 and March 2016, 1,627 CPD members were the subject of five or more misconduct complaints; 350 of those had 10 or more complaints. While there may be innocuous explanations for such complaint numbers for some of these officers, these numbers are high enough to indicate that substantially more than 38 officers should have been enrolled in BIS during this time period.

CPD leadership is aware that these programs are grossly underused. As noted recently by the PATF, CPD "does not use any metrics to measure or assess the effectiveness of the programs." CPD must commit to fixing this broken system with a solution that is well thought out, capable of easy and robust implementation, and supported by all stakeholders.

c. *The lack of a functioning early intervention system, coupled with inadequate supervision, has placed officers and members of the public at risk*

These longstanding, systemic deficiencies in CPD's early intervention systems have prevented CPD from taking two steps that are crucial to ensuring officer safety and wellness, as well as ensuring policing that is effective and lawful. First, CPD does not adequately and accurately identify officers who are in need of corrective action; and second, CPD does not consistently or sufficiently address officer behavior even where CPD identifies negative patterns. Because of these failures, CPD officers are able to engage in problematic behaviors with impunity, which can—and do—escalate into serious misconduct. This has dramatic consequences for the public. It also impacts the health and safety of officers, who either do not get the support and services they need, or are forced to work alongside individuals who are not receiving such support.

In particular, we found that the current EIS does not adequately identify patterns or trends of misconduct related to force and domestic violence. One officer, for example, was the subject of several complaints of domestic violence over the course of just a few years that CPD did not detect or act upon for a significant period of time. After the officer's ex-wife brought four separate allegations of domestic violence and harassment between 2007 and 2008, many of which were closed for no affidavit or deemed not sustained, IPRA finally disciplined the officer for domestic violence, and gave the officer a 15-day suspension. The officer then went on to engage in domestic violence on two more occasions, which resulted in serious injuries to the officer's victims.[44] Likewise, Officer Giraldo Sierra, who killed Flint Farmer in June of 2011, was involved in *three* shootings *within one year*, and three domestic violence allegations in the years prior—yet he was not listed by CPD as an individual who was even considered for enrollment in BIS at any point in 2010–2011. Our review of use-of-force files also found two egregious examples of excessive force where, in each incident, the officers involved had extensive histories of complaints of excessive force but were not on the BIS roster. *See* Report, Section II.B.2. (discussing incident involving officers who used a baton and Taser on a girl at school, and incident involving the forcible removable of 12-year-old boy from his bike). One of the officers involved in the first incident had five separate complaints involving excessive force in the year prior to the incident described; the officer involved in the second incident had ten.

We also reviewed media reports describing a sergeant who was recently involved in his second fatal shooting in three years. This sergeant allegedly was the subject of a BIA investigation in 2004, prior to his promotion, for violating a rule prohibiting CPD employees from owning businesses that sell alcohol. Per CPD policy, this is a rule infraction that could potentially result in termination. *See* Employee Resource E01-11, Secondary Employment, at IV.G (noting that Department members are prohibited from engaging "directly or indirectly in the ownership . . . or operation of a tavern or retail liquor establishment," and that "violation of this policy will result in discipline, up to and including separation."). According to media reports, the individual went on disability leave shortly after that investigation was initiated, and the investigation went dormant as a result. The officer came off disability seven years later in 2011, but the investigation remained stagnant. CPD officials learned of the open investigation after the officer was involved in a fatal shooting of an unarmed man in 2013, but still, the original complaint remained open.[45] The officer was then promoted to sergeant through the merit promotion process, despite the open investigation, and later was involved in his second fatal shooting of an unarmed man. Had there been a functioning, effective EIS system in place, the open investigation could have been caught much earlier—before the officer received a merit promotion, and perhaps before he was involved in his second lethal shooting of an unarmed man.

Finally, we reviewed one investigative file that is emblematic of both supervisors' unwillingness to directly supervise their officers *and* CPD's failure to have a comprehensive EIS. In this incident, a young man was stopped by a CPD officer when he was walking through an alley. After questioning the individual, the CPD officer handcuffed the individual and placed him against the officer's vehicle. In cell-phone video capturing the incident, the officer is seen pushing the individual against the vehicle, as the individual complains repeatedly, in a calm voice, that the handcuffs are too tight and causing pain. The officer repeatedly calls the individual "motherfucker," curses at him, and threatens him, saying "make a move like that at me again, I will fucking show you exactly what I can do." The officer appears to be deliberately provoking the man to "make a move" to give the officer an excuse to use more force. When the individual says that he was not moving, that he had been previously injured in the arm, and the handcuffs were digging into his bones, the officer appears to deliberately push down on the handcuffs, causing additional pain, and continues to repeatedly use profanity while speaking to the man. The individual sought medical attention for injuries he sustained as a result of the incident. An unknown individual eventually filed a complaint with IPRA, and the cell-phone footage of this interaction was posted on Facebook. When the officer involved in the incident saw the Facebook footage, he alerted his lieutenant of the incident and the existence of the video. The lieutenant reviewed the video and, despite the aggressive nature of the interaction and overtly hostile attitude of the officer, sent a letter to his commander saying that he thought the appropriate response would be non-disciplinary intervention. The lieutenant justified this recommendation by saying that the incident did not involve "racially offensive or otherwise inflammatory language" and that the "subject makes no known complaints which are visible in the video"—two statements that are patently false.

This is a clear example of a CPD supervisor neglecting to hold an officer accountable for obvious misconduct. Moreover, if CPD had a functioning EIS at the time of this incident, the supervisor would have seen that the officer had three prior excessive force complaints, some involving similar allegations of the use of profanity and threats, in the prior year-and-a-half. The officer was a clear candidate for BIS, yet no referral was ever made. The IPRA investigation remains ongoing.

d. The City's past reform efforts have been unsuccessful and more is needed to ensure the success of present efforts

The City needs to take a new approach to reforming its EIS system. The City is currently making another attempt to establish a functional EIS system; this effort is described below. But without a focused, determined plan that builds on lessons learned from past unsuccessful reform attempts, it will be difficult for this new effort to succeed.

Previous efforts to create a data-informed, well-structured EIS within CPD have been unsuccessful. For example, in 1994, the City purchased a promising EIS software program called BrainMaker, designed to analyze data points and pick out patterns indicative of problematic behavior and identify officers at risk of being fired from the Department. Use of this program would have put CPD on the cutting edge of EIS technology nationwide. Union leadership felt this system unfairly targeted officers and subjected them to unfair, adversarial questioning from Internal Affairs. The City stopped using BrainMaker after only two years and all the data and reports it produced "went missing."

The City chose instead to rely on the system that CPD still uses today, despite repeated warnings of its shortcomings. The current system came about following the 1997 Report of the Mayor's Commission on Police Integrity. In that report, the Commission urged CPD to implement a meaningful EIS, noting that "small problems become big ones if left unattended." The Commission also recommended that CPD look at unit-wide trends, rather than analyzing only individual officers, and analyzing civil liability judgments in addition to misconduct complaints. At the time, the Commission was hopeful that expanding the behavioral intervention programs would result in more officers being involved in the programs and improved outcomes. According to the PATF's final report, following a grievance filed by the Fraternal Order of Police challenging the inclusion of certain officers in the BIS program, the

City agreed to remove them from BIS, and the program was never expanded as suggested.

More recent studies of CPD's systems reaffirmed the need for reform. A 2007 study noted that nearly 90% of individuals with multiple complaints were never flagged by the EIS, including officers who amassed more than 50 abuse complaints within five years. This study also discussed how, of the 33 officers with 30 or more complaints between 2001–2006, fewer than half had been flagged for intervention. Seven years later, the City was again informed, via the Safer Report, that CPD needed to revise its BIS and PCP programs, including updating the data collection systems to make them more user friendly. In particular, the Safer Report recommended integrating the command staff PRS with systems used by investigative agencies into a single, streamlined case management system. Doing so, according to the study's authors, would eliminate a significant shortcoming of the current system: "the inability to track an officer's conduct throughout her career." Despite these repeated criticisms, the City has not successfully made the changes necessary to improve supervision and accountability in the Department. The PATF Report also highlighted these deficiencies, recommending that CPD develop a structured, tiered EIS system that utilizes appropriate data, supports supervisor training on its use, and provides for evaluation of the program's efficacy.

The City is currently engaging in a promising effort to study and reform the system, but, despite the best intentions of all involved, there are indications that this attempt may not be any more fruitful than past attempts, unless the City lays the necessary groundwork and stays focused until the EIS is fully integrated into CPD culture. The new project is managed by researchers from the University of Chicago, who successfully developed a new EIS system for the Charlotte-Mecklenburg Police Department in North Carolina,[46] and the University of Chicago Crime Lab.

The City launched this partnership in the spring of 2016 to study CPD's data systems and develop a comprehensive EIS tool based on predictive data unique to Chicago. The effort represents an ambitious and potentially transformative approach for the Department. However, CPD has not fully addressed concerns that prevented the success of prior reform efforts. For example, there are plans to involve union representation in the development of the system, but the project managers are taking guidance from the City on how and when to do so—and union involvement has not yet occurred. There is no evidence that the City or CPD engaged with the unions early on, before beginning this new effort, to determine whether CPD's unions will support the new effort.

The City should commit itself to improving its supervision efforts on all fronts: in the systems and management that supports direct, front-line supervisors, and in the data collection and intervention programs that give CPD a high-level view of potential negative behavior patterns. Until both of these areas are meaningfully and permanently addressed, officer morale and efficacy will continue to suffer, and a culture of constitutional policing will never take root.

C. Officer Wellness and Safety

Policing is a high-stress profession. Law enforcement officers often are called upon to deal with violence or crises as problem solvers, and they often are witnesses to human tragedy. In Chicago, this stress is particularly acute for several reasons. CPD officers are confronted with increasing levels of gun violence in some of the neighborhoods they police. Gun violence and neighborhood conditions take their toll on both residents and officers alike. At the same time, the relationship between CPD officers and the communities they serve is strained; officers on the street are expected to prevent crime, yet they must also be the face of the Department in communities that have lost trust in the police. This makes it particularly difficult to police effectively. These stresses animate the interactions officers have with the communities that they serve—both positively and negatively. As one CPD counselor explained, it is the "stress of the job that's the precursor to the crisis." The President's Task Force on 21st Century Policing put it well, noting that "the 'bulletproof cop' does not exist. The officers who protect us must also be protected—against incapacitating physical, mental, and emotional health problems as well as against the hazards of their job. Their wellness and safety are crucial for them, their colleagues, and their agencies, as well as the well-being of the communities they serve."[47]

All of these stressors can, and do, play out in harmful ways for CPD officers. CPD officers grapple with alcoholism and suicide, and some engage in domestic violence. And as explained elsewhere in this Report, CPD officers are part of a Department that engages in a pattern or practice of using force that is unjustified, disproportionate, and otherwise excessive. Although the pressure CPD officers are under is not an excuse for violating the constitutional rights of the citizens they serve, high levels of unaddressed stress can compromise officer well-being and impact an officer's demeanor and judgment, which in turn impacts how that officer interacts with the public. Some officers are able to manage the stress by shifting their focus to working even harder to do their jobs well. For others, it is more difficult. As these officers struggle with the stress of the job, they can close off and push away those they serve and those who want to help. For precisely these reasons, law enforcement agencies can and should do everything they can to support officers' physical and psychological well-being.

Officer wellness in CPD is not an integral part of the Department's operations. Given how officer wellness impacts officer behavior and the especially tense circumstances facing CPD officers each day, CPD officers need greater support. CPD does not have an overarching officer-wellness plan that includes robust counseling programs, comprehensive training, functioning equipment, and other tools to ensure officers are successful and healthy. The resources CPD provides are insufficient to meet Department needs, both because the programs are not robust and because the programs do not account for the needs of the increasing diversity of the officers that make up the Department. Furthermore, Chicago currently lacks an integrated platform of inter-related services—such as integrated training, counseling, and intervention programs—designed to enhance both the Department's organizational health as well as the wellness of personnel.

The Department should reinforce the value of wellness and support a culture that encourages officers to seek assistance when needed. CPD can then better prepare its officers for success, which in turn, will help prevent officers from posing harm to themselves and the communities they serve.

1. CPD must commit to providing officers necessary wellness support

   a. CPD must dedicate more resources to support officers

CPD's support for officers' physical and mental wellness is provided almost entirely through its Professional Counseling Service/Employee Assistance Program (EAP). EAP provides vital services to the Department, but is under-staffed and under-resourced. In contrast to similar-sized departments using the in-service model, which provides professional counseling services through on-staff counselors rather than contracting with independent professional counselors, CPD has devoted fewer resources to support EAP's growth. The ratio of trained counselors available to CPD personnel is considerably less when compared to other departments of comparable size and with similar service delivery models. CPD's EAP is staffed by three clinicians to serve the Department's roughly 13,500 sworn and unsworn personnel.[48] In comparison, the Dallas Police Department also staffs three full-time counselors to provide services for a force that is a quarter of CPD's size (3,400 sworn officers). The Miami-Dade Police Department, while also considerably smaller than CPD with approximately 2,900 sworn officers and 1,700 civilians, has six counselors and one graduate student intern to provide counseling services to its employees. The Los Angeles Police Department, the third largest department in the country, has thirteen counselors available to provide counseling to their roughly 10,000 officers and 3,000 civilian personnel. While CPD does have four certified substance abuse counselors, as well as officers trained to provide peer support services,[49] this staff is insufficient to meaningfully address the needs of a department the size of CPD.

Although the number of professionals necessary for a successful EAP will vary according to the type of program and scope of services provided, the officer wellness consultant we retained to assist with our review of CPD's program found the number of staff dedicated to Chicago's EAP too low to support the programs CPD currently offers. This is especially true given that the EAP in Chicago is intended to provide counseling services to both Department members *and* their families. Indeed, we found that EAP counselors are overextended. EAP reports its accomplishments and activities to the Bureau of Support Services on a monthly basis. At the end of 2015, EAP's three clinicians had provided 7,498 mental health consultations/appointments to Department and family members, including 4,074 clinical interviews, 1,560 informal interviews, and 1,847 telephone interviews. This is laudable, but EAP officials recognize that they could do more, and better, with more resources. One counselor explained that "the problem really is there are so few of us and so much to be done." Every day, counselors check the phones and "triage," many times having to rearrange scheduled appointments, shorten meetings to fit in more people, or cancel others, to address more serious crises. The unmet need is perpetual: EAP offers a one-day stress management program that teaches officers how to manage stress, depression, anxiety, PTSD, and other issues, but according to counselors, there is always a waitlist. The significant strain on the scant resources CPD allocates to officer wellness prevents officers from accessing these services in a timely, meaningful fashion.

> b. *CPD should better encourage and facilitate the use of available employee support programs*

CPD should embrace the concept of officer wellness and support as integral to officer *and* Department well-being. By failing to fully integrate and normalize participation in EAP, CPD risks reinforcing the stigma surrounding seeking help and discouraging officers from using the limited resources currently available.

Even though EAP's small staff is consistently inundated with work, the number of officers who should or could use EAP's services is greater than the number who actually do, primarily because of cultural resistance to accessing these services. Internal CPD culture casts seeking assistance for personal issues as a sign of weakness. As described by one official, "there's still a stigma" associated with going to EAP. Indeed, officers told us that some Department members believe that seeking counseling is a sign of weakness. For the vast majority of officers in need of support, the onus is on them to seek it out, but many will not do so, even in times of need, for fear of being ostracized. Coworkers who see that an officer is in need are equally hesitant to contact EAP on the officer's behalf. One sergeant told us that the burden is on partners to report an officer in crisis, but they will not because they do not want to be seen as "rats." We collected anecdotal evidence from officers who were involved in traumatic incidents such as shootings, and from supervisors, that there is not adequate support from CPD after these incidents.

A former CPD officer who fatally shot an individual, and was shot himself in the incident, told us that his gun was taken away from him after the shooting but was given back to him after his mandatory furlough without any discussion of whether he was ready to carry it again. The officer said that he had also sought assistance from CPD headquarters because he wanted to talk with a psychologist about his experience, but CPD told him that they had no one to recommend. This former officer did not believe that CPD provided him adequate support even though he openly sought help. Beyond shootings, officers have difficult jobs in which they routinely place themselves in danger to help others, and may become witnesses to incidents that cause them to need additional support, such as the death or catastrophic injury of a child. Officers should be provided support services when they experience trauma, whatever the cause.

CPD should better emphasize the importance of officer wellness programs and the value to officers of such programs before, or entirely independent of, being involved in an incident that would result in a mandatory referral. Our investigation found that CPD could better emphasize the importance of officer wellness in several ways. First, CPD does not proactively communicate to officers the services that are available and how using those services can benefit both the officer and the Department. CPD does not provide officers with sufficient information regarding the support services available to them and their families, the practical benefit these services may have, or how to access them. Similarly, CPD misses opportunities to integrate officer wellness principles into existing trainings and promote use of CPD's existing programs. For example, probationary police officers attend stress management training and professional counseling services training. However, the stress management training we observed did not offer any information about EAP or its services.

Relatedly, CPD also does not reinforce the importance of officer wellness through readily available avenues *outside* of the EAP. For example, themes of police legitimacy, procedural justice, and officer wellness could, and should, be woven into all CPD trainings. Trainings on use of force, tactics, and other aspects of CPD operations should capitalize on the opportunity to instruct officers in how to deal with the stressors they will encounter on the job, such as hostile reactions from community members, observing violence or its aftermath, interacting with victims of crime, and policing in communities made up of people with backgrounds that are different than the officers' backgrounds. Likewise, CIT and de-escalation trainings teach officers to identify dangerous behaviors and how to interact with individuals in crisis, which they too can use in their personal life and in identifying coworkers who may be in crisis. CPD does not currently have a template for how these topics should be addressed through trainings.

This lack of cohesive messaging about the services that are available also results in officers misunderstanding how seeking help for stress, including participating in the employee support programs CPD offers, will impact their careers. For example, officers are concerned that if they seek counseling through EAP, they will automatically have their Firearm Owner Identification (FOID) Card taken away, which will prohibit them from having a gun, and therefore working anything other than a desk position in CPD. This is not the case; under Illinois state law an individual's FOID card will be taken away if the person is committed for *in-patient* psychiatric services. An officer's FOID will not be taken away merely for using EAP's services, but CPD's failure to correct this misconception may result in officers not seeking help when needed. Officers also expressed concerns that they would be punished for using EAP or that they would be reported to the Department by the counselors. Union representatives told us that CPD officers need a "safe place to talk out issues" without repercussions, but that is precisely the purpose of EAP. CPD is not publicizing EAP or encouraging its use in a way that would minimize misconceptions and maximize officer participation.

CPD could also develop and implement programs other than EAP that would assist with behavioral intervention. As discussed above, CPD should be monitoring officer conduct to flag officers who might be experiencing personal issues and could be candidates for one of the Department's intervention programs. With a properly functioning EIS that identifies officers who would benefit from the support systems, CPD might be able to provide the assistance necessary to avoid crises, especially in cases where the officers would not seek the help on their own. This, in turn, would increase officer wellness and overall Department health.

In each of these areas, CPD leadership could seize upon critical opportunities to advocate for officer health and wellness, and encourage and guide officers to appropriate and necessary supports. Without prioritizing and planning for officer wellness, officers receive the message from leadership that officer wellness is not valued, which discourages officers who want to succeed but feel overburdened and unsupported in that goal.

    c.   *CPD should adapt its current officer wellness programs to CPD's female workforce*

CPD's current EAP, in addition to being under-resourced, has also not adjusted to the changing nature of policing, or of CPD's police force. The system is set up to provide counseling for CPD members, but the expertise of the current counselors is limited. As currently structured, with only three clinicians with limited expertise, not all officers will be able to access services that are appropriate, tailored, and attuned to their specific needs. Although EAP clinicians make referrals to outside providers, without a more robust, comprehensive counseling program, CPD can and should do more to ensure that all officers in the Department are supported and capable of using CPD's officer wellness programs.

Women officers we spoke with during our investigation noted that they feel particularly unsupported in the Department, both because of its culture and because the available support systems do not take into account the particular needs of female officers. To adequately provide support to all members and their diverse needs, CPD should expand and improve its program to ensure that services provided are culturally appropriate, sensitive to differing circumstances, and attentive to the issues facing all officers.

> d. *CPD should improve other areas of its operations to improve officer wellness, safety, and morale*

While officer support programs are critically important, the protection of officer wellness, safety, and morale depends upon a wide range of practices within the Department, many of which are currently not adequately supportive of officers. We heard from union representatives that restrictions on when and how officers may use vacation and elective leave time hurts morale. Also, CPD sends a negative message to its officers via the Department's deteriorating equipment. Several officers we spoke with described how outdated, malfunctioning equipment not only prevents them from doing their jobs safely and effectively, but makes them feel that the Department is not sufficiently concerned about their safety, efficiency, or professionalism. In particular, officers mentioned that their in-car cameras and computers frequently broke down, making it difficult to complete reports and enter data from the field, or look up information necessary to police their beat. One officer told us that in his district, 11 of the 14 in-car police cameras were broken, and that CPD does not have the sufficient staff to fix the cameras as they break. This impairs the value that cameras provide as a policing tool, and makes officers' jobs more difficult. Others noted problems with CPD's squad cars, saying that there were often not enough cars for a shift, which forces officers to ride three to a car at times. And many of the cars CPD does have are old and run down. A supervisor described CPD's cars as "dangerous and an embarrassment" to the force. These problems with CPD's equipment contribute to officers feeling unsupported in their work, and negatively impact officer safety, effectiveness, and morale, and in turn, community safety.

2. The unaddressed stress that CPD officers face harms officers, their families, and the public

During our investigation we heard that officer suicide and suicide threats are a significant problem in CPD. In fact, when we met with officials from EAP in May 2016, they had just handled an officer suicide threat the night before. One CPD official told us that CPD's rate is 22.7 suicides per 100,000 Department members. The FOP shared figures showing that CPD's suicide rate between 2013 and 2015 was 29.4 per 100,000 based on available information. This would mean that CPD's officer suicide rate is more than 60% higher than the national average of 18.1 law enforcement suicides per 100,000. As a CPD official noted, "in police work, we consider the bad guys the enemies and we have got to change that because it's destructive" and ignores that more officers die of suicide than in the line of duty. Recognizing the prevalence of officer suicide in CPD could help move the Department toward providing better interventions for officers in crisis. Indeed, the FBI credited "an increase in peer support programs, a decrease in resistance to personal assistance, and improvement in proactive mental health checkups" for the decrease in officer suicides nationally in 2012.[50]

Many CPD members also struggle with alcohol and substance abuse. Indeed, EAP served more Department and family members (8,565 consultations) for alcohol and substance abuse than it did for other mental health issues (7,498 consultations). While EAP is serving those officers who seek the help, the Department could do better to alleviate the stresses that may lead to these destructive behaviors, and that implicate public safety, by making wellness central to CPD's culture, from the moment a recruit enters the training academy through an officer's entire time on the force.

Finally, as discussed elsewhere in this Report, IPRA handles many complaints of domestic violence filed against CPD officers. Despite this, CPD does not address officer-involved domestic violence in CPD policies or academy trainings, or proactively inform officer family members how to get help and support if they need it. CPD employs one civilian who serves as a "domestic violence advocate," who can serve as a support person within the Department for victims of officer-involved domestic violence. Moreover, EAP seems particularly ill-suited to deal with domestic violence problems, as EAP officials do not have adequate specialized training or expertise in domestic violence, notwithstanding the fact that this is a known problem at CPD. Nor does CPD offer other robust intervention programs to detect, prevent, and appropriately respond to domestic violence by officers. CPD must institute reforms and dedicate adequate attention and resources to issues of officer wellness so that these and other officer personal and inter-personal issues are addressed appropriately.

D. Data Collection and Transparency

Deficiencies in how the City and CPD collect, analyze, and publish data regarding police activities contribute to the Department's failure to identify and correct unconstitutional policing. These deficiencies also inhibit transparency regarding CPD's practices. For decades, Chicago has failed to develop a comprehensive, integrated system to track and make public basic information about its police force. Instead, information is siloed, inaccurate, and incomplete. In addition, by failing to analyze and use important data, and by not reporting on that data publicly, the City is missing an opportunity to improve public transparency, and in turn, the relationship between CPD and the public.

1. CPD's data collection systems are siloed and disconnected

CPD uses an enormous and cumbersome data collection system to try to document policing activity. The system contains numerous "modules," which are comprised of thousands upon thousands of data-entry fields. When thousands of people (IPRA, BIA, officers, command staff, Human Resources, and more) are inconsistently filling out a few data fields, let alone thousands, the quality of data to support policing services is compromised. And, when police contacts are not properly documented, supervisors are not able to properly review activity, command staff are not able to properly discern patterns and deficiencies, and oversight bodies are not able to properly monitor activity and complaints.

CPD's data collection tools are filled with inefficiencies. CPD primarily relies on a system called CLEAR for its data collection, but there are several discrete, disconnected modules within that system, and information is generally not accessible across these modules. For example, several years ago, CPD used a program called CRMS to collect information about personnel investigations. CPD then migrated to use a program called AutoCR to track complaints against officers; but the rollout of AutoCR was never completed, and now both AutoCR and CRMS contain largely duplicative data, with one system used by IPRA and another by BIA. Both modules remain in CLEAR. Additionally, the TRR and AutoCR modules in the system do not communicate with each other. As discussed elsewhere in this Report, TRRs are supposed to be filled out every time an officer is involved in a reportable use of force. A portion of these force incidents result in a complaint being filed with

IPRA; yet, because the TRR and AutoCR modules are siloed, CPD does not automatically match up TRRs with subsequent complaints. In fact, even though the TRR database includes a field for "CR number obtained," indicating that the TRR is the subject of an IPRA complaint, that field often does not accurately reflect the existence of an IPRA investigation.

Moreover, personnel within CPD often lack access to the data that would help them perform their duties. Commanders reported being able to view only the complaint/disciplinary histories of officers if they are entering a Summary Punishment Action Report (SPAR); otherwise, they believe they do not have the ability to know the histories of their officers and take those histories into consideration when making assignments. Similarly, when an officer is assigned to a new district, the officer's new commander is unable to access the officer's personnel record, complaint record, or other relevant information that would assist the commander with providing appropriate assignments and supervision.

This approach to data collection and maintenance undermines the utility of the data that CPD stores. Command staff are not currently using this data to support or inform officer supervision or officer activity. CPD needs to create a single case management system that will easily allow it to track and share the data it collects. Under the accountability rubric, this data would include CRs, SPARs, TRRs, NDIs, furloughs, medical absences, and related information. Without a streamlined, easy to use data platform, the data CPD collects will remain largely unused, which will continue to impede effective policing and CPD's ability to provide close, well-informed supervision or promote accountability within the Department.

2. The City provides the public with data that is incomplete, inaccurate, untimely, and insufficient to allow the public to determine if CPD is policing constitutionally and effectively

In addition to insufficiently tracking and analyzing data for CPD and the City's own benefit, the information provided to the public regarding the activities of CPD is also woefully inadequate. The City does not consistently provide its constituents with data regarding crime trends, arrests made, case clearances, or other common police metrics. Nor does the City publish sufficient meaningful information regarding officer misconduct. Data that is published is often outdated or incomplete. These deficiencies are impediments to the public's understanding of, and trust in, CPD's ability to detect misconduct, including the use of unreasonable force, and hold officers accountable for misconduct.

CPD has not published an annual report since 2010. In fact, public reporting on crime trends city-wide has not occurred for years; the most recent report covered murder crime trends from 1998–2007. Some statistical reports were historically provided more frequently, but reports have not been issued for the last few years. For example, the most recent "Domestic Violence Quarterly Statistical Report" was released in June of 2014; prior to that, the reports were indeed quarterly. CPD publishes daily crime statistics through a "data portal," but this data is limited to criminal activity. There is no other data published on the website that relates to police-community interactions. Pursuant to a settlement agreement with the American Civil Liberties Union, CPD is required to track and report data regarding investigatory "stop and frisk" practices to a court-appointed monitor, who will issue a public report twice each year. Once this agreement terminates, however, CPD will be under no obligation to report this data, and CPD policy does not mandate data collection and public reporting more broadly. CPD recently stated that it would resume issuing annual reports in 2017, and that the first report would include data for the previous six years when reports were not published. In addition, the Mayor recently issued an end of year "progress report" highlighting the status of Chicago's police reform efforts. These are helpful steps towards greater transparency, but they are not entrenched in policy or otherwise permanent reforms.

The City also should improve public transparency regarding officer misconduct investigations. To be sure, transparency regarding misconduct investigations has greatly improved in recent months, to the credit of the current Chief Administrator at IPRA. Prior to the start of our investigation, until a complaint was fully investigated, the City did not make available the actual allegations filed against officers; police reports that are associated with allegations of criminal misconduct; investigative testimony; or audio or video of incidents where misconduct was alleged. Moreover, until recently, IPRA published only abstract summaries of sustained cases. These abstracts, which were essentially summaries of summaries, did little to illuminate the course of an investigation or the evidence considered. The summaries also covered only sustained cases, leaving the public to wonder how conclusions were reached in the vast majority of cases. Prior administrations also posted redacted summary reports, but only of officer-involved shootings. Under the current administration, IPRA now publishes redacted summary reports, within 30 days of closing the case at IPRA, of all cases, not just shootings, regardless of the investigation's outcome—a positive step towards better transparency. The City also publishes aggregate complaint and investigation data mainly through quarterly reports from IPRA. The reports provide various counts of investigations initiated and completed, such as the number of complaints filed by incident type and the number of complaints that were closed, but this does not provide the public with an accurate picture of police misconduct in Chicago. For example, the reports address only the total number of complaints; they do not account for the total number of *allegations* made against CPD officers. Each complaint could contain several distinct allegations.

IPRA's recent changes to its reporting are improvements, but the City can and should do more to ensure the public has access to as much complete and accurate information as practicable.[51] Indeed, the City's investigative agencies could better report on the types of cases they handle, including the volume, issues involved, and outcomes of those cases. The IPRA quarterly reports also do not provide relevant demographic information of complainants or accused officers. IPRA breaks down the number of incidents filed against each district and specialized unit, but does little else to identify patterns or trends among its data. More specifically, IPRA does not analyze complaint data to identify racial, ethnic, gender, or other disparities that may be present. This prevents the public from seeing how policing is affecting certain communities, and impedes the City's ability to address patterns and root causes of misconduct.

There are also questions about the accuracy, and therefore the usefulness, of the limited data that is reported by IPRA. For example, the Office of Inspector General (OIG) recently concluded that public reporting by IPRA on CPD's use of force prior to 2015 "was inaccurate and incomplete." In particular, the OIG found serious deficiencies and discrepancies in IPRA's reporting of weapons discharges, noting that IPRA's data reported in its quarterly reports "did not match the number of actual incidents in any category during the time periods reviewed." As noted in the Accountability Section of this Report, we found issues with IPRA's investigations that would prevent accurate reporting of misconduct occurring within CPD. Specifically, IPRA consistently miscategorizes complaints and fails to separately investigate all allegations of misconduct that are raised by a complainant. These and other errors in IPRA's data collection and reporting therefore render the quarterly reports useless.

Even where accurate, the limited information given in IPRA's quarterly reports gives an incomplete picture of how misconduct investigations are resolved. IPRA findings can be, and frequently are, challenged by the chain of command and/or set aside by the Superintendent. The information provided by IPRA represents only the first step in resolving a misconduct allegation— the findings of IPRA. However, there is no additional public reporting on how often investigators' recommendations are overturned, or what discipline is ultimately imposed.

Additional layers of review, including arbitration and involvement of the Police Board, may change the ultimate findings and the discipline that is imposed. As discussed elsewhere in this Report, annual reports from the Police Board provide some of this information in aggregate form, but no information is given regarding individual cases. Further, the last report was published in 2014. The information made public by IPRA is therefore misleading, as it does not tell the public how a misconduct complaint was ultimately resolved and what discipline was imposed.

The lack of transparency regarding officer misconduct complaints is not confined to IPRA. BIA and supervisors at the district level barely report publicly *any* information regarding misconduct investigations under their purview, even though, combined, they investigate roughly 70% of all misconduct allegations filed against officers. BIA only publishes a short annual report, consisting of a list of complaint log numbers. It does not publish summary reports or abstracts of any cases it investigates. District command staff publishes nothing on the investigations conducted at the district level—in fact, all of their investigations are conducted and tracked on paper, rather than electronically, thereby making it difficult for command staff to collect, analyze, and publicly report on those investigations. Community members seeking information about the outcome of a particular investigation at BIA or the district are forced to obtain that information through other channels, such as public records requests. The lack of transparency regarding BIA and district investigations leaves broad gaps in the information that is publicly available regarding misconduct investigations.

Complainants themselves are often kept in the dark about the status of their cases. Individuals complaining of officer misconduct do not receive periodic updates from investigators. Several complainants told us that they were left unaware of what was happening with their complaint for months, or even years—and some never heard back at all. At the conclusion of an investigation, complainants typically receive only a form letter stating the finding, i.e., whether the allegation of misconduct was sustained, not sustained, unfounded, or exonerated. No additional explanation is given. Complainants are not told what steps were taken to investigate their claims, leaving them to wonder whether the investigation was sufficient. Chicago also does not tell complainants the discipline imposed as a result of the complaint. And, as discussed elsewhere in this Report, if "mediation" is used to resolve a complaint, the complainant is not involved or consulted before or during that process; they are merely informed at the end that their complaint was resolved. Chicago's failure to meaningfully communicate with complainants at all stages of the investigative process undermines complainants' confidence that their allegations are taken seriously and that appropriate steps are being taken to resolve their concerns.

Finally, as discussed elsewhere in this Report, the City frequently settles civil rights lawsuits brought under 42 U.S.C. § 1983, and loses such cases at trial. In addition to not internally analyzing these lawsuits to identify trends, CPD also keeps the details of these settlements from the public, thereby avoiding public scrutiny of CPD's deficiencies. For most cases, the only transparency provided is a spreadsheet of all judgments and settlements handled by the City's Law Department; this spreadsheet lists complaints against the police, but contains only the plaintiff's name, the amount of the settlement, and a vague description of the claim settled (e.g., "excessive force," or "false arrest"). Until the Chicago Reporter created its database, based on court records and material requested through public records laws, little information about these settlements was publicly available. The City's limited release of information regarding settlements further contributes to public distrust and the perception that the City wishes to keep officer misconduct concealed from public scrutiny.

3. <u>Recent reforms to improve transparency are positive steps, but more is required and changes must be sustained</u>

The City and CPD have taken steps during the course of our investigation to increase transparency, but these changes—both actual and promised—must go further to ensure transparency is permanently supported and encouraged within CPD and IPRA.

The City recently instituted or committed to institute certain measures intended to increase transparency. These welcome reforms are in the initial stages. For example, CPD announced it would resume publication of annual reports, and the IPRA website now contains significantly more information regarding the results of misconduct investigations. CPD and IPRA should continue to publish this type of information regularly. As another example, in early 2016, the City announced a new "transparency policy" at the request of the Police Accountability Task Force. This policy, which was published in draft form, mandates the release of video and audio footage associated with certain incidents of police misconduct within 60 days of their occurrence, "unless a request is made to delay the release." The policy applies to incidents where an officer "discharges his or her firearm, stun gun, or Taser in a manner that strikes, or potentially could strike, an individual, even if no allegation of misconduct is made" and "those where the death of, or great bodily harm to, a person occurs while that person is in police custody."

This policy represents a significant step towards improving the transparency of investigations into CPD misconduct. Pursuant to this new policy, IPRA recently posted materials from 150 open investigations, including videos, case incident reports, tactical response reports, and officer battery reports. While the policy covers incidents that clearly are of heightened public interest, it is nonetheless limited in scope, and the City should apply it to other categories of force and civil rights violations as well. IPRA's website notes that the Mayor has adopted the policy, but a final version of the policy is not posted anywhere on CPD or the City's website, and is not part of CPD's directives system; the IPRA website only links to the policy as recommended by the Task Force. This policy should be finalized and permanently adopted.[52]

Perhaps as importantly, providing true transparency means not just increasing public access to information about problems, but encouraging public involvement in crafting solutions to those problems. The City should continue to meaningfully involve the community in developing proposed reforms. This is particularly important given the potentially monumental changes on the horizon for the City's transparency and accountability systems. We applaud the City's recent efforts to seek public input on proposed reforms, such as the COPA ordinance and CPD's new use-of-force policies. The City should engage in similar efforts for other anticipated reforms, and ensure that the public comments solicited are genuinely considered and addressed. Involving the community in this way will increase public confidence in and cooperation with CPD, which will improve CPD's ability to police safely, constitutionally, and effectively.

There is no dispute that more work is needed to restore the public's faith in CPD. Some of that work may be accomplished through improvements to CPD's data collection, analysis, and publication practices. Above all, to instill meaningful change in this area, any reforms instituted by CPD and the City must be formalized and permanent, so that they survive changes in leadership in CPD and City government.

E. PROMOTIONS

Dedicated, competent leaders are essential to ensuring that CPD promotes safe, effective policing tactics while valuing and respecting the rights of all community members. In Chicago, a lack of transparency around promotional systems and decisions, and years of litigation regarding CPD's promotion process, have created a narrative among the rank-and-file that CPD does not value good leadership, and that current leaders are unqualified to lead. Despite attempts at reform, officers we interviewed continue to view the promotions system with skepticism, which has decreased officer morale and undermined effective supervision. CPD's promotions system should be regularly reviewed, and revised if necessary, with the aim of increasing transparency and ensuring the promotion of candidates who will make CPD better able to police effectively and respectfully, while continuing to abide by court orders put in place to ensure that candidates are not unlawfully excluded from promotions on the basis of race or sex.

1. CPD's current promotions system

Under CPD's current promotions system, candidates interested in a promotion to detective, sergeant, or lieutenant take a two-part test. The first test consists of multiple choice questions testing job knowledge regarding policies and procedures, and is graded on a pass/fail basis. Candidates who pass this qualifying exam then move on to a second part of the exam, which is designed to evaluate the skills and application of knowledge consistent with the promotion position. The second part of the exam is scored and candidates are ranked based on their score on the second part of the exam and placed on a list of individuals eligible for promotion.

Candidates who appear on the list of individuals eligible for promotion to detective, sergeant, or lieutenant, may be promoted in one of two ways. First, candidates are ranked by their score on the second part of the exam, and candidates may be promoted based purely on that rank. At least 70% of promotions for sergeant and lieutenant are made from the individuals who complete both tests and are ranked highly on the lists; at least 80% of the promotions to detective are made this way.

Second, candidates who pass the qualifying exam may be nominated for a "merit" promotion regardless of their score or rank on the second part of the exam. CPD has used a merit system for lieutenants starting as early as the mid-1990s, and for sergeants as early as the late 1990s. The system was created to identify CPD members with supervisory potential who do not necessarily score well on promotional exams, given that previous promotional exams had an adverse impact on minority eligibility for promotions.

Notably, CPD adopted a hiring plan (Hiring Plan) regarding merit promotions in 2011—and readopted a revised Hiring Plan in 2014—pursuant to the Settlement Agreement in *Shakman v. Democratic Organization of Cook County, et al.*, a lawsuit alleging politicized hiring and promotions in several City agencies, including CPD.[53] The *Shakman* orders also gave the City's Office of the Inspector General the authority to audit and monitor compliance with the Hiring Plan. Concurrently, CPD revised its Merit Board to match the requirements laid out in the Hiring Plan, and to provide more structure for the merit selection process.

Under the hiring plan and related CPD policies, for the rank of lieutenant and below, merit nominations can come from chiefs, deputy chiefs, commanders, and directors. A Merit Board consisting of five deputy chiefs and the Director of Human Resources interviews and evaluates the merit nominees. In considering which nominees to recommend to the Superintendent for merit promotions, the Merit Board can review the nominee's complimentary history and performance evaluations, but they can only consider the nominee's disciplinary history as permitted by the nominee's collective bargaining agreement. The Superintendent retains discretion to ultimately select the nominees receiving merit promotions, and is not bound by the recommendations of the Merit Board in making the final decision.

In contrast to this dual-track promotions system for detectives, sergeants, and lieutenants, captains are promoted exclusively by a board and do not sit for an exam. Individuals interested in being selected for promotion to the rank of captain submit application materials in response to a job announcement, are screened by Human Resources to determine eligibility, and then, if eligible, evaluated by the "Captain Screening Board." Individuals who pass the screening board are then evaluated by the Merit Board, similar to the Merit Board's evaluation of candidates for the rank of lieutenant and below.

2.   CPD's promotions system, as a whole, is regarded as unfair

   a.   CPD's tests have been challenged as discriminatory and unfair

The promotional examinations for CPD have been subject to legal challenges under Title VII of the Civil Rights Act of 1964, as amended, 42 U.S.C. § 2000e, *et seq.* (Title VII) for decades.[54] Title VII prohibits an employer from using a neutral employment practice that results in disparate impact on the basis of race, color, religion, sex, or national origin, unless such practice is "job related for the position in question and consistent with business necessity," and there exists no alternative employment practice that would result in less disparate impact and equally serve the employer's legitimate interests. 42 U.S.C. § 2000e-2(k).

The legal challenges of discriminatory impact and allegations of improper exam procedures[55] underscore the continuing need for careful review of the examination's content and procedures. We find the Seventh Circuit instructive in its emphasis of "the City's responsibility to re-examine the promotional process for currency." *Allen*, 351 F.3d at 315. We urge CPD to review its promotional exams and procedures for continued compliance with Title VII in order to ensure the lawful promotion of the best possible candidates in a transparent and fair environment. Ensuring fairness and non-discrimination in promotional testing will help CPD promote the best candidates, which in turn, will ensure that CPD has a cadre of supervisors who are willing and able to provide officers with adequate supervision, guide them on how to police effectively and constitutionally, and hold them accountable when necessary, all of which are critical to preventing, detecting, and appropriately responding to unreasonable uses of force.

   a.   CPD's merit promotions are viewed as political and lack transparency

One of the major complaints from officers we interviewed is that CPD's promotions system lacks transparency regarding the nomination and qualification process for merit promotions. This has led many officers to believe that merit promotions are a reward for cronyism, rather than a recognition of excellence that was overlooked by the testing process. Many of the officers we spoke with—minority and non-minority alike—told us that they feel merit promotions are not truly based on "merit," but rather the "clout" you hold in the Department or "who you know." In other words, officers believe that CPD leadership gives merit promotions to individuals who are unqualified to serve as leaders, merely because those individuals have connections up the chain of command or have advocates in positions of power outside of CPD who call in favors or lobby on their behalf. Female officers in particular feel that they are frequently overlooked for merit promotions. This belief undermines officers' faith in CPD supervisors and their acceptance of CPD's systems of accountability and supervision.

In reality, there are documented instructions and guidance for merit promotion nominators and decision makers, but this information is not widely known. Nominators are required to attend "nominator training" in order to be eligible to make nominations, and are instructed by policy to follow the "Merit Selection Assessment Dimensions" contained in the "Nominator Manual" for the rank being filled. However, CPD has not proactively informed the rank-and-file of those dimensions or the content of the nominator training. The nominator and merit selection manuals are apparently posted on CLEAR, but typically officers we spoke with did not know this information was accessible, and remain unaware of the assessment dimensions used to evaluate potential merit nominees. This leaves officers to speculate about what criteria nominators consider when nominating individuals for merit promotions, which, in turn, increases officer skepticism that truly meritorious criteria are used at all. Finally, although the Superintendent must fill out a written justification memorandum explaining the basis for his or her merit selections, nothing about the reasoning is made public, the justification is often cursory, and candidates who were eligible but did not receive merit promotions are never provided an explanation for why they were not selected.

CPD has moved in a positive direction by establishing the Hiring Plan, allowing oversight by the Office of the Inspector General, and introducing new policies and manuals that, in part, describe the information that may be considered by the Merit Board. However, some of these new policies are written in vague terms that would allow problematic promotions to go undetected, and indeed, we know of at least one example where an individual received a merit promotion based on "clout" rather than merit, even after the new procedures outlined in the Hiring Plan were in effect: a recent inquiry from the City's Inspector General found that, as part of the 2013 sergeant merit promotion process, an officer assigned to the then-Superintendent's security detail was inappropriately promoted to sergeant.[56]

The OIG's current role providing oversight of this process is important to ensuring that the process operates as intended. CPD should also itself continuously review the current nominator manuals, policies, and other materials to ensure the systems are working properly. CPD should also review ways in which it can increase transparency surrounding the process. Given the skepticism expressed to us during our investigation, despite several notable areas of progress, CPD has not sufficiently communicated the details of the merit promotion policies to the rank-and-file.

b. Promotional exams are not offered with sufficient frequency

Numerous officers noted that they lack the chance to be promoted because CPD does not schedule promotional exams with sufficient frequency. For example, the last sergeant's exam was completed in January 2014. Before that, the sergeant's exam was last administered in March of 2006—nearly eight years prior. The last lieutenant exam was given in 2015; prior to that, the last exam was in 2006. Officers reported to us that they had been on the force for nearly a decade without being given an opportunity to make detective; indeed, no detective exam was offered between September 2003 and May 2016. The lack of regular promotional tests increases the frustration and lack of confidence in the promotional system as highly qualified and enthusiastic candidates are forced to wait to take promotional exams for years after they reach eligibility.

The City has recognized this problem and pursuant to the City's new Hiring Plan, eligibility lists must be retired after six years, "unless there is a lack of available funds for testing," in which case the list will be retired "as soon as practicable." City consultants highlighted this problem in 2014, and recommended that the Department administer promotional tests at least every four years. Although the six-year limit contained in the Hiring Plan is an improvement over past practices, CPD should continue to evaluate whether scores on previously administered tests accurately reflect current knowledge and skills, and whether more frequent testing, through validated testing instruments, would result in promotion of the most qualified candidates.

Chief of Staff requested that the commander make the nomination, even though the commander had no knowledge of the officer's qualifications. Human Resources staff did not verify that the officer was eligible for promotion, and despite his failing score, included him on the list of eligible candidates that was forwarded to the Merit Board. The Merit Board nevertheless voted not to recommend promotion, but the Superintendent overrode that recommendation. The Superintendent never submitted a justification memo for this decision, as required by the new policy, but CPD's Human Resources still processed the promotion. The error was not discovered until the newly-promoted sergeant completed supervisor training and the City's own Human Resources department reviewed the hiring materials and discovered that the sergeant was ineligible for that position. The sergeant was then demoted, but the City is now facing a lawsuit over the controversy. The OIG found that, at several steps in the promotional process, the merit promotion policies were either ignored, or there were not enough safeguards in place to catch errors. The OIG recommended several changes based on its review of this incident.

3. CPD must review and revise its promotional exams and merit system as necessary to ensure that the best-qualified candidates are promoted in a fair, lawful, and transparent manner

Despite the long history of litigation and the myriad litigation-initiated reforms, including the addition of the merit promotions system, there remains a broad officer sense that CPD does not promote people fairly. Prior reform efforts have not convinced officers that CPD's promotions system is fair and that the City values strong, quality leadership. Concerns remain about whether the promotion structure as a whole ensures that CPD is promoting the most competent, effective, and dedicated officers to supervisory positions. CPD should engage in regular and careful review of its procedures to ensure that they are fair and sufficiently frequent to result in the promotion of effective, ethical, and otherwise highly qualified officers.

Further, as noted above, CPD should take concrete steps to enhance the transparency of the promotions system. Some recent efforts, including the expansion of the OIG's role, are laudable, and should be expanded and sustained. We note that previous attempts to create transparency in the merit promotion process were scaled back or rescinded following changes in leadership. For example, one former Superintendent published a list of command staff who nominated officers for merit promotions alongside the names of the individuals they nominated. This measure was intended to increase accountability; officers would be aware of whether or not they were nominated, and command staff who nominated individuals for political rather than meritorious reasons could not hide those nominations from public scrutiny. However, the policy of publishing this information was rescinded immediately when the next administration took over. It is imperative that steps taken towards transparency through the 2014 changes be maintained and built on, rather than reversed.

V. CPD MUST BETTER SUPPORT AND INCENTIVIZE POLICING THAT IS LAWFUL AND RESTORES TRUST AMONG CHICAGO'S MARGINALIZED COMMUNITIES

❧

True community policing is an overarching ethos that creates both direction and space for officers and communities to treat each other with respect and with trust. This relationship serves as the foundation for working together to establish crime prevention priorities and develop solutions to public safety problems. Implemented correctly, community policing helps people feel neither over- nor under-policed, and incentivizes and empowers many people to work with the police—and others to at least not work against them. To be successful in this way, community policing must be supported not just by an entire police department, but by an entire city.

Within the past several months CPD and the City have announced ambitious plans to revive community policing in Chicago. Superintendent Johnson has formed a Community Policing Advisory Panel, comprised of national experts, police command staff, and local community leaders, to develop strategies for enhancing community policing within CPD. The Superintendent has pledged to remake the Department's Chicago Alternative Policing Strategy (CAPS), the formerly robust CPD community policing initiative. The Department also recently issued a directive establishing the "Bridging the Divide Program," focused on improving youth-police relationships, in eight districts, with further expansion planned. As part of this approach, Superintendent Johnson has said that "the job of every officer is to reduce crime and help restore trust." CPD has several additional community policing related initiatives underway.

We commend CPD for its renewed emphasis on community policing. This policing approach, when implemented with fidelity to all its tenets, has been shown to be effective at making communities safer while incentivizing a policing culture that builds confidence in law enforcement. As such, it is a promising path that can lead to eliminating the patterns of unlawful conduct our investigation found, increasing community trust in CPD, and reducing crime in Chicago.

The importance of community trust in reducing crime can be seen in homicide clearance rates. In 2016, CPD was able to identify a suspect in only

29% of all homicides, which is less than half the national rate for 2015. Identifying suspects in homicides is recognized as an important factor in preventing future homicides. And there is broad consensus, including throughout Chicago, that increasing community trust and confidence in CPD is necessary for CPD to be able to clear more homicides. As Superintendent Johnson recently stated, "The first thing we have to do is improve our trust with the community—especially the minority community and CPD—that will help raise the clearance rate, because those individuals will be more comfortable in coming to us and giving us the information we need to hold these individuals accountable." We heard this same message during many of our conversations with residents of Chicago's high-violence neighborhoods. As one woman told us, "You can get a lot of things done if I have a relationship with you and I can trust you, then I can tell you some stuff. But if I can't trust you, I can't tell you anything . . . [CPD] need[s] to build relationships with the people in the community."[57]

Chicago was formerly a leader in advancing community policing and continues to recognize the promise of this approach. As the Mayor has stated, "Chicago is where the whole idea of community policing began. . . . It remains the best and most comprehensive approach we have in changing the everyday conditions that breed crime and violence and then breed mistrust." CPD's Superintendent Johnson has repeatedly called community policing his "core philosophy."

Notwithstanding this recognition, community policing as a true CPD ethos and driving force fell away many years ago, and past attempts to restore it have not been successful. To be successful this time, CPD must build up systems throughout the Department, to support and bolster this community-focused approach to policing. Community policing will struggle to be successful in Chicago if it remains a series of disconnected initiatives, no matter how well-meaning and well-executed. As stated in the report from the Task Force on 21st Century Policing, community policing must be "infused throughout the culture and organizational structure" of a police department.

A. CPD'S MOVE TO RESTORE TRUE COMMUNITY POLICING WILL BE DIFFICULT BUT IS PROMISING

Infusing community policing throughout City and police systems—from training and supervision to transparency and accountability—while dismantling practices that undercut this effort, will be a lengthy endeavor requiring sustained commitment and focus. Once achieved, however, this trust-building approach to policing will better promote both public safety and respect for constitutional rights.

1. <u>CPD has many officers who are already policing in a community-focused manner</u>

CPD has the officers to make community policing work. During our investigation we observed many instances of diligent, thoughtful, and selfless policing, and we heard stories of officers who police this way every day. While on a ride along, we observed officers patiently talk to a troubled young man until they convinced him to remove a belt from around his neck. During an interview with a patrol officer, we learned that he had paid for and installed a koi pond at the school where he works because he "wanted to do something for the kids here." This same officer volunteered to coach the girls' cross-country team at a local school when no one else would take the role.

Chicago residents provided us with story after story of officers who care deeply about the community, are affected by the violence they see individuals commit against each other, and work hard to build trust between the community and the Department. We heard about officers who are well-respected and beloved in the neighborhoods they patrol. We were told about a district commander who knew and interacted with all of the community groups in his district and handed out his personal cell-phone number to residents. We know there are many more like him. Many of the officers with whom we went on ride-alongs took the time to stop and talk with kids or shopkeepers who obviously knew them and were happy to see them. We saw a field training officer and his probationary police officer walk around the neighborhood frequently during our ride-along with them, taking the time to visit with children at a community center and shop. We spoke to officers who organized and secured officer attendance for a CPD-sponsored daddy-daughter dance, to step in for those fathers who, for whatever reason, were absent from their children's lives. We spoke with "Purpose over Pain," an advocacy and support group committed to ending gun violence. The group—run by one of its founders who began the group with her then-husband, a CPD officer—related to us that CPD officers attend its events and are deeply involved in its mission. We were impressed by the attitude and efforts of the CPD officer who led the "Building the Divide" program, a program that promises significant strides in humanizing officers and residents to each other. The Department is currently planning to restart this program in eight districts.

Another of the many examples of such policing that we observed personally occurred while on a ride-along with an officer in the Fifth District. The officers we were with responded to a call in one of Chicago's public housing projects. We observed an officer deal with a potentially volatile incident with skill and patience. By treating both parties with dignity, compassion, and respect, the officer was able to resolve the incident successfully rather than having it escalate, which might have occurred had the officer approached the situation differently, as we have seen from other CPD officers. This officer told us that the resolution was not atypical for him, and that he believed most situations like that could easily be defused with patient and respectful interactions by police officers. Throughout our time with this officer, it was clear he had a warm rapport with the people in the neighborhood he patrolled. He had grown up in the area and knew many people in the neighborhood. It was clear that this officer knew the importance of connecting, on a real and personal level, with residents. He told us that he considered establishing those relationships as one of the keys to success for an officer working his or her beat. As a result of Chicago's requirement that officers live within the City, many officers talked to us, with pride and concern, about policing in the same neighborhoods they grew up in.[58]

From these observations and others, it is clear that many Chicago police officers help community members every day in meaningful and tangible ways. Most of these efforts never make the news because they are part of an officer's daily routine: watching carefully to detect wrongdoers before they can do wrong, diligently patrolling, notwithstanding the disrespect and cold stares that are too often part of the job, and risking their lives to protect complete strangers.

2. <u>For community policing to be successful it must be infused throughout CPD's policing strategies and tactics</u>

Of course, the realities of police work can create challenges to policing with care for even the most well-meaning and dedicated officer. For community policing to be successful within CPD, the Department and City will need to take a holistic approach that will translate the discrete programs and initiatives currently underway into a department-wide ethos that resets the CPD culture. This will require both a sustained shift of resources to systems and initiatives consistent with a community-based policing focus, and a transformation of many of the CPD systems discussed elsewhere in this Report, including Training, Supervision, and Accountability.

Inculcating community policing throughout CPD will also require a remaking of CPD's existing community policing structure. Examining the shortcomings of these current community policing efforts may be helpful in bringing about greater success moving forward.

From 2000 to 2010, Chicago's commitment to community policing waned. Even as CPD's overall budget went up, its budget for CAPS was cut. Community policing within CPD began to be implemented half-heartedly and superficially to the point where, today, community policing is largely seen as illegitimate by many officers and community members.

In recent years, community policing in Chicago has been relegated to a small group of police officers and civilians in each district. CAPS typically has a sergeant, two police officers, and a civilian in each district responsible for setting forth a community policing agenda and coordinating community policing activities in the entire district. The officers receive little training on how to accomplish their mandate, and there is little to no involvement by patrol officers or commanders in planning and implementing community policing strategies. Community policing efforts are also poorly funded. Districts receive approximately $9,500 a year to carry out all of CAPS' work if the district is in a high crime area, and $8,000 if not.

Approximately half of the money is budgeted for community meetings and events while the other half is budgeted for youth programs and events. This money is far less than what is needed to cover the expenses staff incur in organizing events, so CAPS staff either rely on donations from businesses or pay out of their own pockets. We were told by community policing staff that funding was an "enormous challenge" in developing community policing strategies and events.

Given the lack of resources and emphasis put on community policing, CAPS for the most part focuses on hosting community meetings. But these meetings are not effectively advancing community policing within CPD. Effective community policing is responsive to residents' input regarding community needs, and seeks residents' insights into the best way police can help address those needs. At its core, community policing "takes seriously the public's definition of its own problems." Chicago has attempted to meet this tenet of community policing by sponsoring regularly scheduled meetings in each of CPD's districts. But as currently run, these meetings generally are not an effective way for CPD to learn about neighborhood problems or the concerns of the spectrum of residents who make up each neighborhood. According to some residents, the meetings "are not a place to go if you have an agenda other than what the police want to discuss." This was consistent with our observations. From our interviews with community policing staff and observations of several meetings, it became clear that the purpose of the meetings was to discuss neighborhood criminal activity to the exclusion of broader issues involving the police that are also of importance to the community. One community policing staff person said that community meetings are not meant to address citizen concerns about officer use of force or explain Department policy, telling us that residents should "raise it with someone else." For example, complaints received by community policing officers at the meetings were frequently referred to the saturation, tactical, and gang teams for enforcement—teams by whom some in these communities felt victimized and dehumanized. In one CAPS meeting we saw, an officer was actively antagonistic to community members, responding with hostility after misinterpreting an attendee's statement, and getting increasingly louder and more aggressive as the attendee tried to defuse the situation.

Not surprisingly, CAPS meetings are not generally well-attended and do not reflect a broad spectrum of residents. Although several CAPS sergeants stated that the community meetings were well attended, at the meetings we observed, there were usually only a handful of residents attending. Given other priorities such as jobs, school, and child care, as well as transportation challenges and concerns about possible retaliation, these meetings may not attract large numbers of residents every week. There is a need for CPD to be more creative in finding ways to more meaningfully connect with those who will likely rely on its services the most. The Department has a long way to go in this respect: one young man told us that one CPD officer's reaction upon recognizing him while he was working at the young man's church internship this summer was to say, "You're one of those motherfuckers who sits in CAPS meetings and complains." Statements like this, particularly alongside the conduct of officers described elsewhere in this Report, reinforce the broadly held view among some in Chicago that CPD's approach to community policing is not genuine, and mostly operates as a "surveillance" tool to assist the Department in executing its enforcement strategy.

To be successful moving forward, CPD also must better recognize, reward, and encourage positive community policing efforts. Most community policing officers we spoke to told us that their work is given low priority within the Department. We were mostly met with amused smiles when we asked if their work was recognized by CPD. One community policing officer told us, "*We* acknowledge the work that we do." CPD officers outside CAPS with whom we spoke were generally dismissive of CAPS and community policing, calling it "not effective." One patrol officer told us he makes an effort to go to CAPS meetings "when he can;" another officer told us that, due to constant enforcement initiatives, officers didn't have time to attend community events. In addition to being disheartening—officers should make the time to connect with residents in the neighborhoods they patrol—the many comments like this that we heard reflect officers' understanding of the Department's priorities. Similarly, the Department's "Bridging the Divide" program was very popular with community members when it was launched, but suffered from poor participation by officers. The Department recently issued a directive requiring participation in this program in eight districts. This effort is laudable, but will not likely be successful if CPD cannot tap into and incentivize the many good officers who are eager to build genuine positive connections with Chicago's youth and families.

B. CPD MUST CHANGE PRACTICES TO RESTORE TRUST AND ENSURE LAWFUL POLICING

To turn around policing in Chicago, CPD and the City must focus their efforts on improving relationships within neighborhoods that have Chicago's highest rates of crime, poverty, and unemployment, and with communities that are otherwise marginalized. These efforts include recognizing that Chicago's policing practices have had an unnecessarily negative impact on these communities, and working to change practices to increase police legitimacy and community trust.

Chicago recognizes that it must focus on changing the way it polices, particularly in these communities, and that it must rebuild trust in light of past experiences of both community members and police officers. As Superintendent Johnson has stated publicly, "We recognize that we did treat certain parts of this City inappropriately. And that was our fault. So we have to correct that."

We commend Chicago for recognizing the critical importance of this effort, and urge them to continue and redouble their efforts.

1. <u>CPD must do more to ensure that officers police fairly in neighborhoods with high rates of violent crime, and in vulnerable communities</u>

Any effort to restore trust and ensure lawful policing in Chicago must focus on Chicago's predominantly black and Latino neighborhoods, especially those with high rates of violent crime. Many individuals in these communities experience policing in a fundamentally different way than do white individuals and white communities. Restoring trust and bringing about effective policing will be difficult unless CPD eliminates unnecessary, harmful differences in how people in these communities are treated, and takes affirmative measures to demonstrate its dedication to treating the residents of these neighborhoods fairly.

a. CPD must ensure it is responsive to victims of crime in Chicago's high-crime neighborhoods and other vulnerable communities

Strikingly, residents of Chicago's most challenged communities consistently expressed concern to us about their treatment when they or their family members are the victims of crime. An oft-repeated concern was that officers do not put sufficient emphasis on solving more significant crimes, or at least do not convey their concern to victims of such crimes.

Black and Latino residents in particular told us of feeling disregarded by CPD when they tried to get help after being victimized by crimes. One middle-aged man told us that after being assaulted and having his nose broken outside a store, he reported the crime and told the police there was video footage, but the police told him to go to the store himself to retrieve the video. An Englewood resident told us that a CPD sergeant told him flatly she would not help him get rid of a drug house on his street. One student we met with told us how he once tried to flag down an officer for help, but the officer just drove by. Many residents in predominantly black or Latino areas complained about response times when they call the police for assistance.

The many family members of homicide victims with whom we met similarly expressed a lack of confidence in CPD because of how they had been treated. Their experience with CPD, after a family member had been murdered, had made them feel that CPD does not genuinely care about the murders of young black men and women, and do too little to investigate and resolve those homicides. A young man told us how, after his brother was killed, he would go to the station to talk to someone about the investigation and officers would roll their eyes and say dismissively, "we're working on it." Families told us of detectives not interviewing key homicide witnesses or suspects, declining to obtain relevant video footage, and failing to update parents on the status of investigations, or even return their calls. One woman said that the Department switched the detective who was handling her son's homicide investigation without telling her. Another woman stated that she has to resort to getting information "on the street" about her son's case instead of from the detective, who told her that she "calls too much." This same woman told us that it took a week after her son was killed before anyone at CPD reached out to her. One mother told us that she felt CPD did not think her child was worthy of having his homicide solved. Yet another mother complained that police did not investigate the murder of her son, but sent her a bill for the cleanup of his body. Undoubtedly, many CPD detectives, like many other CPD officers, including those who helped start and participate in the aforementioned support group for those affected by gun violence, care deeply about victims of homicides. Our conversations with scores of family members of homicide victims made clear that CPD needs to do more to convey their commitment and care to these communities.

We also heard many concerns regarding CPD's investigation of potential hate crimes or hate incidents. CPD's Civil Rights Unit is charged with investigating all hate crimes and hate incidents in Chicago, yet has only two investigators.[59] Under CPD's current policy, officers are to notify the Civil Rights Unit when there appears to have been a hate crime or other criminal or quasi-criminal incident motivated by hate. An official familiar with the investigative process explained that the Civil Rights Unit must be notified before the Unit can run a parallel hate crime investigation. This official told us that front line officers need better training to recognize potential hate crimes, or these crimes will go uninvestigated. Indeed, the Civil Rights Unit did not learn about a rash of anti-Semitic and anti-Muslim graffiti in the Rogers Park neighborhood over the summer until there was a televised news report. We were also told that the Unit sometimes has to push to investigate crimes that appear to be hate-motivated because detectives minimize the seriousness of such crimes, saying things like, "a crime is a crime," or "so they got called a name."

Advocates and members of the Latino, Muslim, and transgender communities each separately raised concerns with us about Chicago's response to potential or apparent hate crimes against members of their communities. For example, a Latino church in the Pilsen neighborhood was vandalized numerous times over the past year with anti-immigrant messages stating "Rape and Kill Mexico" and drawings of swastikas. While CPD eventually investigated the incidents as a hate crime, church members were distressed that the church was vandalized six times before CPD acted. The church had installed a security camera after the fifth incident, and it was not until there was a video of the perpetrator that CPD seemed to take the incidents seriously. The church told us that it had been a "struggle . . . to get anyone in authority to hear us and to do work to protect us. We fear we won't be heard until a tragedy occurs." Advocates from the Muslim community voiced similar concerns and frustrations, telling us that in their view CPD is "reticent about looking at potential hate crimes." A Muslim advocacy organization told us that they receive around 200 discrimination complaints per year, and estimates that up to 30% could be hate-related. Yet, CPD reported only three hate crimes against Muslims between 2013 and 2015. Leaders in the transgender community are likewise concerned by the investigations of the murders of several transgender women in recent years. The Civil Rights Unit was not asked to open a hate crime investigation into any of these murders. Not only are members of this community upset that these crimes were never investigated as hate crimes, but they are also concerned that CPD's failure to solve any of the murders reflects a lack of commitment to these cases.

Indeed, CPD needs to work harder and more effectively to address concerns of all Chicago communities, including Chicago's transgender residents who voiced concerns about their treatment by CPD officers. CPD updated its General Order governing interactions with transgender individuals in December 2015, which is commendable. However, the community has expressed concerns about the policy, including that it fails to ensure that transgender individuals are classified by their gender identity and does not require officers to ask an individual their preference regarding the gender of the officer to conduct a search. CPD might have more effectively addressed these concerns had CPD's outreach to the transgender community been more extensive. For example, the Department only has one LGBT liaison, which is insufficient to ensure collaboration and ongoing partnership with this community.

Several CPD officers told us that some people in these neighborhoods and communities seem accustomed to crime. These officers seemed not to recognize the role that police can play in normalizing crime if they fail to respond vigorously to violent crime no matter how often it occurs. The high incidence of violent crime in these neighborhoods and the effects that it has on entire communities make it more important, not less important, that CPD respond seriously to these events. Failing to do so creates the perception for some that crimes committed against those living in these areas are not important to CPD. Indeed, we heard from other officers that CPD leadership responds with greater interest to crimes in some parts of the City, with one commander telling us that he will "catch holy hell" if a "white woman has her iPhone stolen" in the wealthy part of Chicago he commands. CPD must ensure it consistently makes clear to officers that crime does not matter more if it is committed in more advantaged communities.

b. Many residents of Chicago's high-crime neighborhoods experience policing as overly harsh and unfair

Proactive policing is an important part of public safety, when implemented consistently with constitutional and community-oriented policing principles and as part of a thoughtful public-safety plan. However, where proactive tactics are used in a manner that seems dismissive of community concerns, such tactics erode community trust, endanger citizens and officers, and encumber crime solving, particularly over time, as distrust creates an intractable unwillingness to aide investigations.

Even as many residents feel that CPD is not sufficiently concerned when they are victims of crime, they often feel that CPD polices too harshly in their neighborhoods, and too often assumes that they are the perpetrators of crime. This sense may be due in part to CPD's reliance on specialized units to conduct "hot spot" type policing in these neighborhoods, rather than beat officers. These specialized teams, such as the tactical (TACT), gang, saturation, and narcotics units, do not answer service calls, but aggressively seek out problematic activity by conducting traffic stops, making contacts, and effecting arrests. Many of these officers drive unmarked vehicles and do not wear the traditional police uniform. They instead wear either plainclothes or a uniform consisting of a black shirt, khaki pants, and black boots. This attire sends the message that these officers are not meant to be neighborhood police officers, but instead operate outside CPD's normal police channels. As CPD officers put it, the saturation teams "are jump out squads." Officers also told us of a policing "tactic" of randomly stopping their police vehicle and opening one door: if anyone runs, an officer will get out and give chase; if no one runs, they will close the car door and drive on. In addition to the unnecessary, dangerous situations this approach can get officers into, discussed in the Force Section of this Report, policing like this does little to promote community confidence or efficiently address crime. As one of our police experts put it, in some respects, Chicago's policing strategy in these neighborhoods seems to involve little more thought than having officers go out and "stir stuff up."

CPD incentivizes this tactical-oriented policing approach by elevating members of specialized units to special status. According to officers, being a member of a specialized unit or team carries prestige, and is considered as a "step up" for those uninterested or unable to obtain promotions to sergeant or other command positions. A TACT sergeant told us that officers are selected for TACT teams based on their "aggression, hustle, and effort," and "a patrol officer who rides around and just answers calls is not aggressive. Aggressive officers seek out crime between their radio assignments." This officer told us that his TACT officers "like to hunt" for offenders. One TACT officer we spoke to proudly touted the 1,300 arrests he had made in 11 years. The quality, impact, or even legitimacy of those arrests appeared generally unimportant to most of those that we spoke with throughout CPD. At one COMPSTAT meeting we observed, officers were told to go out and make a lot of car stops because vehicles are involved in shootings. There was no discussion about, or apparent consideration of, whether such a tactic was an effective use of police resources to identify possible shooters, or of the negative impact it could have on police-community relations.[60]

While people in Chicago's downtown areas only rarely see this type of policing, this is how residents in certain segments of the City experience policing on a daily basis. As a result, many residents in those neighborhoods feel, as we were told often in conversations with community members, as if CPD is an occupying force. One youth told us that the nature of the police presence in his neighborhood makes him feel like he is in "an open-air prison." One resident told us, "they patrol our streets like they are the dog catchers and we are the dogs." One officer told us that the law is unquestionably enforced differently in some neighborhoods: when "kids" on the North Side of Chicago get caught with marijuana, they get a citation; kids on the South Side get arrested. This officer's commander confirmed this approach when he told us that his policing philosophy in areas with violence is to make arrests because that was how he "was brought up."

In addition to feeling unduly harsh to residents of these neighborhoods, this type of policing has resulted in many residents, especially young people, feeling unfairly targeted and stereotyped by police. Young people we spoke with individually and during community meetings told us many stories of officers who, while unwilling or unable to help them when they needed help, followed and "harassed" them as they went about their daily lives. Young people told us of being stopped and searched by police, handcuffed, and having background checks conducted before being let go, while doing everyday things like walking to the store. A young woman told us of being stopped and frisked on her way to her father's funeral. People also told us that even programs nominally put in place to protect them, such as CPD's Roadside Safety Checks and DUI Saturation Checks, are conducted in ways that make the programs feel like excuses to search residents and their cars.

Young black residents told us they are commonly stopped and suspected of engaging in criminal activity, or of being gang members, based solely on their appearance. As one resident told us, "they see you with [certain types of clothing] and they think you are a criminal. Wear dreads and you get stopped." A young girl stated that "[they are] always think[ing] [we're] gangbangers." Residents with whom we spoke were very concerned about the presumption of gang affiliation, not only because of the assumptions it made about people, but because it also provides a false narrative that can follow these individuals in future interactions with the police and the criminal justice system.

Latino residents of these communities voiced similar concerns. As one Latino resident stated, "there is guilt by association." Latinos stated that there is a tendency for officers to "lump everyone together." One Latino outreach worker told us that he was pulled over multiple times, mostly by TACT teams or non-uniformed officers. During these stops, officers would search the vehicle, and after finding nothing, would let the outreach worker and any passengers in the car go. These stops became so prevalent that the outreach worker's employer eventually had several conversations with CPD to try to stop these needless intrusions.

Of particular concern to us were officers who did not appear to recognize when profiling was unlawful. One *sergeant* told us that "if you're Muslim, and 18 to 24, and wearing white, yeah, I'm going to stop you. It's not called profiling, it's called being pro-active." CPD's own officers, especially, but not only, its black officers, acknowledge profiling and harassment by CPD. A lieutenant told us, "I'm a black man in Chicago, of course I've had problems with the police." Black CPD officers shared stories of being profiled by their own Department. One black officer said that he has been stopped many times by police in the Englewood neighborhood for no reason other than he is a black man in a nice car. Another black officer told us that when she lived in Englewood, she was profiled and stopped many times by officers. Another officer acknowledged that sometimes officers harass youth, but stated that sometimes what looks likes harassment may on occasion be officers interjecting themselves out of concern, such as officers who try to "clear a corner" out of concern for kids when they have information that the corner may be targeted for a shooting. Officers recognize the impact this type of policing has on residents and their perceptions of CPD. We were informed that when officers encounter black men on the street, men sometimes lift their shirts without being asked.

During our meeting with members of Chicago's Arab American Police Association, officers raised similar concerns about cultural sensitivity and the treatment of Muslims in particular. They explained that many times non-Muslim CPD officers will offend cultural norms unintentionally because of "ignorance and lack of training."

This may not be how CPD intends policing to be conducted or perceived in these neighborhoods, but these experiences offend and humiliate people and diminish residents' willingness to work with law enforcement. Nor can these consequences be excused by the rates of violence in some of these communities. As it endeavors to better partner with the residents of these communities, CPD must do a better job—*especially* in these communities—demonstrating that it presumes community residents to be allies rather than suspects, absent individualized evidence to the contrary. Practices that facilitate and support officers gaining close familiarity with the people and dynamics of the neighborhoods they police is an important aspect of encouraging this mindset. More broadly, CPD must ensure that it is incentivizing and rewarding conduct by all personnel—whether specialized units, beat officers, or CAPS staff—that builds community trust.

2. The City must address serious concerns about systemic deficiencies that disproportionately impact black and Latino communities

CPD's pattern or practice of unreasonable force and systemic deficiencies falls heaviest on the predominantly black and Latino neighborhoods on the South and West Sides of Chicago, which are also experiencing higher crime. The impact of these widespread constitutional violations, combined with unaddressed abusive and racially discriminatory conduct, have undermined the legitimacy of CPD and police-community trust in these communities. Many low-income black neighborhoods suffer the greatest harm of violent crime in Chicago, and therefore have more police contacts. As a result, residents in these neighborhoods suffer more of the harms caused by breakdowns in uses of force, training, supervision, accountability, and community policing. Our investigation also found that CPD has tolerated racially discriminatory conduct that not only undermines police legitimacy, but also contributes to the pattern or practice of unreasonable force. As CPD works to restore trust and ensure that policing is lawful and effective, it must recognize the extent to which this type of misconduct contributes to a culture that facilitates unreasonable force and corrodes community trust. We have serious concerns about the prevalence of racially discriminatory conduct by some CPD officers and the degree to which that conduct is tolerated and in some respects caused by deficiencies in CPD's systems of training, supervision and accountability. In light of these concerns, combined with the fact that the impact of CPD's pattern or practice of unreasonable force fall heaviest on predominantly black and Latino neighborhoods, restoring police-community trust will require remedies addressing both discriminatory conduct and the disproportionality of illegal and unconstitutional patterns of force on minority communities.

a. *The pattern or practice of unreasonable force disproportionately burdens minority communities*

As described throughout this Report, our investigation found that Chicago's black residents collectively have a very different experience with CPD than do Chicago's white residents. Many low-income black and Latino neighborhoods suffer the greatest harm of violent crime in Chicago. Residents in these neighborhoods, not surprisingly, have more frequent police interactions. With these interactions come the harms of unreasonable force that arise from CPD's systemic deficiencies outlined here and throughout this Report. The result is that Chicago's black and Latino communities experience more incidents of unreasonable force. These are the very communities who most need and call on the police to fight violent crime, and where police and community trust and cooperation is most important.

Blacks, Latinos, and whites make up approximately equal thirds of the population in Chicago, but the raw statistics show that CPD uses force almost ten times more often against blacks than against whites. For example, of all use-of-force incidents for which race was recorded between January 2011 and April 18, 2016, black individuals were subject to approximately 76% (19,374) of the uses of force, as compared to whites, who represented only 8% (2,007) of the force incidents. In some categories of force, blacks were even more overrepresented: black individuals were the subject of 80% of all CPD firearm uses and 81% of all Taser contact-stun uses during that time period. CPD's data on force incidents involving youth also showed stark disparities: 83% (3,335) of the incidents involved black children and 14% (552) involved Latino children.

These data strongly support what we repeatedly and consistently heard from both law enforcement and community sources: Chicago's black and Latino communities live not only with higher crime, but also with more instances of police abuse. Starting from a young age, black and Latino people, especially those living in Chicago's most challenged neighborhoods, have a vastly different experience with police than do white people. These negative, often tragic, interactions form the basis of minority communities' distrust of police.[61]

*b.   Recurrence of unaddressed racially discriminatory conduct by offi-
cers further erodes community trust and police effectiveness*

Our investigation found that this pattern or practice of misconduct and systemic deficiencies has indeed resulted in routinely abusive behavior within
CPD, especially toward black and Latino residents of Chicago's most challenged neighborhoods. Black youth told us that they are routinely called "nigger," "animal," or "pieces of shit" by CPD officers. A 19-year-old black male
reported that CPD officers called him a "monkey." Such statements were confirmed by CPD officers. One officer we interviewed told us that he personally
has heard co-workers and supervisors refer to black individuals as monkeys,
animals, savages, and "pieces of shit."

Residents reported treatment so demeaning they felt dehumanized. One
black resident told us that when it comes to CPD, there is "no treating you
as a human being." Consistent with these reports, our investigation found
that there was a recurring portrayal by some CPD officers of the residents
of challenged neighborhoods—who are mostly black—as animals or subhu-
man. One CPD member told us that the officers in his district come to work
every day "like it's a safari." This theme has a long history in Chicago. A
photo from the early 2000s that surfaced years later shows white CPD officers Jerome Finnegan and Timothy McDermott squatting over a black man
posed as a dead deer with antlers as the officers hold their rifles. Finnegan
was later sentenced to 12 years in prison for being part of a corrupt group in
the Department's Special Operations Section that carried out robberies and
home invasions in predominantly black neighborhoods, while McDermott
was fired when the photo surfaced. This mindset has desensitized many officers from the humanity of the people of color they serve, setting the stage for
the use of excessive force.[62]

We reviewed data related to complaints of racially discriminatory language and found repeated instances where credible complaints were not adequately addressed. Our review of CPD's complaint database showed 980
police misconduct complaints coded as discriminatory verbal abuse on the
basis of race or ethnicity from 2011 to March 2016. Thirteen of these complaints—1.3%—were sustained. We found 354 complaints for the use of the
word "nigger" or one of its variations. Four, or 1.1%, of these complaints
were sustained.

Generally, these complaints were sustained only where there was audio,
video, or other irrefutable evidence. One of the four sustained complaints
was sustained because the officer admitted using the racial slur; another was
sustained because there was an audio recording of the officers using the slur.
The third sustained complaint was sustained because the victim's husband
was a police officer in a neighboring municipality who took extraordinary

measures to document the incident. In that case, the officer was suspended for 15 days for the incident, which involved an altercation with the victim at a dog park that involved the officer telling her: "Fuck you, you fucking nigger, you should keep your big mouth shut." When the woman's husband told the officer that the officer should not speak that way to the woman, the officer responded: "Why? Because she's pregnant? I don't care if she's pregnant. I'll beat her fuckin' ass too." As a police officer himself, the woman's husband knew to call the police, request contact cards, get witnesses' information, and go directly to the district station to file the complaint.

The fourth sustained complaint had been generated internally by a lieutenant when she learned of a recording of a police officer yelling, "Don't move nigger!" at a man he was chasing during a foot pursuit. The slur had been broadcast over the police radio. The allegation against the officer was sustained, as were allegations of failing to report misconduct against a lieutenant and another officer. These results are the exception, rather than the rule; most racially charged language used by CPD officers is neither recorded nor directed towards another member of law enforcement who knows how to respond in a way that will ensure the officer is held accountable.

Chicago has settled several lawsuits that alleged racially discriminatory treatment by CPD officers. In one suit, the victim asked the officers why he was under arrest to which they responded, "We got something for big mouthy niggers like you" before beating him. In 2013, a CPD officer arrested a Chinese-American citizen working at a massage parlor and used excessive force. A video of the incident captured an officer screaming, "I'll put you in a UPS box and send you back to wherever the fuck you came from," and another officer hitting her in the head while she was on her knees.

Finally, we found that some Chicago police officers expressed discriminatory views and intolerance with regard to race, religion, gender, and national origin in public social media forums, and that CPD takes insufficient steps to prevent or appropriately respond to this animus. While CPD policy prohibits Department members from using social media to convey "any communications that discredit or reflect poorly on the Department, its missions or goals," this policy is apparently not well-enforced, even against supervisors. For example, one officer posted a status stating, "Hopefully one of these pictures will make the black lives matter activist organization feel a whole lot better!" with two photos attached, including one of two slain black men, in the front seats of a car, bloodied, covered in glass. Several CPD officers posted social media posts contain disparaging remarks about Arabs and Muslims, with posts referring to them as "7th century Islamic goat humpers," "Ragtop," and making other anti-Islamic statements. One CPD officer posted a photo of a dead Muslim soldier laying in a pool of his own blood with the caption: "The only good Muslim is a fucking dead one." Supervisors posted many of the discriminatory posts we found, including one sergeant who posted at least 25 anti-Muslim statements and at least 43 other discriminatory posts, and a lieutenant who posted at least five anti-immigrant and anti-Latino statements. Given these statements, our observations and conversations with officers during the course of our investigation, and other publicly available commentary, such as the comments posted anonymously on popular CPD officer blogs, it appears that more CPD officers have made similarly derogatory statements, often without repercussion.

Even when CPD learns of overtly discriminatory statements, its response reflects a lack of sufficient concern about such conduct. For example, in June 2015, Chicago learned about an officer who had posted racist comments and had called for a race war on social media forums after a reporter from ABC 7 News contacted IPRA and sent the agency the posts. The investigative file indicates that the case was still pending as of December 2016. Indeed, underscoring both the inadequacy and impact of CPD's response to overtly racist behavior, we found nearly 100 troubling public posts made by the same officer as recently as June 2016, many exhibiting racial animus.

In response to our question about what changes he would like to see among Chicago police officers, one black teen responded, "act as if you care." This simple request from a young Chicago resident encapsulates the kind of policing we heard people asking for in the hundreds of conversations we had, and in the scores of community meetings we attended during our investigation. People living in Chicago's marginalized neighborhoods want policing that demonstrates that CPD has genuine concern about the safety and well-being of all Chicago residents, no matter where they live or what they look like.

The conduct of those officers who have engaged in the racist and abusive behaviors described here, unchecked due to the systemic and cultural failings described in this Report, hurts the many well-intentioned officers. CPD will not be able to convince residents in these neighborhoods that it cares, no matter how earnestly it launches community policing initiatives, if it does not take a stronger, more effective stance against unnecessarily demeaning and divisive officer conduct.

3. <u>CPD must stop using dangerous practices, such as "guns for freedom," to coerce people into providing information</u>

During our investigation, we heard allegations that CPD officers arrest individuals and attempt to gain information about crime using methods that undermine CPD's legitimacy and may also be unlawful. In some instances, we were told that CPD will attempt to glean information about gang activity, the locations of weapons, or drug activity, and refuse to release the individual until he provides that information. In other instances, CPD will take a young person to a rival gang neighborhood and either leave the person there or display the youth to rival members, immediately putting the life of that young person in jeopardy by suggesting he has provided information to the police. Our investigation indicates that these practices in fact exist.

We commend the CPD officers who are working *with* community members to protect the public from gun violence, including by removing illegal guns from the streets. However, when officers use unlawful arrests and detentions or improper intimidation tactics to coerce information, they erode community trust and undermine the work of CPD and the community to rid the City of violent crime.

We were told by many community members that one method by which CPD will try to get individuals to provide information about crime or guns is by picking them up and driving them around while asking for information about gangs or guns. When individuals do not talk, officers will drop them off in dangerous areas or gang territories. We reviewed a publicly available video that appears to capture one instance of an officer displaying a youth in police custody to a group of individuals gathered in a rival gang territory. The video shows CPD officers standing around a marked CPD vehicle with the back doors wide open and a young male detained in the rear. Officers permit a crowd of male youths to surround the car and shout at the adolescent. The crowd can be seen flashing hand gestures that look like gang signs and threatening the cowering teenager in the backseat. One of the males in the crowd appears to have freely recorded the interactions all while CPD officers stood beside the open vehicle doors. The video does not show any legitimate law enforcement purpose in allowing the youth to be threatened.

Residents told us that this has happened for years, with several individuals recounting their personal experiences. A young black man told us that when he was 12 or 13 years old, he and his friends were picked up by CPD officers, dropped off in rival territory, and told to walk home. Another black teen told us that his brother was picked up in one location, dropped off in another location known for rival gangs, and told: "Better get to running."

We also talked with several individuals who gave credible accounts of being detained by CPD officers for low-level offenses (for example, failure to use a turn signal) or on false pretenses, and then were told that they would not be released until they brought the officers guns. We heard community members refer to this practice as "guns for freedom." One man told us of an incident that happened within the past few months, in which he was arrested for driving on a suspended license and told by officers that "everything would go away" if he brought the officers two guns. Officers released him on bond and told him he had one week to bring the officers the guns. They warned him that if he did not bring the guns they would put him away "forever." This person told us of a friend who had a similar experience several years ago.

Other individuals with whom we met during community meetings told us similar stories of CPD officers offering to release them from custody if they provided officers with a weapon. A pastor at a Latino church told us that his congregants reported being picked up by CPD officers seeking information regarding guns or drugs, but when they either could not or would not provide such information, the officers removed the congregants' shoelaces and dropped them off in rival neighborhoods. Another man told us that he saw officers surround his seven-year-old niece seeking information about who sold drugs and which gangs were running in their neighborhood.

A recording from November 2015 appears to capture part of a "guns for freedom" incident on video. The video is part of a case in which an individual alleges that police coerced him into producing weapons to gain his own release and the release of a friend. According to the individual who produced the gun, police first required him to tell them where guns were located, and then demanded that he bring them a gun. The man claims he had to buy the gun he brought to the police. The video recording appears to show the man placing the gun in a trash bin and police officers retrieving the gun later that day. The officers' incident report does not mention any arrest and instead claims that the man directed them to "the location of multiple firearms being hidden in the 5th and 22nd district."

In addition to the likely illegality of this conduct, its impact on community trust cannot be overstated. The fear and anger created by these practices was obvious when we talked with individuals who reported these experiences. As the attorney for the man in the November 2015 incident noted during a media interview, "if there was any trust that's built up by officers on the street, that trust is clearly and quickly destroyed." His words underscore what we found more broadly throughout our investigation: when practices like this are allowed to persist, CPD allows abusive officers to set the culture, undermining the hard work of CPD's many good officers.

Our review of CPD's misconduct investigations revealed more than 100 complaints of similar conduct; these complaints were only very rarely sustained, even when internally generated complaints arising from the same incident were sustained. In other cases, investigators failed to follow through on the investigation despite possible corroborating evidence.

Through the publicly available videos noted above, the conversations we had with community members, and the hundreds of complaints that have been made about this conduct over the past few years alone, it is clear that this is a concern CPD should address. Indeed, CPD TACT officers complained to us that while supervisors' direction now is to stay out of trouble, previously the guidance from supervisors was: "If you get me a gun, we'll take care of you."

There may be circumstances in which giving an arrestee who is lawfully arrested based on probable cause leniency or even immunity in exchange for recovering illegal firearms is appropriate. Such practices should be pursued, however, under policy and supervision to ensure they are safe, effective, and within constitutional limits. CPD must ensure that officers consistently police in a manner that builds and preserves police legitimacy.

C. A TRUST-BUILDING, COMMUNITY-FOCUSED APPROACH TO POLICING WILL BETTER PROMOTE LAWFUL POLICING AND PUBLIC SAFETY

When community policing was more fully supported and broadly implemented in Chicago in the 1990s, studies found it had a substantial impact on public safety and community confidence in CPD. Researchers found, for example, that blacks experienced a 22% decrease in fear of crime in their neighborhoods, and a 60% decrease in perceived social disorder. At the same time, blacks, Latinos, and whites all reported better relationships with police officers.

In the last decade, community-focused policing has worked to bring down crime and rebuild trust in other cities—including big cities and cities with high rates of violent crime. New York has reduced its crime rate while at the same time lowering the number of stops and arrests it makes. Community policing can also be instrumental in bringing about the relationships that are helpful in bringing up homicide clearance rates, one of the most critical problems currently facing Chicago.

No police department is perfect, but other police departments, and Chicago's own history, have shown that it can better support lawful policing, gain legitimacy in the eyes of the public, and more effectively address crime, if it roots out unlawful and divisive practices and infuses its systems with a community-focused approach.

VI. RECOMMENDATIONS

Throughout this Report, we make several recommendations to the City and CPD related to our findings. These recommendations are gathered and offered in more detail below. Through the changes we have identified, CPD will be better poised to police constitutionally and effectively, and improve trust between officers and the communities they serve. We look forward to working cooperatively with the City and CPD on how to best craft and implement these recommendations.

A. USE OF FORCE

CPD should re-orient officers' approach to the use of force to avoid using force except when necessary, and should provide officers with the policy guidance and training to develop and maintain proficiency in de-escalation. CPD should also implement a system of force reporting and investigation to better detect and respond to instances of unreasonable or unnecessary force. Additionally, providing officers with the tools and training to better respond to persons in physical or mental health crisis and those with intellectual disabilities will help avoid injuries, increase community trust, and make officers safer. CPD should:

1. Adopt use of force practices that minimize the use of force.

a. CPD has begun the process of revising its force policies to better reflect the sanctity of human life, the need to avoid the use of force, and de-escalation and force mitigation consistent with officer safety. CPD should continue this process to ensure these concepts are incorporated throughout CPD's force policies, including its canine and Taser policies, and that policies provide sufficient guidance to officers;

b. CPD has begun training officers in safely using de-escalation methods so that force may be avoided. CPD should continue this process and should incorporate these concepts throughout CPD training;

c. Develop, train and implement a foot pursuit policy that makes clear that foot pursuits are dangerous and that sets forth guidelines for foot pursuits that balance the objective of apprehending the suspect with the risk of potential injury to the officer, the public, and the suspect. The policy also should address unsafe foot pursuit tactics to ensure the risks of foot pursuits are not increased;

d. Ensure that officers are trained in sound tactics to avoid unnecessarily exposing officers to situations in which deadly force may become necessary;

e. Revise and reinforce policies against shooting at or from a moving vehicle, and provide additional training on avoiding dangerous vehicle maneuvers;

f. Revise Taser policies consistent with best practices, including implementing restrictions on the use of Tasers in drive-stun mode; limitations on Taser use in situations that pose inordinate risk to the suspect; limitations on Taser use on vulnerable people (e.g., the elderly, pregnant women, people in mental health crisis); restrictions on Taser use to situations in which it is necessary and proportional to the threat or resistance of the subject; and discouragement of the use of Tasers in schools and on students, and requiring officers to factor into their decision to use a Taser a child's apparent age, size, and the threat presented for proportionality and appropriateness. CPD should emphasize in training that Tasers are weapons with inherent risks that inflict significant pain and should not be viewed as tools of convenience;

g. Prohibit the use of retaliatory force, force used as punishment, force used in response to the exercise of protected First Amendment activities (e.g., filming), and force used in response to speech only rather than in response to an immediate threat;

h. Equip officers with appropriate first-aid supplies, train them in their use, and require officers to render aid to injured persons consistent with the officer's training;

i. Equip all patrol officers and supervisors, and officers who regularly interact with the public, including tactical officers, with body cameras, and develop a body camera policy delineating officers' responsibilities regarding the consistent and appropriate use of body cameras and the retention and review of body camera footage.

2. Change the reporting and review of force to accurately capture the totality of the circumstances in force incidents.

a. Develop and implement use-of-force reporting requiring officers to complete a narrative force report that describes with particularity the force used and the circumstances necessitating that level of force, including the reason for the initial stop or other enforcement action. Witness officers should also complete reports for serious uses of force (e.g., firearms discharges and other forms of deadly force). Injuries to officers and persons against whom force was used should be photographed;

b. Develop and implement supervisory review of force that requires the supervisor to conduct a complete review of each use of force, including gathering and considering evidence necessary to understand the circumstances of the force incident and determine its consistency with law and policy, including statements from individuals against whom force is used and civilian witnesses;

c. Develop and implement a system for higher-level, inter-disciplinary review of incidents involving all types of firearms discharges, successful canine deployments, Taser uses, use of chemical weapons, and force resulting in injury to the person against whom force was used;

d. Discipline or otherwise hold accountable officers who fail to accurately report their own uses of force, officers who fail to accurately report another officer's use of force when policy requires it, and supervisors who fail to conduct adequate force investigations;

e. Collect and analyze data on uses of force to identify racial and other disparities in officer uses of force.

3. **Revise the initial response to officer-involved shootings to prevent collusion and the contamination of witnesses.**

a. Adopt a policy requiring that IPRA investigators participate in the preliminary assessment during the immediate aftermath of an officer-involved shooting to the same extent as the CPD commander in charge and CPD investigators conducting administrative or criminal investigations;

b. Adopt policies and practices that preclude involved and witness officers from speaking with one another, or with civilian witnesses, about the shooting incident until after they have been interviewed by IPRA investigators, except to the extent necessary to ensure public safety. To that end, require that, where possible, involved officers, witness officers, and civilian witnesses be transported to the station separately and their conversations be monitored to avoid contamination prior to interviews;

c. Except to the extent necessary to ensure public safety, prohibit involved officers and witness officers from using cell phones before they speak with the on-scene commander;

d. Consider prohibiting involved officers, witness officers, and civilians from viewing footage from dashboard cameras, body cameras, surveillance cameras, or cell phones before their interview with IPRA. In all cases, inquire of witnesses and officers whether they have viewed any recordings prior to the interview;

e.   Require that interviews with involved officers and witness officers be recorded and IPRA investigators be present (except that an officer may speak with his or her attorney in private) and that interviews with civilian witnesses be recorded unless it would interfere with investigation. In cases where interviews are not recorded, the reason for failing to record the interview should be documented;

f.   Revise CBA provisions or other restrictions on how soon officers may be interviewed following an officer-involved shooting; and

g.   CPD and IPRA should develop appropriate protocols to conduct concurrent, bifurcated investigations with specific measures to ensure that the integrity of criminal investigations is not compromised.

4.   Implement policies and develop training to improve interactions with people who are in crisis.

a.   Devote appropriate resources to improve CPD's existing CIT program. Develop and implement policy and training to better identify and respond to individuals with known or suspected mental health conditions, including persons in mental health crisis and those with intellectual or developmental disabilities ("I/DD") or other disabilities;

b.   Screen and designate volunteer officers who have expressed an interest in becoming CIT specialists and are well-suited to this work. CPD should continue to offer CIT training for officers who wish to develop crisis intervention skills, but reserve participation in the CIT program to the selected officers;

c.   Provide crisis intervention training to CIT-designated officers, who will respond to critical incidents involving persons in crisis. This training should include how to identify and respond to common medical emergencies that may at first appear to reflect a failure to comply with lawful orders (e.g., seizures, diabetic emergencies);

d.   Ensure that there are enough CIT officers on duty throughout the City and throughout the day to help ensure a CIT officer is available to respond to calls involving an individual in crisis;

e.   Require that, wherever possible, at least one CIT officer will respond to any situation concerning individuals in mental health crisis or with I/DD where force might be used;

f.   Improve the quality of the current CIT 40-hour training program, which will in turn require obtaining sufficient CIT training staff and resources so that training can focus on requiring CIT candidates to demonstrate competency in the necessary skills;

g. Collect data on CIT calls to allow CPD to make informed decisions about staffing and deployment so that a CIT officer is available for all shifts in all districts to respond to every CIT call;

h. Develop a CIT reporting system (apart from the use-of-force reporting system) so that each deployment of a CIT officer is well documented. CIT officers should submit narrative reports of their interactions with persons in crisis so the appropriateness of the response can be evaluated in an after-action analysis; and

i. Implement an assessment program to evaluate the efficacy of the CIT program as a whole and the performance of individual CIT officers. A portion of a CIT officer's performance review should address skill and effectiveness in CIT situations.

B. Accountability

A well-functioning accountability system (in combination with effective supervision) is the keystone to lawful policing. The City and CPD must create impartial, transparent, and effective internal and external oversight systems that will hold officers accountable in a timely manner for violations of law, CPD policy, or CPD training. To that end, the City and CPD must:

1. Improve the City and CPD's accountability mechanisms for increased and more effective police oversight.

a. Work with police unions to modify practices and procedures for accepting complaints to make it easier for individuals to register formal complaints about police conduct;

b. Adopt practices to ensure the full and impartial investigation of all complaints, and assessment of patterns and trends related to those complaints;

c. Revise IPRA/COPA mediation policies and procedures to: 1) require complainant notification of and participation in mediation; 2) incorporate principles of restorative justice; 3) create clear, objective standards for referring cases to mediation; and 4) prohibit mediation for resolving certain categories of complaints, including use of force and domestic violence complaints;

d. Revise BIA policies and procedures to require that investigators record interviews and include transcripts of all interviews with victims, witnesses, or suspect officers in every file. CPD policy should dictate that summaries of interviews will be accepted only where obtaining a recorded or transcribed interview is not feasible;

e. Enforce CPD policies prohibiting officers from falsifying reports and providing false information or testimony during interviews by providing strict disciplinary penalties, up to and including termination, for those officers who violate them; and

f. Put systems in place that ensure administrative charges are fully and timely investigated, even where CPD and the State's Attorney's Office are investigating potential criminal charges, or have decided not to pursue criminal charges, for the same conduct.

2. Ensure investigative agencies have the appropriate resources, training, and structure necessary to conduct investigations thoroughly, efficiently, and fairly.

a. Conduct a staffing analysis, and create a staffing plan based on that analysis, to ensure that both BIA and IPRA/COPA have the staffing and resources to perform their responsibilities effectively;

b. Improve the timeliness and quality of BIA/IPRA/COPA investigations through the creation of case management protocols, including streamlined procedures and target deadlines for the completion of investigations; and

c. Develop and implement mandatory and comprehensive training for BIA/IPRA/COPA investigators, Police Board members, and hearing officers on police practices, civil rights law, evidence collection and assessment techniques, interview techniques, and other pertinent issues. The training for IPRA/COPA investigators should also include training on implicit bias and proper witness interviewing techniques. Investigators tasked with investigating domestic violence and sexual misconduct complaints should receive specialized training on the dynamics of those incidents and interview techniques for domestic violence and sexual misconduct victims.

3. Implement changes to the City's discipline and discipline review systems, including the Chicago Police Board, to ensure disciplinary decisions are fair, timely, and transparent.

a. Revise how disciplinary decisions are made, including streamlining the number of disciplinary decision makers and the layers of review of disciplinary recommendations, to facilitate quicker final resolution of complaints;

b. Revise CPD's disciplinary matrix to ensure that it provides meaningful guidance to those making disciplinary recommendations and findings;

c. Consider moving the Police Board's police commission and civilian oversight duties to another entity (such as a Community Oversight

Board), to allow the Police Board to focus on its critical function of reviewing Superintendent/IPRA misconduct and disciplinary findings;

d. Create a cadre of trained and experienced attorneys within IPRA/COPA to advocate before the Board;

e. Modify CPD and IPRA policy, and address related provisions in the CBAs, to ensure that the Board has access to the information necessary to make a fair and informed decisions;

f. Ensure selection criteria for Police Board members and hearing officers include requisite competence, impartiality, and expertise;

g. Post all Police Board materials, including video recordings of hearings, on the Board's website in a timely manner; and

h. Track and publish more detailed case-specific and aggregate data about Police Board decisions, and make this information available in a timely manner.

C. TRAINING

Training is the foundation for ensuring that officers are engaging in effective and constitutional policing. To that end, CPD should:

1. Provide training that is comprehensive, organized, based on adult-learning principles, and developed with national best police practices and community policing principles in mind.

a. Revise Academy curricula and lesson content to ensure consistency with CPD policy and current law, particularly with respect to the use of force, and revise lesson-delivery methods to include lessons that are consistent with adult learning principles and include more scenario-based trainings;

b. Revise end-of-course Academy evaluations to ensure recruits graduate the Academy with sufficient knowledge and skill to police safely and lawfully;

c. Revitalize CPD's Field Training Program by increasing incentives provided to FTOs in order to ensure a sufficient number of high-quality FTOs; improving the training provided to FTOs and, in turn, the quality of supervision and guidance that FTOs provide; creating a standardized curriculum for each FTO to use when training PPOs; increasing the rigor of FTO evaluation of PPOs; creating better supervision of FTOs and regularly evaluating the Field Training Program to identify areas in need of improvement; and

d. Implement a mandatory in-service training program, based on a comprehensive evaluation of Department needs, that includes high quality training through live, scenario-based trainings; provides updates on law and Department policy; and presents officers and supervisors with opportunities to refresh important skills and tactics.

2. **Take steps to ensure the creation of a well-planned, comprehensive training program that is carefully tailored to Department needs and is properly resourced.**

   a. Formalize CPD's creation of a training committee in CPD policies, including outlining the committee's goals, membership, responsibilities, and deliverables;

   b. Recruit, hire, and train additional instructors, and develop and implement rigorous testing, evaluation, and training of all instructors to ensure subject-matter competency and skill in instruction; and

   c. Improve CPD's physical training facilities and equipment.

D. SUPERVISION

Patrol officers must receive proper supervision and guidance in order to ensure that they are engaging in constitutional and effective policing and that they are held accountable if they engage in misconduct. This requires that patrol supervisors receive the tools, training, and support they need to perform their supervisory duties effectively. To that end, CPD should:

1. **Reform CPD's supervisory structures and incentives to provide all officers with meaningful direction and oversight.**

   a. Develop and implement policies that establish clear requirements and provide specific guidance to ensure the appropriate supervision of all officers;

   b. Ensure that supervisors closely monitor officers under their command, review officer uses of force, and direct and guide officers to use force only where necessary, in a manner that is safe, and that comports with the principles and values set forth in CPD's revised force policies;

   c. Hold supervisors accountable if they fail to report misconduct that they observe, fail to accept and refer to IPRA a misconduct complaint, or otherwise fail to take appropriate steps to ensure officer accountability;

   d. Implement appropriate span-of-control ratios in all districts and reform shift scheduling to allow for unity of command;

   e. Re-examine the responsibilities of supervisory staff at districts to allow supervisors to maximize time spent providing mentorship, oversight, and accountability of officer activities;

   f.   Provide new supervisors with adequate training on supervisory skills, including leadership and management, and provide all supervisors with regular training on issues relevant to their supervisory responsibilities; and

   g.   Incentivize and reward supervisors who provide close and effective supervision.

2. Ensure CPD supervisors have the appropriate tools and information necessary to provide meaningful supervision.

   a.   Commit to putting in place a new and fully integrated EIS system that will allow for early identification of problematic behavior trends and appropriate interventions, and involve all relevant stakeholders in the process early on to ensure its ultimate success; and;

   b.   Ensure that data collection and tracking systems are adequate Department-wide to support this effort, and audit their use to ensure that these systems are used consistently and appropriately.

E. OFFICER WELLNESS AND SAFETY

Officers must receive the support they need from the Department to perform their policing responsibilities well and safely, and to address the stressors related to their work. To better support its officers, CPD should:

1. Evaluate and respond to the needs of CPD officers.

   a.   Conduct a needs assessment to determine what additional resources officers desire or need to reduce the stressors of their jobs;

   b.   Expand the Employee Assistance Program by hiring additional counselors, substance abuse specialists, and other staff with specialized training and skills in certain topics, including post-traumatic stress disorder, domestic violence, women's issues, and depression;

   c.   Coordinate a communication strategy to inform all CPD members of the services available through the Employee Assistance Program and ensure that references to the range of available counseling and support services are included in Academy trainings, including the stress management and wellness trainings;

   d.   Explore alternative methods for providing officer support, including anonymous support hotlines and group meetings; and

   e.   Revise and implement new protocols for evaluation and treatment of officers involved in, or who witness, traumatic events, not limited to officer-involved shootings.

2. Incorporate officer wellness principles into all facets of CPD operations.

   a. Explore and evaluate other methods to increase officer access to employee supports and services, including how using those services can benefit CPD officers, and encourage officers to use these programs; and

   b. Conduct a Department-wide technology and equipment audit to determine what equipment is outdated, broken, or otherwise in need of replacement, and develop a plan with timelines for repair or replacement of equipment as needed.

F. DATA COLLECTION AND TRANSPARENCY

To increase transparency and community trust, it is critical that the City improve its data collection systems and publicly report and release information relevant to its policing and accountability efforts. Accordingly, the City, through CPD and IPRA/COPA, should:

1. Improve City data collection systems.

   a. Examine and evaluate current data collection mechanisms and technology to determine where there are gaps and inefficiencies;

   b. Create a plan to improve and synthesize City and CPD data collection systems by dates certain; and

   c. Develop systems to ensure that data is appropriately and timely analyzed to identify trends or patterns in policing activities, including officer use of force and police misconduct complaints. The City and CPD should use data collection systems to track and identify patterns or practices of constitutional violations, so that corrective action can be taken where necessary.

2. Increase transparency regarding CPD and IPRA/COPA activities.

   a. Seek input from community members regarding the type of data and information they believe is important for CPD and IPRA to disseminate;

   b. Develop and implement policies mandating regular public reporting of crime trends and CPD policing activities;

   c. Develop and implement policies mandating regular public reporting of misconduct investigations, including investigations handled not just by IPRA or COPA, but also BIA and the districts. These policies should cover regular reporting on complaint patterns and trends, investigation outcomes, and discipline (both recommended and imposed);

d. Finalize and formally adopt, as part of CPD and IPRA policy, the video release policy, with consideration of expanding the universe of complaints the policy covers; and

e. Develop and implement policies that would increase transparency related to City settlements of police misconduct complaints.

G. PROMOTIONS

To ensure constitutional and effective policing, CPD must promote competent, capable leaders, and ensure confidence amongst officers that deserving, well-qualified candidates will be selected for promotions. CPD must review its promotions systems to ensure all qualified candidates have a chance to be promoted, and improve transparency around the promotions process to better inform officers of how promotional decisions are made. To that end, CPD should:

1. Ensure promotions are fair.

a. Continue to review promotional exams to ensure they are valid and fairly administered;

b. Schedule promotional exams with sufficient frequency to allow qualified candidates frequent opportunity for promotion throughout their careers; and

c. Review and revise, as necessary, the merit promotion process, to ensure that policies and procedures are followed, and that the system is working as intended.

2. Increase transparency around the promotions process.

a. Devise and implement mechanisms for teaching officers about the policies and procedures guiding the merit promotion process;

b. Develop mechanisms for improving transparency regarding those who receive merit promotions, and the reasons those candidates were selected; and

c. Continue, and potentially increase, oversight of the merit promotions process through the Chicago Office of the Inspector General, and ensure that the OIG's role in overseeing this process is communicated to both officers and the public.

H. COMMUNITY POLICING

CPD should adopt, and incorporate in its policing approaches, an ingrained and permanent community policing philosophy that humanizes officers and residents to each other and builds trust between the community and the police; incentivizes police-community partnerships; and effectively uses these partnerships to solve crime and address community concerns. To that end, CPD should:

1. Develop community policing as a core component of CPD's policing strategies, tactics, and training.

a. Develop and implement, with the help of community members from Chicago's diverse groups, comprehensive recruit and in-service training to officers on how to establish formal partnerships and actively engage with diverse communities, to include understanding and building trust with minority communities, Muslim communities, immigrant and limited English-proficiency communities, persons with disabilities, and lesbian, gay, bisexual, and transgender communities;

b. Incorporate community policing and problem-solving principles into Academy training, and require regular in-service training on topics such as procedural justice, de-escalation, bias-free policing, diversity and cultural sensitivity;

c. Create liaison officers in each district that will be responsive to, and specifically address, the concerns of minority communities, including LGBTQ individuals, Muslims and other religious or ethnic minorities, individuals with limited English-proficiency, and individuals with disabilities. District liaison officers should have monthly meetings to coordinate Department-wide outreach efforts and strategies;

d. Develop systems that encourage and facilitate opportunities for officers to actively engage with communities while on patrol and gain more familiarity with residents through one-on-one interactions;

e. Increase opportunities for officers to have frequent, positive interactions with people outside of an enforcement context, especially groups and communities that have expressed a high level of distrust of police; and

f. Measure, evaluate, and reward individual, supervisory, and agency performance on community engagement, problem-oriented-policing projects, and crime prevention.

2. **Ensure that officers police fairly and compassionately in all neighborhoods, including in those with high rates of violent crime and in minority communities.**

   a. Develop and implement a policy that specifically and comprehensively addresses and prohibits discriminatory policing and biased-based policing;

   b. Provide initial and recurring training to all officers that sends a clear and consistent message that bias-based profiling and other forms of discriminatory policing are prohibited, and ensures that officers are capable of interacting with and providing services to all communities;

   c. Provide training to supervisors and commanders on detecting and addressing bias-based profiling and other forms of discriminatory policing;

   d. Provide safeguards for officers who report bias-based profiling and other forms of discriminatory policing;

   e. Provide training to supervisors, detectives, and officers on how to detect and report potential hate crimes or hate incidents;

   f. Work with community members from Chicago's diverse racial, religious, ethnic, gender, and disability groups to create and deliver cultural awareness training in partnership with CPD, and to inform and suggest the development of additional measures that may improve police-community relations;

   g. Enforce Department rules regarding appropriate language, respect, and social media use;

   h. Collect and analyze enforcement data (including use of force data) to identify patterns of unequal enforcement on the basis of race or ethnicity, and devise and implement operational changes based on this analysis. Publish stop, search, arrest, and force data bi-annually with the analysis of trends, and the steps taken to correct problems and build on successes; and

   i. Capture and track complaints alleging racial and other bias-based profiling or discrimination, along with characteristics of the complainants. Analyze this data to identify and correct any patterns of discrimination.

ENDNOTES

❦

1. Throughout this Report, we use the terms "unreasonable" and "excessive" interchangeably; both terms refer to force that exceeds constitutional limits, or in other words, is disproportional in light of the threat posed to officers or others, the level of resistance, and the severity of the crime suspected. When using the term "unnecessary," we instead mean that force was used when the incident could have been resolved without resorting to the amount of force used.

2. Anthony J. Pinnizzotto Et Al., *Escape from the Killing Zone*, fbi law enforcement bull., March 2002, at 1.

3. U.S. Customs and Border Protection, Use of Force Review: Cases and Policies6, 8 (Police Executive Research Forum, 2013), available at https://www.cbp.gov/sites/default/files/documents/PERFReport.pdf; USE OF FORCE: CONCEPTS AND ISSUES PAPER 7 (IACP National Law Enforcement Policy Center, Rev. 2006), available at https://www.documentcloud.org/documents/370261-iacp-use-of-force-concepts-and-issues-paper-2006.html.

4. During our review of officer-involved shootings, we saw shootings at dogs that appeared to be unnecessary, retaliatory, or reckless. We also observed that there were many complaints from community members that officers unnecessarily or recklessly killed their dogs and that, like other civilian complaints, these complaints were not adequately investigated. These deficiencies in investigation of civilian complaints are discussed elsewhere in this Report.

5. The shooting was of concern for other reasons as well. The first officer claimed the suspect had turned his body to point his weapon at the second officer, prompting him to warn his partner and then pull the trigger. The second officer contradicted this account, claiming the suspect never turned his body and never pointed the weapon. IPRA never pursued the inconsistency and did not mention it in its final report.

6. "Taser" is the brand name of electronic control weapons manufactured by Taser International, Inc. CPD uses Taser brand electronic control weapons and refers to these weapons in their policies and forms as "Tasers."

7. Tasers can be used in drive-stun or probe mode. Taser probes shot from a short distance incapacitate a person by causing them to lose control of their muscles. Drive-stun mode requires direct contact between the Taser and the person and simply causes pain. Many agencies restrict the use of Tasers in drive-stun mode because it is less effective in minimizing threats and has a high potential for abuse. *See, e.g.,* Directive 10.3: Use of Less Lethal Force: The Electronic Control WEAPON (ECW) 9 (Phila. Police Dep't, Sept. 18, 2015) ("Personnel must be aware that using an ECW in Drive Stun is Often Ineffective in Incapacitating a subject."), available at https://www.phillypolice.com/assets/directives/PPD-Directive-10.3.pdf; Att'y Gen., Supplemental Policy on Conducted Energy Devices § V.4., at 7 (N.J. Attorney General, Rev. March 3, 2016) ("An officer shall not use a [Tas-

er] in drive stun mode unless the officer reasonably believes based on the suspect's conduct that discharging the device in drive stun mode is immediately necessary to protect the officer, the suspect, or another person from imminent danger of death or serious bodily injury."), available at http://www.nj.gov/oag/dcj/agguide/directives/2016-3-3_Supplemental-Policy-on-Conducted-Energy-Devices.pdf.

8. 2011 ELECTRONIC CONTROL WEAPON GUIDELINES 21 n.27 (Police Executive Rese. F. & Community Oriented Policing Serv.'s, March 2011), available at http://www.nccpsafety.org/assets/files/library/2011_Electronic_Control_Weapon_Guidelines.pdf.

9. CIT is a distinct program, different than other mental health awareness training. CPD's recruit training includes a 14-hour mental health module, and officers are now being provided eight hours of CIT training as part of CPD's newly designed force-mitigation training. However, this basic training does not equip officers with the specialized skills needed for crisis intervention. Similarly, CIT overlaps in some respects with de-escalation training, but CIT training is distinct from and more expansive than CPD's current eight-hour de-escalation training.

10. *See, e.g.*, CIT International, *CIT is More than Just Training. . . . It's a Community Program*, available at http://www.citinternational.org/Learn-About-CIT.

11. *Id.*

12. RANDY DUPONT ET AL., CRISIS INTERVENTION TEAM CORE ELEMENTS (U. of Memphis Sch. of Urb. Aff. and Pub. Pol'y, Sept. 2007), available at http://cit.memphis.edu/pdf/CoreElements.pdf.

13. *Id.*

14. KELLI E. CANADA ET AL., CRISIS INTERVENTION TEAMS IN CHICAGO: SUCCESSES ON THE GROUND, (J. Police Crisis Negot. 2010, Jan. 1, 2011), available at https://www.ncbi.nlm.nih.gov/pmc/articles/PMC2990632/#R4.

15. Officers are not required to report the use of escort holds, pressure-compliance techniques, and firm grips that do not result in an injury or allegation of injury; control holds, wristlocks, and armbars utilized in conjunction with handcuffing and searching techniques that do not result in injury or allegation of injury; that force necessary to overcome passive resistance due to physical disability or intoxication that does not result in injury or allegation of injury, or the use of force in an approved training exercise. *See* GENERAL ORDER 03-04-05: INCIDENTS REQUIRING THE COMPLETION OF A TACTICAL RESPONSE REPORT (Chi. Police Dep't October 30, 2014).

16. Pursuant to City ordinance, supervisors are required to report all Taser uses to IPRA. *See* CHAPTER 2–57, INDEPENDENT POLICE REVIEW AUTHORITY (IPRA) 2-57-040(c) (IPRA chief administrator has power and duty to "conduct investigations into all cases in which a department member discharges his or her . . . stun gun, or Taser in a manner which potentially could strike an individual, even if no allegation of misconduct is made"). Notwithstanding this ordinance, unless the supervisor specifically requests additional investigation, IPRA does not investigate Taser discharges. We saw

several instances where the supervisor did not notify IPRA that a Taser discharge had occurred, despite being required to do so.

17. "Sustained" means the complaint was supported by sufficient evidence to justify disciplinary action. "Not sustained" means the evidence was insufficient to either prove or disprove the complaint. "Unfounded" means the facts revealed by the investigation did not support the complaint (e.g., the complained-of conduct did not occur). "Exonerated" means the complained-of conduct occurred, but the accused officer's actions were proper under the circumstances. *See* IPRA RULES § 4.1.

18. The City's new Police Accountability Ordinance narrows IPRA's jurisdiction over Taser discharges, as discussed elsewhere in this Report.

19. IPRA's use of "mediation" to resolve domestic violence disputes is problematic because it minimizes the serious, repetitive nature of this abuse and allows abusers to avoid meaningful punishment, which may empower them to continue the cycle of abuse. Using even true mediation (as opposed to IPRA's current plea-bargain mediation) to resolve domestic violence allegations against police officers would be inappropriate, given the dynamics of domestic violence.

20. We note that a significant amount of alleged officer misconduct involves officers working secondary employment. While we did not fully investigate CPD's oversight of officers' secondary work, the review that we did undertake indicated that there is a need for a thorough review of the policies and accountability measures related to officers' secondary employment.

21. We discuss the problems associated with IPRA's decision to delay officer interviews pending a prosecutor's determination in greater detail below.

22. *See* IPRA STANDARD OPERATING PROCEDURES MANUAL SECTION E, *Accused Members,* § C.6. (Rev. Jan 1, 2015).

23. We analyzed CPD's complaint data by comparing the race of the complainant and the findings outcome. A single complaint can include multiple allegations, and each allegation will have a separate finding. We deemed a complaint sustained whenever at least one allegation was sustained. Thus, for example, if a complaint included five allegations, one of which was sustained and the others unfounded, then the complaint was noted to have had at least one allegation sustained.

24. After our investigation began, the State's Attorney's Office announced it had begun reviewing cases in which officers' testimony had been questioned by judges and had begun issuing "disclosure notices" notifying criminal defense lawyers that a judge has discredited an officer's testimony. This is a positive step for the CPD accountability system and the Cook County criminal justice system but will require oversight to ensure that this program is effective and that it continues when public focus turns elsewhere.

25. CPD and IPRA also do not sufficiently gather or make use of the audio and video showing misconduct that is available. This problem is discussed separately in this Section.

26. As part of its role deciding certain disciplinary matters, the Board is assigned the responsibility of resolving disagreements between the Superintendent and IPRA over the recommended discipline for officers found to have committed misconduct. Where there is a disagreement, the Superintendent bears the burden of overcoming the IPRA Administrator's recommendation. *See* Chicago Police Board Rules Of Procedure, Section VI (April 16, 2015). The frequency of such disagreements has varied over time, and the Board reportedly has overwhelmingly refused to overturn IPRA's recommendations. There have been no such disagreements since 2014, and in 2014 there was only one.

27. Officers and supervisors may request Board review of a suspension of 30 days or less where the union decides not to arbitrate an officer's grievance.

28. The Police Board's decision can be appealed only to Cook County Circuit Court via petition for administrative review. Either party may appeal the Circuit Court's decision to the Appellate Court of Illinois. The Court will overturn the Board's findings of facts only where they are against the manifest weight of the evidence. The Court presumes the Board's findings of fact to be *prima facie* true and will find them contrary to the manifest weight of the evidence only where the opposite conclusion is "clearly apparent." The Court will overturn the Board's imposition of discipline only where the decision was arbitrary or unreasonable, taking into account the Board's "wide latitude" to determine what punishment was appropriate to "punish the conduct of the officer . . . and deter future conduct by other officers." *McDermott v. City of Chicago Police Bd.*, 2016 IL App (1st) 151979, ¶ 35.

29. In another five cases the officer resigned, and one case was otherwise dismissed prior to decision. The Board was more likely to uphold the Superintendent's suspension cases in 2014, upholding two of the three cases it heard, and, in an unprecedented decision, discussed below, recommending an increase in the penalty in a third case.

30. It is unclear how dependent this change is on the individuals currently on the Board. As discussed below, there are several structural changes that can be made to the Police Board to improve its functioning at an institutional level, and increase officer and public confidence that its decisions are fair and impartial.

31. Several Police Board officials with whom we spoke expressed concern in particular about IPRA's handling of allegations against officers of domestic violence, including IPRA's failure to sustain such allegations and to "mediate" a resolution. Both of these topics are covered elsewhere in the Accountability Section of this Report.

32. 65 Ill. Comp. Stat. 5/10-1-18.1 (1992).

33. *Castro v. City of Chicago Police Board,* 2016 IL App (1st) 142050, ¶ 42.

34. The Board process itself adds significant delay to the accountability process. As per the Board's 2014 Annual Report (the most recent available), in 2013 and 2014 the median number of days from the Superintendent filing charges to Board decision was 198, or over six-and-a-half months. According to the Police Accountability Task Force Report, in 2015 this median was 209 days. In our review of 2016 cases (excluding cases in which the officer resigned) the median was 266 days, and it took

the Board an average of 301 days after the Superintendent filed charges to render a decision. The Board should develop and implement a plan to reduce the length of time it takes it to resolve the cases that come before it.

35. The City's ostensible reason for not releasing videos is that witnesses might not be willing to testify if they knew video of their testimony would be released. This argument is unpersuasive, as it ignores the availability of image- blurring technology and the ability to redact witness names, and the fact that the City currently makes no attempt to redact the names of witnesses from the transcripts it releases. It also ignores that the Board's hearings are already open to the public.

36. During the course of our investigation, the City acknowledged problems with CPD's training systems and sought immediate input from our investigative team on potential reforms. In response, we assisted CPD with securing immediate substantial technical assistance from another large city agency. The City also hired an independent consultant to conduct a full review of CPD's training program to identify deficiencies and potential solutions. At the City's request, our team spoke with this consultant to share our observations in order to assist his review. At the conclusion of the consultant's review, the City agreed to let us meet with the consultant to discuss his recommended reforms but did not provide a copy of the consultant's report or relate the conclusions he reached that justified the reforms he recommended.

37. SUE RAHR, ET AL., FROM WARRIORS TO GUARDIANS: RECOMMITTING AMERICAN POLICE CULTURE TO DEMOCRATIC IDEALS (New Perspectives in Policing Bull., April 2015), available at https://www.ncjrs.gov/pdffiles1/nij/248654.pdf; Seth Stoughton, *Law Enforcement's "Warrior" Problem*, 128 HARV. L. REV. F. 225 (2015), available at http://harvardlawreview.org/2015/04/law-enforcements-warrior-problem/.

38. Like many of the other recent training reforms noted above, the City apparently recognized the significant problems attendant to providing training without any strategic plan or guiding committee. The City recently informed us that it established a new "Training Oversight Committee" chaired by the First Deputy Superintendent. This committee is reportedly responsible for establishing, implementing, and overseeing all CPD training, creating strategic plans, and conducting periodic needs assessments. The formation of this committee is an important step. However, as discussed more fully below, additional steps are necessary to ensure the work of the committee is widely accepted and that its goals and objectives can, and will, be met.

39. American Civil Liberties Union of Illinois, *Landmark Agreement Reached on Investigatory Stops in Chicago* (Aug. 7, 2015), available at http://www.aclu-il.org/landmark-agreement-reached-on-investigatory-stops-in-chicago/.

40. A second facility used for scenario training is on a public street, in close proximity to an elementary school. Conducting scenario trainings in such a setting puts the public at risk.

41. *See, e.g.*, ROBIN SHEPARD ENGEL, HOW POLICE SUPERVISORY STYLES INFLUENCE PATROL OFFICER BEHAVIOR (Nat'l Inst. of Justice, June 2003), available at https://www.ncjrs.gov/pdffiles1/nij/194078.pdf (a study of leadership styles in urban police departments that found that an active leadership style "was more likely than the

others to influence officer behavior" and that this "influence can be either positive or negative; for example, it can inspire subordinates to engage in more problem-solving activities, or it can result in more frequent use of force").

42. STEPHEN J. GAFFIGAN, POLICE INTEGRITY: PUBLIC SERVICE WITH HONOR 36 (Nat'l Inst. of Justice & Cmty. Oriented Policing Serv.'s 1997), available at https://www.ncjrs.gov/pdffiles/163811.pdf (comments of former Metropolitan Police Department Captain Swope).

43. The one exception is that officers with three "not sustained" excessive force complaints in one 12-month period may be referred to BIS.

44 Following the fifth and sixth separate incidents of this nature, which involved physical abuse of the officer's wife and children, CPD and IPRA sustained the complainant's allegations of domestic violence. To CPD's credit, given the severity of the misconduct, the Superintendent recommended termination from the Department. However, the Police Board reversed this recommendation and instead suspended the officer for a period of days, during which the officer was required to attend counseling and evaluation through the Employee Assistance Program. *See In re Edward Feliciano*, No. 12 PB 2824, available athttps://policeboard-production.s3.amazonaws.com/uploads/case/files/12PB2824_Decision.pdf. As noted elsewhere in this Report, the counselors who work in that program have no specialized training in domestic violence, and are ill-equipped to address these issues. *See* Report, Section IV.C. The Police Board's ability to overturn the recommendation of the Superintendent in this case is also illustrative of how Chicago's Police Board can undermine accountability more generally. *See* Report, Section III.H.

45. According to CPD's chief spokesman, in response to this revelation the Superintendent ordered an audit of why the 2004 complaint was never investigated to completion. However, the spokesman noted that the audit would be conducted by Internal Affairs—the same agency that lost track of the complaint. *See* Jeremy Gorner, *Discipline of cop involved in 2 fatal shootings fell through the cracks*, CHI. TRIB., Dec. 12, 2016, available at http://www.chicagotribune.com/news/local/breaking/ct-chicago-police-shootings-john-poulos-met-20161212- story.html.

46. University of Chicago, Center for Data Science and Public Policy, *Building Data-Driven Early Intervention Systems for Police Officers*, available at http://dsapp.uchicago.edu/public-safety/police-eis.

47. FINAL REPORT OF THE PRESIDENT'S TASK FORCE ON 21ST CENTURY POLICING 62 (Office of Community Oriented Policing Services, May 2015).

48. This is approximately a 1:4,000 counselor-to-officer ratio, and does not account for family members or retired officers who are also entitled to EAP's counseling services. *See* E06-01, III (D): CHICAGO POLICE DEP'T, EMPLOYEE RESOURCE (Chi. Police Dep't, Feb. 21, 2016), *available at* http://directives.chicagopolice.org/directives/data/a7a57be2-12aaf135-2a912-aaf1-37fbc7d8d466f49f.html ("All of the services offered by the Professional Counseling Service/EAP are available to Department members, a member's immediate or extended family, and retired sworn members."). While we found no published guidelines for the appropriate ratio in the police context, the

Employee Assistance Professionals Association's (EAPA) standards and guidelines state: "EAP staffing patterns, and the number of professionals, vary according to the type of program and the scope of services provided. Whether the EAP is internal or delivered by external contractors, the number and qualifications of EAP professionals should match program needs." EAPA Standards and Professional Guidelines for Employee Assistance Programs at 14 (2010). EAPA recommends considering the size and distribution of the workforce, the diversity of the employees, and the scope and design of the EAP, among other factors when determining the necessary staffing levels for an EAP. *See id.*

49. CPD's Peer Support Program has 300 volunteer members who do not offer counseling, but will offer support to officers in times of need and will also refer officers to clinicians or drug and alcohol counselors.

50. Brian R. Nanavaty, *Addressing Officer Crisis and Suicide: Improving Officer Wellness*, FBI LAW ENFORCEMENT BULL. (Sept. 8, 2015), available at https://leb.fbi.gov/2015/september/addressing-officer-crisis-and-suicide-improving-officer-wellness.

51. In the past, IPRA also produced Annual Reports. However, IPRA has not released an Annual Report since 2012. *See* IPRA, *Publications: Annual Reports*, available at http://www.iprachicago.org/category/annual-reports/ (last accessed Jan. 12, 2017).

52. It is also worth noting that on June 6, 2016, CPD's officer union filed an "unfair labor practice charge" with the Illinois Labor Relations Board, challenging IPRA's release of video as a violation of the union's collective bargaining agreement. The dispute is set for a hearing in early 2017.

53. *See* City of Chicago's Unopposed Motion for Entry of an Order Approving a City of Chicago Police Department Hiring Plan for Sworn Titles, *Shakman v. Democratic Org. of Cook Cnty.*, Case No. 69-C-2145 (N.D. Ill. Oct. 14, 2011).

54. Several of these lawsuits claimed that CPD's promotional exams discriminated against African-American officers, Latino officers, and female officers, and were not consistent with Title VII requirements. *See, e.g., Banos v. City of Chicago*, 398 F.3d 889, 890 (7th Cir. 2005) (minority sergeants challenged 1998 promotions to lieutenant); *Allen v. City of Chicago*, 351 F.3d 306, 307 (7th Cir. 2003) (minority officers challenged 1998 promotions to sergeant); *Bryant v. City of Chicago*, 200 F.3d 1092, 1094 (7th Cir. 2000) (minority sergeants challenged 1994 promotions to lieutenant); *United States v. City of Chicago*, 549 F.2d 415, 420 (7th Cir. 1977) (plaintiffs alleged discrimination against African-American, Latino, and female officers in hiring and promotions). White officers have also sued, claiming the tests discriminate against them. *See, e.g., Majeske v. City of Chicago*, 218 F.3d 816, 818 (7th Cir. 2000) (non-minority officers challenged 1989 detective promotions); *Barnhill v. City of Chicago*, 142 F. Supp. 2d 948, 950 (N.D. Ill. 2001) (white male officers challenged 1998 promotions to sergeant).

55. Separate from, and in addition to, litigation concerning the tests' discriminatory impact, promotional examinations also have been tainted with allegations of cheating or cronyism in the exam's preparation or administration. A 1998 promo-

tional exam was heavily criticized when groups of officers allegedly conferred with one another during bathroom breaks and subsequently changed their exam answers, and some test takers were given exams that were copied poorly, leaving portions of the questions unreadable. The City Inspector General is also currently investigating allegations that three recently promoted lieutenants were coached by a high-ranking official who helped develop the August 2015 lieutenant exam. Although the investigation is ongoing, allegations of improper exam procedures make CPD officers doubt the fairness of the exam process.

56. The officer was, in fact, ineligible for a merit promotion, because the officer had failed the sergeant's exam. The officer was nominated by a commander who had worked for CPD for only two weeks, after the Superintendent's Chief of Staff requested that the commander make the nomination, even though the commander had no knowledge of the officer's qualifications. Human Resources staff did not verify that the officer was eligible for promotion, and despite his failing score, included him on the list of eligible candidates that was forwarded to the Merit Board. The Merit Board nevertheless voted not to recommend promotion, but the Superintendent overrode that recommendation. The Superintendent never submitted a justification memo for this decision, as required by the new policy, but CPD's Human Resources still processed the promotion. The error was not discovered until the newly- promoted sergeant completed supervisor training and the City's own Human Resources department reviewed the hiring materials and discovered that the sergeant was ineligible for that position. The sergeant was then demoted, but the City is now facing a lawsuit over the controversy. The OIG found that, at several steps in the promotional process, the merit promotion policies were either ignored, or there were not enough safeguards in place to catch errors. The OIG recommended several changes based on its review of this incident.

57. Our discussion of the importance of trust in clearing homicides is not meant to diminish the importance of other factors. Many other factors, including the number of detectives assigned to the unit investigating homicides, and to each homicide case, as well as the timeliness of detective response to the scene of a homicide, are important factors in increasing clearance rates. Further, as discussed below, how CPD handles homicides is itself an important factor in building community trust and confidence in law enforcement.

58. Media reports of course include many additional accounts of officer dedication to the community, as well as officer heroism. For example, CPD officers operate a youth baseball league in one of the most challenged neighborhoods in Chicago, with several officers volunteering their time to coach 9–12 year olds in the league. CPD's "Shop With a Cop," an established annual event that occurs every holiday season, gives children the opportunity to spend a day shopping, eating, and bowling with police officers. News stories also recount stories of officers assisting people changing flat tires in the middle of the night; buying groceries for elderly neighbors; pulling people and dogs from building fires; pulling a teenage boy from the bottom of a pool and saving him from drowning; and many instances of officers assisting individuals with gunshot wounds—sometimes being credited with saving their lives.

59. The New York City Police Department's Hate Crimes Task Force has 26 officers (including 20 detectives plus additional supervisory staff) and two civilians assigned to it.

60. CPD is currently working on a relaunch of COMPSTAT that is intended to improve its utility and reputation within CPD. We encourage CPD to ensure that COMPSTAT incorporates integrity and constitutional policing components, as well as community insights, into its use.

61. Devon W. Carbado, *From Stopping Black People to Killing Black People: The Fourth Amendment Pathways to Police Violence*, 1 CAL. L. REV. 102 (forthcoming 2017) (discussing how police interactions expose people "not only to the violence of ongoing police surveillance, contact, and social control but also to the violence of serious bodily injury and death").

62. *See* Phillip Atiba Goff et al., *The Essence of Innocence: Consequences of Dehumanizing Black Children*, 106 J. PERSONALITY & SOC. PSYCH. 526 (2014).